"I've seen Bob successfully tackle business challenges both at Procter & Gamble and at Microsoft. In *The Fiefdom Syndrome*, he identifies a critical business problem in the corporate world that very few have been able to solve—until now. It shrate America."

—JAMES I. ... essor of Business
Administ... chool of Business

"A vitally important business book. As Bob Herbold, longtime COO of Microsoft, makes clear, the battles over territory and turf stem from basic human behavior. Uncontrolled, they can be incredibly destructive, yet they are inherent in every organization. In *The Fiefdom Syndrome*, Herbold shows how fiefdoms can hamstring a company's operations, and how to break through them. I strongly urge people of all organizations, large and small, profit and nonprofit, to read this book."

—JOHN CHAMBERS, President and CEO, Cisco Systems

"*The Fiefdom Syndrome* is a must-read for any executive who faces the pervasive and crippling challenge of turf battles. All institutions need a clear, unified mission and Bob Herbold's new book will help managers achieve it."

—HANK PAULSON, Chairman and CEO,
The Goldman Sachs Group, Inc.

"*The Fiefdom Syndrome* tackles a pervasive and seldom-discussed problem, namely, why organizations tend to become slow-footed, fragmented, and mediocre. Herbold provides valuable insights into cutting through the fiefdom syndrome, allowing you and your team to make the most of your talents, improve your organization, and avoid stalled careers."

—JOHN DOERR, partner,
Kleiner Perkins Caufield & Byers

"Bob Herbold takes on the bureaucracy and turf battles that can undercut any company's agility—the kinds of problems Sam Walton fought his whole life to overcome. I strongly recommend it."

—ROB WALTON, Chairman of the Board,
Wal-Mart Stores, Inc.

"I have seen many organizations with strategy or profitability problems where the core issues blocking their progress are the types of fiefdom-like behaviors Bob describes. The reader will highly value the powerful, useful learnings in this book, told via great 'war stories' by a very experienced practitioner. I strongly recommend *The Fiefdom Syndrome*."

—ADRIAN SLYWOTZKY, author of the acclaimed books *Value Migration, The Profit Zone*, and *The Art of Profitability*

"Fiefdoms, turf wars, and bureaucracy are often related to getting out of balance on centralization or decentralization. Bob Herbold provides valuable insights on how to achieve the proper balance and how to recognize and then avoid the pitfalls of decentralization that goes too far, i.e., fiefdoms."

—DICK KOVACEVICH, Chairman and CEO, Wells Fargo & Company

"In this day and age, turf battles and bureaucracy are practically synonymous. As one who has seen these battles up close, both in the public sector and private sector, I was intrigued by *The Fiefdom Syndrome*. Bob not only analyzes the causes, he offers compelling suggestions on how to overcome them. Whether you are in business, government, education, or the nonprofits, I urge you to read this book, and, more importantly, to take its advice and put it to good use."

—JACK KEMP, co-founder of Empower America and former candidate for Vice President of the United States

"The book has an important message for all organizations and individuals: there are some basic human behaviors that lead to performance-damping, career-crushing insularity and mediocrity. *The Fiefdom Syndrome* alerts you to the causes and the cures. This is a must-read for everyone, not just business people."

—WALTER HEWLETT, independent software developer and Chairman, The William & Flora Hewlett Foundation

THE
FIEFDOM
SYNDROME

THE TURF BATTLES THAT UNDERMINE CAREERS AND COMPANIES—AND HOW TO OVERCOME THEM

ROBERT J. HERBOLD

CURRENCY
DOUBLEDAY

NEW YORK   LONDON   TORONTO   SYDNEY   AUCKLAND

A CURRENCY BOOK
PUBLISHED BY DOUBLEDAY
a division of Random House, Inc.

CURRENCY is a trademark of Random House, Inc., and DOUBLEDAY
is a registered trademark of Random House, Inc.

The Fiefdom Syndrome was originally published in hardcover by Currency in September 2004.

Book design by Tina Thompson.

Cataloging-in-Publication Data is on file with the Library of Congress.

ISBN 0-385-51068-3
Copyright © 2005 by Bob Herbold
All Rights Reserved

PRINTED IN THE UNITED STATES OF AMERICA

All trademarks are the property of their respective companies.

SPECIAL SALES
Currency Books are available at special discounts for bulk purchases for sales promotions or
premiums. Special editions, including personalized covers, excerpts of existing books, and corporate
imprints, can be created in large quantities for special needs. For more information, write to
Special Markets, Currency Books, specialmarkets@randomhouse.com.

10 9 8 7 6 5 4 3 2

This book is dedicated to my incredible wife, Pat, with whom I have shared almost forty years of marriage. I also want to acknowledge the support of our three children: Donna, Jim, and Greg. Throughout my almost four decades in business, I have had more than my share of fun, and none of that would have been possible without their ongoing encouragement and feedback as they listened to my stories and reacted to my experiences as they were happening.

CONTENTS

INTRODUCTION

RECENTLY, ON AN airplane returning home to Seattle from a consulting job with a large corporation, I realized that, once again, I was seeing the same kind of problems in the company I was working with that I had seen many, many times before. Over the course of my thirty-six years in business, I have come to realize there is a set of behaviors that people exhibit that remind me very much of the feudal fiefdoms of the Middle Ages. Individuals and groups tend to isolate themselves from the larger organization, and worry more about defending their turf and protecting the status quo than in moving the organization forward. I call such behavior the Fiefdom Syndrome.

I've found this syndrome in nonprofit organizations, K-12 school systems, universities, and governments, as well as in private industry. The behaviors that characterize the Fiefdom Syndrome lead to a culture where ego and bureaucracy consistently trump common sense and innovation. They lead to turf wars. And they are almost always destructive.

It's not that people who exhibit fiefdom tendencies are mischievous or unethical. These behaviors are simply natural human tendencies that emerge as people try to exercise control over their workplace environment, protect their domain, and avoid change that might upset the present order.

After retiring from the position of chief operating officer at Microsoft, where one of my chief tasks was to break through corporate fiefdoms and help to streamline the company, I decided to write down what I'd discovered about fiefdoms for general business readers. To a greater or lesser extent, fiefdoms have been a part of every organization I've ever encountered—and they can absolutely hamstring an organization's effectiveness, far more so, in fact, than any cyclical downturn or economic recession.

Turf wars can cause employees and managers to focus more on the size of their staff, the scope of their responsibilities, and their ability to manage their own affairs, than on the larger goals of the organization. The net result of such battles is that too many efforts are directed inward, instead of outward on the products and services the company is providing. We've all encountered such battles over turf, whether it's the department head who is a constant roadblock to efforts to change the way things are done, or the executive secretary or assistant who, in acting as gatekeeper, decides he or she is more important than the position justifies.

The observations in this book are the distillation of what I've learned through my many accumulated battle scars in the business world, as well as my involvement in nonprofits, schools and universities, and my interactions with government over the years. I've been fortunate to work with two world-class companies: Procter & Gamble for twenty-six years and Microsoft for nine years. Within those organizations I've seen a lot of the behaviors I decribe in this book. More important, I learned how these behaviors could be dealt with in an effective manner. My consulting activities with companies over the last three years have confirmed how prevalent these human behaviors are, and how detrimental they can be.

In some of the examples and anecdotes in the book, I name the organization and the people involved, to point out the problems and show how they were fixed. In many other examples, to avoid embarrassing the individuals or companies involved, I've disguised or altered their identities and changed the settings, while remaining true to the core experience and the insights to be gained into what the problems are and how to overcome them.

I believe that conquering the fiefdom syndrome is one of the most important things a company can do to improve its profitability. Being aware of the dangers of fiefdoms can be immensely valuable in shaping one's individual career, as well.

I would like to thank my administrative assistant, Kim McGee, whose incredible efforts were instrumental in helping to put my thoughts down on paper, and who was tireless in the revision process. Also, I am deeply grateful to Wes Neff of The Leigh Bureau, who encouraged me to tackle this project and contributed much to making it a reality. Last, but certainly not least, I want to thank Chuck Martin, who assisted in writing this book. Together we made a great team, and his experience really helped in creating an insightful manuscript. We also had a lot of fun doing it, because we were convinced that what we were doing was something that could *really* help organizations and individuals.

PART I

THE FIEFDOM SYNDROME

1 THE PROBLEM WITH FIEFDOMS

THERE IS A potentially infectious condition inside virtually all organizations that can cause more damage than economic downturns, management upheavals, or global business shifts. Until now it has had no name. But this condition has been an enormous problem in all facets of business. It has impacted some of the world's leading companies, including Procter & Gamble, IBM, Coca-Cola, and Microsoft.

I call it the "fiefdom syndrome," and it happens to all organizations, large and small, profit and nonprofit. It occurs at the individual level as well. And it can significantly decrease an individual's, and a company's, effectiveness. In extreme cases, it has shaken entire industries and taken down major corporations.

The problem begins when individuals, groups, or divisions—out of fear—seek to make themselves vital to their organizations and unconsciously or sometimes deliberately try to protect their turf or reshape their environment to gain as much control as possible over what goes on.

It is a natural human tendency, probably dating back to the origin of our species. But if this human tendency isn't managed properly, the damage caused by these "fiefdoms" can begin to undermine an organization. Left untouched, fiefdoms can toll the death knell of what should have been a strong and vital organization.

The fiefdom syndrome stems from the inclination of managers and employees to become fixated on their own activities, their own careers, their own territory or turf to the detriment of those around them.

People who create fiefdoms can become dangerously insular, losing perspective on what is happening in the world outside their own control. They also lose their ability to act consistently on behalf of the greater good, or in a way that enhances the effectiveness of the larger organization. They often resist new situations and change.

People who create fiefdoms tend to hoard resources. They are determined to do things their own way, often duplicating or complicating what should be streamlined throughout the company, leading to runaway costs, increased bureaucracy, and slower response times. Organizations infected with fiefdoms tend to kill off or stifle individual creativity, leading to what I call the "freeze factor": when organizations become frozen or stuck in place, letting competitors pass them by.

The term "fiefdom" first arose in the Middle Ages. Back in the time of William the Conqueror, before the establishment of a strong monarch or central government in Europe, feudal lords controlled most territories and governed the lives of the people in those territories.

Today, organizational fiefdoms exist in companies large and small. Geographical and product-based divisions can grow into impenetrable fiefdoms. But fiefdoms also emerge in nonprofit organizations, government agencies (which today are almost synonymous with the word "fiefdom"), and franchises. Fiefdoms can be found all the way to the CEO's office. Some are even sanctioned by top management, such as when an executive has a pet project or division he or she protects from reality. Motivated by self-interest or greed, fiefdoms can wittingly or unwittingly cause an organization and its shareholders great harm.

Because the fiefdom syndrome has its origins in basic human nature, the challenges it poses are universal. The fiefdom syndrome is not tied to good or bad economic conditions or to particular managerial approaches. It can emerge in any environment. But the good news for organizations and individuals is that there are ways to deal with the fiefdom syndrome. And deal with them you must. For fiefdoms can:

▪ Lead to inefficiency and ineffectiveness within a company, causing it to lose market share and reduce its profitability

- Stifle creativity and innovation
- Result in staleness and insularity
- Hinder execution or follow-through, which can lead to organizational mediocrity

FIEFDOMS AT MICROSOFT AND IBM

In the early '90s, Microsoft's sales subsidiaries in most major countries were feeling very confident in their abilities to run their businesses. They enjoyed impressive revenue and profits. When Microsoft started these subsidiaries in the 1980s, they were intentionally made independent to ensure they could grow fast, unencumbered by directives from Redmond, Washington, headquarters. It was the perfect environment for fiefdoms to take hold.

By the early 1990s, these subsidiaries were growing quickly. This led them to argue for their own resources in a variety of areas.

- Microsoft's Italian subsidiary, which was hiring a fair number of new employees each year, argued (successfully) that they needed additional human resources (HR) personnel to emphasize quality training, as well as several HR generalists to help manage the growing staff.
- At Microsoft UK, the company launched several creative marketing efforts that later were utilized successfully by other countries. Before long, the subsidiary had hired a surprising number of additional marketing people.
- In Germany, Microsoft was especially strong in information technology. Microsoft Germany set up a small data center designed to show customers how they could successfully use Microsoft software. It seemed like a great idea at the time. Over time, however, this evolved to a major data center, complete with its own information systems; the subsidiary felt these systems were necessary to run their business in their market.

What was going on in these Microsoft subsidiaries was the basic human tendency to take on more and more resources. Those additional resources may look worthwhile at the time. But as the divisions grow, they consume more manpower and balloon costs. By the mid-1990s, Microsoft's German subsidiary had a staff of more than seventy IT professionals. Their data center and systems were extremely independent, duplicating countless resources already available at headquarters in Redmond, Washington.

Some countries "staffed up" in the technical public relations arena, since a key marketing tool in the information technology sector was making sure that the trade press reported on the performance of Microsoft software versus competition and on publicizing successful case studies of companies benefiting from the use of Microsoft software. The subsidiaries wanted publicity in their countries to properly reflect Microsoft's achievements and perspective. So they hired additional staff to make sure that happened.

The same kind of thing happened in finance as well. Subsidiaries came up with their own ways to analyze their business, methods that tended to emphasize how well they were doing. They institutionalized those new measures and used them to report on their business. Spain, for example, might decide they need to develop their own general ledger, or "chart of accounts," one that was different from that used by Microsoft's corporate headquarters, in order to properly reflect the nuances of their particular business.

This sort of thing was happening to one extent or another in all of Microsoft's subsidiaries. In one country, the managers decided that costs related to marketing materials directed to the distribution channel were sales costs; in another country, they were classified as marketing costs. In one country, employees' personal computers might be charged to the department in which the employee works, while in another country, they might charge all PCs to the information technology group. In some countries, revenue was certified and officially booked on a weekly basis and each month started with the closest Monday to the start of the month and ended with the closest Friday to the end of the month. In another country, revenue might be booked on a monthly basis that began with the first day of the month and ended with the last day of the month. Comparing the performances of the subsidiaries was like comparing apples and oranges. Getting all of this data sorted out at the end of a quarter to form uniformly defined corporate financial figures was a nightmare.

What was going on at Microsoft in the early to mid-1990s was not that different from the experiences of most other multinational corporations. General managers of company subsidiaries of many corporations perceive themselves as "kings" in their countries. They want to act and be treated totally independently; each GM wants to be perceived as the CEO or president of the company in his or her country. They often argue that this puts them on par with their peers in other industries, as well as with the heads of competing companies in their country. The top executive in each country frequently argues that each market is different and that the "uniqueness" of their country requires that it have its own financial measures and systems. From the country's perspective, this is not only logical but also incredibly efficient. After all, they reason, executives in the United States could not possibly understand the economic cycles and local nuances of conducting business in France, Germany, or whatever the specific country might be.

This kind of thinking was going on in most of the Microsoft subsidiaries, and it was resulting in some major challenges for the company. At the end of the quarter, the subsidiaries would send in their spreadsheets and reports, often defining terms differently than Microsoft's corporate finance department. You can imagine what a mess this created for the corporate finance folks at the end of the quarter. The number of frantic phone calls and e-mail messages flying back and forth between the subsidiaries and the corporate controller and his department was phenomenal.

I remember during the first week of January 1995 walking into the office of one of the financial analysts who was trying to pull together all the European results. I had been at Microsoft for only a few months, and as the new chief operating officer, I was making the rounds to see how the place operated. The analyst was on a speakerphone in the midst of a screaming match with the Italian subsidiary about why they seemed to change each quarter how they categorized marketing costs for shipping promotion materials and what they classified as cost of goods sold. He was trying to pinpoint exactly what definitions they used this period so that the right cost could be put in the right financial bucket.

After listening in on this conversation between the Italians and Microsoft's corporate finance people, it was clear to me that there was no discipline in the system. The Italians weren't trying to be difficult— they felt that they were running their business smartly. The problem was that the corporate folks didn't have a focused, disciplined approach toward the basic elements of the company's financial structure.

It would drive Bill Gates nuts that it took weeks for the company to figure out what the quarter was going to look like. Not that Bill was overly interested in the short-term financial results. In fact, he absolutely wasn't; he was focused on designing and developing great software. But he was *very* concerned that we didn't have the information systems in place to make the financials fall into place in a timely manner. After all, we were the world's foremost software company. He expected the company to have superb systems.

A couple of weeks after the end of the October–December 1994 quarter, I was meeting in my office with Mike Brown, Microsoft's chief financial officer. Bill stuck his head in and said, "So where are the results? I know you must have the raw data by now. Come on, guys, do you want me to go in there and figure out how to piece it all together myself? Do you want me to write the code? I'll do it over the weekend."

This undisciplined behavior on the part of Microsoft's overseas subsidiaries was not unique to Microsoft. I saw the same kind of behavior at Procter & Gamble, where I had worked for twenty-six years. The heads of the sales organizations in the various countries eventually positioned themselves as president of the company in their respective countries. And clearly a president needs his own finance, HR, and IT personnel. Before long, they were developing their own marketing efforts, often out of sync with the overall strategic and marketing direction of Procter & Gamble's products and services.

Shortly after I became head of marketing at Procter & Gamble, I recall sitting in the office of the general manager of Procter & Gamble Germany and listening to him describe how Procter & Gamble Germany ranked with respect to other companies in Germany. He explained in great detail all of the various components of his "company." I sat there thinking that this man feels that he's a stand-alone company, one that requires the full resources of a company in all functional areas, when he is actually a sales manager for Procter & Gamble Germany.

Human nature is such that we are always trying to convince ourselves that we are more important than the rest of the group, company, or world believes we are. It is not so surprising that the head of Procter & Gamble in Germany, after years of successfully running that business, inflated his role in his own mind in terms of what he represented to the larger company.

These are examples of fiefdoms at their most grandiose. They are expensive in that they can result in enormous duplication of people and equipment. And they can slow down or paralyze the inner workings of the company. They create turf wars and needless bureaucracy. They rob the organization of profitability by adding untold dollars to a company's operating costs.

Fiefdoms spring up like weeds in all organizations. In his best-selling book *Who Says Elephants Can't Dance?*, retired IBM CEO Lou Gerstner wrote that when he joined the company in 1993, "the geographical regions, for the most part, protected their turf and attempted to own everything that went on in their region. The technology divisions dealt with what they thought could be built, or what they wanted to build, with little concern about customer needs or priorities."

During Gerstner's first few months as CEO, he paid a visit to IBM's European operations. Upon returning, he said: "I returned home with a healthy appreciation of what I had been warned to expect: powerful geographical fiefdoms with duplicate infrastructure in each country. Of the 90,000 employees in Europe/Middle East/Africa, 23,000 were in support functions."

Those fiefdoms had become rigid, and their financial systems were a mess: "Other IBMers practically had to ask permission to enter the territory of a country manager. Each country had its own independent systems. In Europe alone, we had 142 different financial systems. If we had a financial issue that required the cooperation of several business units to resolve, we had no common way of talking about it because we were maintaining 266 different general ledger systems."

At Microsoft, the true impact of the geographical fiefdoms that had grown up over the years and the financial challenges they posed to the company hit home when Microsoft had to embarrassingly make excuses to its customers when they asked to see how Microsoft managed its financial systems. Our customers were expecting to learn the best practices from a global leader in information technology. After all, they reasoned, a totally networked high-tech company with offices throughout the world must have the most sophisticated financial reporting system on the planet, right? Later in this book, I'll describe what Microsoft did (in record time) to break up its fiefdoms and truly turn itself into an incredible showcase of financial-systems excellence. Today the company can close its books each quarter in a couple of days.

CUTTING THROUGH FIEFDOMS!
SAM WALTON AND HIS DREAM

Back in 1987, when I was the chief information officer at Procter & Gamble, Sam Walton invited a Procter & Gamble executive team to Bentonville, Arkansas. He told them that he had heard so much about their tremendous effort behind "total quality" that he wanted his executive team to be exposed to their wisdom. Sam went on and on about how much he admired Procter & Gamble's knowledge on this subject and how he hoped that Wal-Mart would be able to learn from their experiences.

Naturally, this made the Procter & Gamble people proud of their total quality efforts. They jumped at the opportunity to go to Bentonville to present a one-day training program to Sam's executive team. This was the same one-day training effort that Procter & Gamble had been implementing internally with its own people. Upon hearing that the training required a full eight-hour day, Sam was a little bewildered. But he continued to move forward with the plans to have the Procter & Gamble crew come to Bentonville.

The P&G team walked into the meeting room in Bentonville with a stack of transparencies to be used with an overhead projector. Sam looked at that stack and once again got a bewildered look on his face.

The training session began, and Sam impatiently fidgeted in his chair as the trainer painstakingly droned through the material.

About an hour into the meeting, Sam got up and said to the Procter & Gamble folks: "Look, boys, I'm not so sure we need to go through all those transparencies. I think we are all beginning to get the idea behind this total quality stuff. What I'd really like to talk about is how Procter & Gamble and Wal-Mart can do business together with a lot fewer people involved and with a much higher rate of overall efficiency in both of our organizations. What we need is to just have you guys ship us product as automatically as possible and we'll settle up at the end of the month and things will be real simple."

Now it was the Procter & Gamble people's turn to look bewildered. The total quality trainer jumped up and indicated that he was confident they could tackle that problem as a group exercise once they got through the transparencies and understood some of the nuances of total quality that he claimed easily applied to Sam's problem. The total quality presentation resumed, and Sam took his place and again fidgeted around like a hyperactive kid.

After another hour, Sam popped up and said: "Look, we don't want to get too loaded down with theory here. I think I see where you are going with this total quality material, and I want again to suggest that we interrupt the meeting and just jump right in to making it simpler for our two companies to get P&G products through our warehouses and stores and off to the customer."

The P&G folks tried to get Sam to back down, but there was no stopping him now. He took the felt-tip pen and started drawing boxes on the flip chart that represented P&G computers, Wal-Mart computers, Wal-Mart distribution centers, P&G warehouses, and Wal-Mart stores. He then proclaimed, "Why can't we just have your computers and our computers talk every night and place the order for P&G products to be shipped to Wal-Mart distribution centers automatically?" Again, the P&G folks tried to get Sam and his group to back off, but Sam prevailed. This time he got a bit more emotional: "You boys have about seven operating divisions that all offer separate products and all have different business practices. Each of those divisions sends their salespeople and their fancy cars to park in our lot and sit in our lobby and wait for our buyers. We have to have buyers for every one of those salespeople, and these sellers and buyers get all set in their ways and believe they are very important and have their own ways to do the business and it costs us all in time and money. Let's just see how simple we can make this stuff."

Sam was asking that we break up the P&G sales fiefdoms and that he break up the Wal-Mart buyer fiefdoms that had developed to meet with the P&G fiefdoms. He was convinced P&G didn't need all those salespeople and all those cars those salespeople drove and all the appointments they made with his buyers. He was convinced that his buyers had formed their own fiefdoms to protect their "profession" and that all the sellers and buyers had avoided the potential of technology for fear of it replacing them.

Sam Walton was a student of logistics. He was always probing for ways to make products flow more efficiently and effectively within the distribution channel. He would spend hours roaming around in Marks and Spencer stores in London, asking clerks how they could have such fresh produce and such fresh flowers. He asked them if he could go into the back room and talk to the stock clerks about where the products came from and how long they remained in the store before customers walked out with them.

At the meeting with P&G executives and their total quality people, Sam described his dream and charged me, as the chief information officer at Procter & Gamble, to work with Bobby Martin, the CIO of Wal-Mart, to take one brand, Pampers, and put it on what he called "continuous replenishment." The intent was that every evening P&G computers would receive from Wal-Mart distribution centers the data on the movement of Pampers out of each distribution center in the previous twenty-four hours. The system then would check availability of the various Pampers items at warehouses and manufacturing centers of Procter & Gamble and develop an order that replenished the distribution centers in the most economical manner, as well as select the trucking company that fit the needs most economically. Early the next morning at P&G, one clerk would check the order as soon as he came to work. That was the only human intervention involved.

Sam demanded at the end of the total quality meeting that the group get together again in two months to see "if our boys can come up with this system that I dream about every night and report to us the kind of results they are seeing." This was Sam at his best. He knew his logistics well. He demanded a no-frills approach that could be implemented in weeks, not months or years. The secret was to have the CIOs of the two companies dedicate only a few highly skilled people to the task, who could make things happen quickly and in a high-quality manner.

The system for the experimental product, Pampers disposable diapers, was built in six weeks. Sam picked Pampers because it was bulky to handle and occupied significant warehouse space in the Wal-Mart distribution centers and stores. Minimizing inventories would create a big gain for Wal-Mart.

When the companies got together 8 weeks later, the teams reported that the new continuous-replenishment system was up and running. As a result of this system, Pampers moved from a rate of 20 turns per year to 110 turns per year (a turn is the length of time between the moment the product is received by a retailer like Wal-Mart until a consumer takes it out the door in a shopping cart). In the old system, it took an average of 18 days (365 days a year divided by 20 turns) to get a box of Pampers from the receiving dock at a Wal-Mart distribution center into the hands of a Wal-Mart customer. Eighteen is actually a respectable number and would be the envy of some supermarket chains. The new continuous-replenishment approach reduced that 18-day period to 3 days (360 days divided by 110 turns). That is a sensational result.

I'll never forget the childlike grin on Sam's face when he saw those results. He said to the Procter & Gamble team: "You boys are probably noticing that your products are in our distribution centers and stores only about three or four days before we get paid for them by our customers, but we don't have to pay you for ten days. I know you are sitting there thinking: 'Sam's running his business on your money.'" He then pointed out that it would only be fair to take some P&G items that Wal-Mart didn't stock and see if they could make those a big success in the continuous-replenishment system. That would do some good things for Procter & Gamble (finally getting Wal-Mart to stock some of these items they had wanted them to stock) while getting great financial results for Wal-Mart.

Over the next year, most of the Procter & Gamble products were moved to continuous-replenishment, and enormous savings were achieved both by Wal-Mart and Procter & Gamble. The reduced inventory by both parties was stunning. In addition, P&G needed dramatically fewer sales personnel, and Wal-Mart needed fewer buyers to interact with Procter & Gamble.

So what had happened here? Sam had spotted fiefdoms at work, and he wanted to break them up. He was able to move the business ahead significantly by doing so.

While you can observe fiefdoms in a huge variety of situations, they generally fall into six major categories: personal, peer, divisional, top-tier, group, and protected. Each can cause varying degrees and different types of negative impact on an organization.

THE PERSONAL FIEFDOM

A fiefdom of one, if the person's impact is broad, can affect coworkers, workgroups, entire departments, and even the actions of the entire company.

At one company for which I consulted, I ran into an in-house employee benefits specialist in the human resources department who was giving people fits by blocking creativity in the employee benefits area. The woman, whom I'll call Melissa, had been the benefits specialist for almost twenty years and was associated with the design of most of the key benefit programs of the company, such as the 401K, employee stock purchase program, and healthcare plans.

Melissa had a very strong personality and was extremely protective of her turf (i.e., her areas of expertise). Because she had developed the legal and regulatory basis of most of the company's benefit programs with some of the veteran HR people who weren't around anymore, she felt it was her job to protect those gems.

Melissa was awfully hard to deal with. Even her superiors were afraid of her because of her incredibly brash demeanor. They didn't want to upset her because they assumed that her long tenure in the job meant she had deep expertise in the area of employee benefits. The HR people under her dreaded going into her office. She would give them that "cold stare" over her glasses as she folded her arms, ready to repel just about any new ideas that might be thrown in her direction.

The situation came to a head when the organization decided that it needed to make some dramatic changes in the healthcare area; it wasn't satisfied with its current vendor, and it couldn't put up with the sky-rocketing costs. A small group of human resources people was pulled together and given responsibility to fix the healthcare cost problem. They were told that the HR benefits specialist would be their resource for all employee, legal, and regulatory issues.

Melissa viewed the committee as a potential threat to her authority and consequently did everything possible to hinder progress and make it clear that she was the person who had to approve any recommendation for changes. She was determined to protect her turf at all costs. After all, this had been her area for years.

HR management described to me one major blowup between the new group and Melissa. Apparently, the group didn't believe she was completely up-to-date on the government regulations as to what they could and could not do. So they went outside and consulted with a corporate benefits attorney. As a result, they came back with several points of view different from those of the company's HR benefits specialist. Melissa exploded in anger. Then she ran to the head of HR and complained that the group was out of control and that he needed to make it clear that no risks were to be taken in any legal and regulatory areas that contradicted her own advice. The head of HR, intimidated by Melissa's claim regarding inappropriate risks, supported her view.

After several similar blowups, Melissa realized that she was going to have to become a participant in the process because the health costs were clearly a major issue within the organization. Consequently, she began to give ground on a few points, and eventually the committee reached a solution, though one that was far less than optimal.

Soon after the healthcare effort was completed, a couple of young HR specialists in the benefits area came forward and claimed they had found a new vendor for the company's 401(k) program, one that could provide employees far better services and some unique new features. HR management directed them to Melissa to get her opinion and advice. Her ego had been a bit bruised by the healthcare exercise, and she really came down hard on this group. She lectured these "youngsters," I was told, for two straight hours on the regulatory risks associated with changing any aspect of a 401(k) program, while giving the team the clear impression that she was the authority in this area and may veto any aspect of their work.

The team made several attempts to talk with Melissa, as there were clear advantages being offered by this new vendor. She, on the other hand, had great relationships with numerous people associated with the current vendor and wasn't about to budge an inch. Throughout the process, she projected an "all of this is too complex for you to understand" attitude and basically told them to let her tell them what they could and couldn't do. One thing she did do was relay back to the current vendor a couple of changes that it should make in the administration of its program to make it easier for company employees to interact with them. She suggested to the HR team that they focus on the current vendor and work things out.

The result was that the team that had the creative ideas about the new vendor became frustrated. In the end, the current vendor did generate some improvements, but they were not nearly as significant as those the new vendor could have offered.

It was a clear example of a fiefdom created by a single person who caused huge turf battles and stifling bureaucracy. Melissa had a negative impact on the entire organization, blocking new thinking and ideas, even those pursued at the urging of top management. Fortunately for the company, a new head of HR was appointed, and after working with Melissa for about nine months on the tough problem of the continuing escalation of healthcare costs, he had the nerve to confront the fiefdom. Melissa opted for an early-retirement package to avoid experiencing the demise of her fiefdom.

Personal fiefdoms can create major blockages within an organization. They occur in every type of organization, including for-profit businesses, not-for-profits, government organizations, and school systems. We have all seen them at work in small ways and in large ways. Fiefdoms control information, stifle creativity, and are unwilling to cope with change. The organization can have difficulty recognizing a fiefdom at times because of the esoteric nature of the work involved. But they should be watched for. After all, personal fiefdoms are a real problem everywhere.

THE PEER, OR NETWORK, FIEFDOM

Fiefdoms can sprout up at the peer level as well, with similar groups in an organization each operating as a fiefdom. When taken together, these parts can affect how an organization conducts business in a given market.

In his best-selling book *The Profit Zone*, Adrian Slywotzky describes how Coca-Cola, in its early years, formed an independent-bottler network to serve its needs. Throughout the period from the 1920s through the 1960s, Coke would select a bottler in a region, make it its exclusive agent, supply Coca-Cola syrup at a standard price for all bottlers, and help the bottler get off the ground financially.

By the late '70s, these independent bottlers were acting very independently, to the point that each had become a fiefdom with exclusive rights to the bottling of Coke within its region and virtually no other commitments to the Coca-Cola Company. Many of them became very set in their ways and saw little need to change because they were financially successful and because they were the only source of Coca-Cola to the retailers in their area. In essence, it was a network of peer fiefdoms.

Unfortunately for Coca-Cola, in the late 1970s and in the '80s, national supermarket and mass-merchandiser chains began to emerge. Organizations like Kroger, Safeway, Kmart, and Wal-Mart wanted to execute national Coca-Cola promotions with an aggressive target national feature price. For example, over a Fourth of July weekend, they wanted to work with Coca-Cola to execute a 99-cent special on the Coke 64-ounce plastic bottle.

For Coca-Cola to execute such a promotion meant it had to work with each of its individual bottlers and "ask" them to participate, requiring the bottler to supply unusually large quantities at the retail outlets to meet the spike in demand. It also needed to set up point-of-purchase marketing materials and product displays in the retail outlets, making the marketing theme highly visible to shoppers. While there was a small amount of merchandising money for the bottler to cover its additional work, the whole effort was quite disruptive to its normal business. Given that they were already hugely successful, the bottlers didn't warm up to the idea of "taking orders" from Coca-Cola to do special promotions that required more labor and coordination.

Moreover, Coca-Cola lacked the authority to issue directives to the bottlers. There was no chain of command. Bottlers had basic contracts with Coke, and that was it. As a result, executing a promotion with marketing materials that needed to be handled with precise timing in a certain way required an immense amount of interaction by Coca-Cola. Getting each of the bottlers to execute in a timely manner was very difficult. The sole tool Coca-Cola had to encourage compliance was to structure the merchandising funds in such a way that if the promotion was not executed well, payments were withheld from the bottlers.

The problem was that these bottlers had become quite satisfied with their place in life. They had become insular and resistant to change. They wanted no part of the random marketing campaigns that the Coca-Cola Company was trying to implement with its national promotions. They simply wanted to be left alone in their individual fiefdoms, enjoying the fruits of their past success. Why perform cartwheels to meet the needs of some supermarket chain if they didn't need to?

In contrast, Pepsi had none of these problems. It had control over its bottlers and offered national deals and implemented them across the country at aggressive prices. Pepsi worked carefully with its bottlers to ensure they understood the opportunities of larger volume and the merchandising allowances that Pepsi's promotions offered them. They worked hard to make sure the bottlers understood how good it would be for the entire Pepsi organization to execute these promotions well.

Given the growth of large regional and national supermarkets and national mass merchandisers during the '80s, Coca-Cola's inability to mobilize its bottlers was emerging as a distinct competitive disadvantage. Coke simply lacked the ability to plan or execute such national offerings. The fiefdoms that had emerged with the independent bottlers were hurting Coke's business.

The problem that Coca-Cola had to tackle in the 1980s is an excellent example of the dangers of peer fiefdoms. Coca-Cola had to break up the peer fiefdoms to compete in a changing marketplace. It began to buy back or take a controlling financial position in the bottlers, forming Coca-Cola Enterprises. Its formation gave Coke control over its distribution chain, enabling it to interact successfully with the large national supermarkets and the national fast-food chains that were emerging.

DIVISIONAL FIEFDOMS

In larger organizations with multiple product lines, growth adds complexity over a period of time. This can lead to divisional fiefdoms, where each product line or division of an organization ends up acting as its own entity, without the necessary synergy or interaction with the rest of the organization, its external distribution channel, or its customers.

In the late 1990s, a good friend of mine consulted with a large food company that had six product divisions, each with different lines of food products. Yet the company had one sales organization, which sold the products of all six divisions.

As the product divisions gained strength and their individual product lines became more successful, they developed into six individual fiefdoms. Each had formed its own individual merchandising and marketing organization, which developed different types of promotions for customers and separate terms for selling its products.

The company did not have a strong central sales organization to oversee the individual business units and to question the sanity of the various merchandising approaches the six divisions used. In addition, top management was insulated from its customers and had grown accustomed to reasonable revenue and profit growth per year. Management had no real energy to search for ways in which dramatic improvement could be achieved.

The salespeople who had to call on the company's customers had the most difficult task of all. Each of the six business units had different promotion schedules for the calendar year. One had the year broken into thirteen promotion periods of four weeks' duration each; another had six promotion periods of eight weeks each. To make matters worse, each of the divisions sold to the same customer. One salesperson, whom I'll call Joe, had to meet with the customer's buyer and present the promotions for each division that were to be active in the next month or so. He literally had to explain six completely different approaches to merchandising and attempt to get the account excited about ways to manage all of the initiatives.

Joe might go in at the beginning of one month and explain that none of the business divisions had any active promotions over the next four to six weeks. A month later, five of the six might be running promotion offers, and he had to request that the customer merchandise all five of the promotions simultaneously.

Joe was continually making excuses for the business divisions as to why they were executing the way they did. The customer saw what was happening and felt treated like a second-class citizen whose own needs were ignored by the company.

A relatively new salesperson, whom I'll call Rick, called on a retail outlet and asked it to run three different promotion themes in its weekly circular that went out to its customers. The buyer for the retail outlet got so incensed at the absurdity of the practices and Rick's request that he chased him out of the office and called the company's VP of sales, demanding that he be fired. The buyer had a good point. It was ridiculous for a retail outlet to have three different promotion themes in its weekly circular. Retailers want to make it simple for customers. They try to have one general theme per circular that they can drive home to get people to come to their store that week. Rick was not putting himself into the shoes of the retailer. He was simply trying to push out the door what was being pushed down upon him from the independent business units.

Eventually, the company's competitors recognized the company's administrative and executional mess. They designed programs across their product lines to make it extremely easy for customers to deal with them. They formed customer-focused teams composed of one sales representative for each of their business units. Each of these sales representatives reported to the head of sales of their business unit, but represented the company as a member of the team. They had the authority to go back to the individual business unit they sold for and demand change. These competitors used their new strategy to gain leverage with the customers.

As the food company began to suffer declining revenues, the CEO finally woke up and began to listen to the impassioned pleas of the sales representatives who had to call on the company's customers. But when he tried to implement changes, the divisional fiefdoms pushed back, and the CEO was unsuccessful in pulling the company out of its tailspin. He was replaced after experiencing two years of dismal results. The irony is that during those two years the business units continued to act as fiefdoms and continued to cite how strong their product offerings were compared to competitors. They blamed the company's revenue problems on the sales organization. The fiefdoms, by preventing the CEO from coordinating across the business units, unwillingly hamstrung their company in the marketplace.

THE TOP-TIER FIEFDOM

One of the easiest fiefdoms to spot, and most difficult to alter, is the top-tier fiefdom, where the person at the top of the organization cuts himself off from the marketplace to such an extent that he becomes immune to the realities of the business. Market forces often correct this type of fiefdom naturally, but the organization can generate some ugly problems until that happens.

Let me give an example from the world of the fine arts. A well-known, prestigious West Coast arts organization was on a roll throughout the 1990s. It attracted great talent for highly publicized events, was constantly mentioned in the press for its controversial views, and was constantly launching international junkets to associate itself with "big name" European and Asian organizations and artists.

The organization's flamboyant and controversial director, whom I'll call Max, had become a wildly popular figure in the arts world and the topic of fierce debates. He also developed an incredible fiefdom. Max treated the organization's board very graciously but kept them in the dark on details. They really had little idea of what was happening.

From 1994 through the late 1990s, Max made a number of joint agreements with similar organizations around the world and formed multiple partnerships. Those efforts were often very expensive, with artists and materials being shipped around the world, budgets being blown, and revenues falling short of their targets. Let me give you a few examples.

In 1994, Max set up an arrangement with the director of a similar arts organization in the U.K., where each visited the other's facilities twice during the year and was referred to as a visiting lecturer. This seemed to feed the ego needs of both these individuals, and they anticipated easily covering their travel and housing costs via revenue from the lectures they would schedule. While it no doubt added another impressive-sounding entry into each of their résumés, there was really minimal interest in these lectures, and the revenue expectations were substantially missed. It does reveal the inflated self-assessment that Max had of himself.

In 1995, Max developed a partnership with a similar arts organization in Japan and one in South Korea to fund a traveling group who had agreed to visit all three of the organizations. This was an expensive proposition, and here in the U.S. it was inadequately marketed and led to very disappointing turnouts. Frankly, Max seemed most interested in the very positive publicity of achieving such an impressive international arrangement; he showed minimal interest in ensuring excellent execution of the eventual events.

In the summer of 1997, Max organized a trip to Europe that included London, Madrid, and Paris. The purpose was to nail down the details of some emerging partnerships. In London, he met with his counterpart. Each brought along numerous staff. The resulting large group held a two-day meeting at the very luxurious Le Meridien Grosvenor House, located on ritzy Park Lane in London. Nothing was too good for this egocentric director; Max wanted to make sure that his European counterparts realized how cosmopolitan and upscale he was. The costs, needless to say, were out of sight.

The same thing happened in Madrid, this time at the five-star Hotel Melia Madrid Princesa. Again, the group enjoyed nothing but the finest food and wine and stayed in the hotel's finest suites. Max repeated this scenario in Paris at the prestigious Hôtel Royal Monceau near the Arc de Triomphe on the Champs-Elysées. Upon his return to the U.S., the board was eager to find out what kind of revenue potential existed from these three partnerships. Unfortunately, he had come back with nothing concrete. But he had one astronomical bill as a result of this incredible junket. In fact, the budget of this arts organization more than doubled from 1995 to 1998; the program was out of control.

In 1998, the organization named a new chairman of the board. Yet he and the other board members remained outside of the director's fiefdom. They were somewhat in awe of Max's reputation and personality and the prestige of the organization in the arts world. The new chairman frankly enjoyed having his picture in the paper next to Max, who had achieved almost rock-star status in the arts world.

By 2000, however, the organization had exhausted its financial reserves and was depending on future gifts, which were far from certain. Its profligate ways came to a head in September 2002, when the director proposed to the board of trustees an aggressive new spending plan for 2003. At last, the chairman blew his stack. Arts organizations around the country had not been faring well, given the soft economy of 2000 to 2002 and the country's fears post–September 11. The organization awoke to a huge financial crunch by the end of 2002 as the number of visitors, particularly from abroad, plummeted, along with contributions from patrons.

The chairman at last was forced to confront the top-tier fiefdom that Max had created. In essence, Max was told: "Either you bring this organization's financial affairs into order or start looking for another job." A few months later, the chairman told me: "What we had was an institution that was overly aggressive and a board that enjoyed the notoriety and didn't get into the details. We became overly impressed by our success, and we began to think we were better than we were and tended to ignore the basics of revenue and cost."

Max came back with a revised budget that was half the budget of

2000 and specified several major cuts as well as a reallocation of funds to clear up old debts. At last, the board had broken through Max's fiefdom and worked with him on how to manage the budget affairs and the activities of the organization into the future.

But it took action at the board level to take apart this top-tier fiefdom.

THE GROUP FIEFDOM

Perhaps the most harmful and common fiefdom in business today is the group fiefdom, where a relatively small group of people forms around some common task, responsibility, or objective. There are examples in recent years of group fiefdoms that were extremely harmful to the organization in which they resided.

At Enron, a small group of people in finance engineered incredibly intricate financial structures and formed an impenetrable fiefdom around its activities. In their book *The Smartest Guys in the Room*, Bethany McLean and Peter Elkind go into great detail about this group fiefdom and how it shielded its activities from most other groups in the company, including the very top management as well as the board of directors.

The incredible aggressiveness of this fiefdom and its desire for independence is illustrated in the following from the McLean and Elkind book. It describes how the Enron finance team convinced Enron executives as well as their board to agree to an exemption from Enron's code of ethics and to allow members of the finance team to significantly benefit from these private partnerships (even though they tried to play down the amount they would benefit):

> On the morning of Friday, June 18, 1999, Skilling (the president and COO at the time) and Fastow (the CFO) walked over to Ken Lay's office (the chairman and CEO at the time) for a discussion of the deal that would give birth to LJM (the first of the private partnerships). Fastow's role in the new private partnership would require an exemption from Enron's code of ethics, which barred employees from profiting from any company that did business with Enron but allowed the CEO

to waive the provision if the arrangement "does not adversely affect the best interest of the company." Lay agreed to grant the waiver but wanted the board of directors to ratify his decision.

Ten days later, LJM was brought before a special meeting of the Enron directors; most participated by phone. As Fastow explained it, his personal involvement in the new partnership was an active altruism, an unfortunate but necessary ingredient to attract outside investors to LJM. In materials that had been sent to the directors, he insisted that even though he would serve as LJM's general partner, he would person- ally receive "no current or future (appreciated) value" from the Enron stock it held; if Enron's shares continued to rise, those gains would all go to his limited partners.

Fastow did note, however, that he would receive a $500,000 annual management fee plus more than half the returns on any assets in LJM. Fastow also told the board that PricewaterhouseCoopers would be issu- ing a fairness opinion affirming that the deal was fair to Enron. (Fas- tow neglected to mention that the firm was also being paid by LJM to work on the deal.) With nary a dissenting vote—or even any discussion of how to monitor the conflict—the directors passed a resolution exempt- ing Enron's CFO from the company's code of ethics. Even with several other items on the agenda, the meeting was over in just an hour.

To show how protective it was of its activities and any detailed data describing those activities, McLean and Elkind report the following concerning an Enron board finance committee meeting just prior to the Palm Beach, Florida, October 2000 board meeting:

Enron had generated 3,000 separate corporate entities, more than 800 of them in off-shore jurisdictions like the Cayman Islands. Enron's cor- porate tax return for 2000 ran to 13 volumes.

But such details weren't of concern to the Enron board. In Palm Beach, Fastow didn't hand out any documents or approval sheets to the directors, as he routinely did on Enron deals—and none of the board members demanded any. He didn't mention the size of LJM3 (the most recent private partnership—a billion dollars) or discuss the returns or his personal compensation from the first two private partnerships. But he did explain how Enron had "largely mitigated" his conflict—and would do so in the future.

It is amazing that this amount of complexity was left unprobed by the board. On the other hand, you also see how this small fiefdom of financial personnel was making it very difficult to do any kind of probing. The authors McLean and Elkind cite additionally in their book:

Much later, Enron's top executives and directors insisted that certain key information about the Raptors (another one of the special purpose entities developed by the finance group)—information that would have set off alarms—was deliberately withheld from them.

Enron is unfortunately not the only large organization that ended in a catastrophe due to small groups of individuals forming impenetrable fiefdoms and taking the company's livelihood in their own hands. A huge amount has been written about Arthur Andersen and how a small group of its employees eventually caused the destruction of the company. It appears from the reports in the popular press that the situation at WorldCom was similar.

Before these group fiefdoms were identified and dismantled, catastrophic damage was done to shareholders, to the brands, and to investor confidence. A huge number of jobs were lost, investors lost billions of dollars, and a dark shadow of shame touched all of business as these organizations collapsed.

THE PROTECTED FIEFDOM

Protected fiefdoms occur when a top executive or a board sanctions, harbors, or even creates a fiefdom and provides long-term protection of the fiefdom by sheltering it from financial or strategic scrutiny and, in general, ensuring a hands-off approach to it.

To be clear, a protected fiefdom is different from a top-tier fiefdom. In the latter case, one individual at the top of a particular organization is running the show and keeping his management out of things and is truly the feudal lord of the fiefdom. With a protected fiefdom, you have an individual who is not really involved in the activities of the fiefdom; however, people reporting to him or her are, and they make sure that their fiefdoms operate as they wish. The leader, therefore, is not the feudal lord; but by allowing fiefdoms run by other feudal lords to exist, he or she is, in fact, enabling their continued growth.

In a Fortune 500 general merchandising retailer whom I am familiar with, an overbearing and flamboyant vice president whom I'll call Mark stepped forward in 1998 and convinced the company to launch an Internet service that would make all the products the retailer stocked in its stores available online. The new business unit reported to Mark, who claimed the Internet business unit was the future of the company and, as such, deserved massive investment.

The Internet business unit hired employees mostly with backgrounds in information technology as well as MBA degrees. Like so many Internet-focused business ventures in 1998 and 1999, the newly formed group was massively overconfident.

This group recommended that a huge data center be built with the capacity to handle the volume they were expecting three and four years into the future. Of course, the projections were based on nothing more than the Internet hype that was so prevalent at the time. Mark lacked knowledge of information systems; therefore, he was afraid to challenge some of the technology-related proposals being generated by the "youngsters" in his group who were driving the business venture.

In addition, Mark's logistics folks were arguing for increased warehouse space. They proposed three additional facilities: one on the East Coast, one in the Midwest, and one in California. Betting on the revenue and volume projections cited earlier, they took the point of view that their business model was completely different from the existing retailing business and, consequently, they needed to build completely separate warehouses from those of the ongoing retailing business. With every step down this expensive path, Mark's ego got larger (and it was already enormous to begin with). He began to genuinely believe that Internet-savvy marketing, logistics, and information-technology wizards would be the saviors of the company as the world transitioned to online.

Vis-à-vis marketing, the MBAs argued that they needed their own trademark, while also using the trusted trademark of the parent in the background; they asked that the company spend whatever it would take to make the new trademark well known on a national basis. They advocated spending almost two hundred million dollars over a four-year period to establish a recognizable brand. Again, Mark didn't want to ruffle the feathers of his prima donnas (and challenge their fiefdoms). He figured they had a much better sense of the Internet phenomenon than he did (although he would never admit that). Consequently, he backed their proposal and confronted top management with this incredible budget request.

As you can see, Mark acted as the group's protector from the common-sense questions of top management, and he certainly wasn't doing the questioning himself. His people were clearly a protected group; and given all the hype about the Internet swirling around business at the time, the business unit was doing whatever it wanted to do.

When the Internet bubble began to burst in mid-2000, Mark continued to protect the Internet business unit by convincing top management that this was good for the company. He argued that as new firms in Internet retailing fell by the wayside, they would leave the business open to their Internet efforts because of the trusted trademark name of the long-established parent company.

Mark got away with protecting this group for another year before top management lost patience. The Internet business unit was losing increasing amounts of money, and top management finally decided that they had had enough. The Internet group was closed down, and Mark was let go. It was an extraordinarily expensive and painful lesson to learn.

I have seen other examples where the protector of a fiefdom is the CEO. In one instance, the fiefdom was a group of high-flying scientists who the CEO felt were about to make an important breakthrough in the world of fuel cells. Nothing materialized over the next ten years except the generation of bad morale in R&D. The protected scientists spent most of their time out on the academic lecture circuit, convincing others and themselves of their importance. The CEO finally had to give in to the senior VP of R&D and allow him to dismantle the group.

Each of these six categories of fiefdoms results from some very basic human behaviors or tendencies. Each of them can damage the company, sometimes to a surprising extent. But the fiefdom syndrome *can* be controlled.

2 FIEFDOMS AND HUMAN NATURE

I BELIEVE THERE are three basic human tendencies hardwired in every human being that seem to result in fiefdoms.

1. We have an innate need to control the data or information that reflects on our work.
2. We have a natural desire to be independent and in control of our destiny.
3. We have a natural tendency to exaggerate the quality of our work and its importance to our organization.

It's crucial to understand how fiefdoms come to be in order to be able to spot tendencies in the workplace early on that can lead to fiefdoms, and institute practices to discourage them from growing.

Fiefdoms can pose serious problems for both individuals and organizations: Costs can explode, performance can be compromised, and employee potential can be stifled. By identifying behavior that can lead to fiefdoms, managers can create a system of checks and balances to prevent such behavior from taking hold.

BEHAVIOR #1: CONTROLLING THE DATA

The majority of people want to do well in the workplace. They want their organizations to do well too. As a result, they are highly motivated to be involved in the generation of data or information that reflects on their performance within the company. That desire to do well is good as long as the information about performance remains objective. Unfortunately, that's where problems can occur.

To demonstrate that they are doing well, employees naturally look for ways to control the information about them that is used to evaluate their success, or that of their group or division. In talking about their performance with superiors, they tend to want to present information that shows them and their group, division, or company in a good light.

Fiefdoms at times emerge when people place more energy and emphasis on demonstrating that they are doing well than on changing their behavior to improve their actual performance.

At Procter & Gamble, during my years in brand management, one of my early assignments was working in a four-person brand group to market Sure deodorant/antiperspirant. Our job was to be the advocate for that brand within the company. The brand group is responsible for developing strategy, product direction, and marketing ideas to grow market share and revenue. In essence, the brand groups act as advocates for the brand to top management, which makes the decisions on what to fund, based on their goals for the entire company.

When you're an advocate for a particular brand, you are very sensitive to any negative comments about the business success of the brand. I remember one month we got the disappointing news that the Sure brand market share was flat versus the previous year. We hadn't grown our market share a whit! Naturally, top management began asking all kinds of questions about what we were going to do to get the brand growing again.

We reacted very defensively. We had generated all kinds of data that demonstrated that we were making good progress in the areas of our business that we felt were most important.

For example, we were growing market share on the Sure stick form, the smallest but fastest-growing segment in the antiperspirant market. Of course, we also were losing market share on the aerosol spray—the largest, but rapidly declining, part of the market. Our large but slowly declining share of the antiperspirant-spray segment basically canceled out our small but fast-growing share of the stick segment.

You can predict what happened after our brand group reported that flat market share. We were called to the group vice president's (whom I'll call Harry) office to have a chat about the Sure business. We were given one day's notice. We madly pulled together all the charts that supported the fact that the antiperspirant/deodorant market was moving to the stick form as the preferred method of application. We documented how sprays were declining and tossed in a few charts showing that the roll-on segment was small and probably wasn't going anywhere. We sliced and diced the data in any number of ways to put our best foot forward in showing how we were managing the brand.

The Sure brand group was part of the health and beauty aid division that had been reporting to Harry for several years. He was a seasoned Procter & Gamble veteran and a gracious but tough businessperson. He had been through the regulatory wars associated with aerosol sprays in the antiperspirant/deodorant industry and was instrumental in getting key changes made to the propellants to make them environmentally safe. Bottom line, Harry really knew the aerosol business. I'm sure he viewed the stick business as a distraction at that time.

To our surprise, he listened intently to all we had to say, and I think he was even a bit impressed at some of the charts we had developed to demonstrate the growth of Sure in stick form.

After going through all of our exhibits, he sat back in his chair in his paneled office and said, "You know, ladies and gentlemen, you're making this too complicated. All I want to know is when does the total market share of Sure get out of the doldrums and start to grow significantly?" The brand manager of the group, as well as the division vice president, fumbled around for an answer, but to be honest, we had no fancy exhibits to address this critical point. We said we would get back to him with a memo that outlined our plans to get the Sure business growing, and we humbly exited the office.

Basically, our brand group had been exhibiting fiefdom-like tendencies. We didn't want to hear people say we weren't doing well or that our market share was flat. We all were working very hard, convinced that based on our data, we were doing much better than management believed. The truth was, however, that we were flat compared to the previous year, and that was all that mattered. We needed to grow the Sure brand somehow, and we weren't doing it. We were hunting for excuses so that we could feel good. Thank goodness Procter & Gamble had aggressive, hands-on management that wouldn't let us off the hook with our complicated explanation of why we thought we were doing what we should.

If the brand group had controlled *all* the data (which it didn't), we probably could have gotten away with our explanation of our progress, and we wouldn't have been as driven to grow our market share. We would have convinced ourselves that we were doing the right thing by growing market share of the stick segment, and we might have dismissed concerns about losing market share in the spray segment.

In order to control fiefdoms, companies need company-wide dissemination of data and information among their key employees. The same key measures of performance must be available to the troops and to top management. Top management should demand improvement in those key areas while guiding the troops on how to use the detailed data to see where they should be generating improvement.

The problem with fiefdoms that control key data is they make it difficult for top management to figure out what is going on in the organization. When a fiefdom controls all the data, it will present the pieces that show as positive a picture as possible. As a result, it will be hard to get a clear read of how the company, or a specific division, is doing. When fiefdoms control key data and present too rosy a picture, they effectively eliminate the sense of urgency needed to generate change and improvement that some of those key measures might suggest.

KEY BUSINESS DATA AND PERFORMANCE MEASURES

In every organization, it is important to share key information and measurements across the enterprise. When the right information is widely available, the leaders of the organization can easily see what is going on in each of their businesses. Subsidiaries or divisions in other parts of the country or world can be compared to one another. More important, a company's businesses can be compared to its competitors'. The CEO or boss can determine whether or not operations are running on all cylinders, while leaving the responsibility for generating growth to the individual business units.

I'm not suggesting a company centralize everything. Rather, I'm arguing that vital data and standards to measure performance must be available to the business units as well as to top management, so that everyone can understand the overall progress of the company. This will benefit all stakeholders. Individuals can see how their unit is doing and what they must do to improve its performance; top management can see the performance of the various groups.

Fiefdoms tend to emerge as a result of the natural human tendency to control information. This is precisely what happened at Microsoft's international subsidiaries, as I discussed in Chapter 1. Their goal wasn't to deceive management; it was to better present their business, consistent with their biases. It satisfied their need to believe they were successful and had sound plans in place.

This is similar to what Lou Gerstner observed when he joined IBM. Why does this happen? It's only natural that when a group controls the information about its performance, it has a chance to look it over and determine how to best present it or piece it together. If necessary, a group can generate alternative measures that better accentuate its success.

MARKETING CONTROLS THE DATA

In the early '90s, when I was a senior vice president of marketing at Procter & Gamble, we had several truly global brands. However, P&G's marketing plans were created and executed country by country. Top management determined certain elements of the marketing of the company's global brands, but much of the marketing was the responsibility of the individual subsidiaries, who understood the local needs of their country. Each subsidiary knew it was responsible for coming up with ways to grow these global brands, and each knew that top management would compare the progress of these brands country by country.

As I would go from country to country and ask about, say, Head and Shoulders shampoo, I was struck by the incredible creativity used by each subsidiary to convince me that the brand was doing well.

In Italy, when I asked the folks in the marketing department about Head and Shoulders, they gave me a detailed presentation that showed new ratings on various attributes of the product from one of their market research studies. They were extremely proud that compared to a year ago, their rating on "controls dandruff" was still higher than their competitors'. And their ratings on "great-looking hair" and "hair not dry or brittle" had each gone up about eight points. They had still not reached the levels of the pure cosmetic shampoos, but they were within striking distance, which certainly wasn't the case a year earlier. They went on to show me the television advertising that they had been using over the last ten months. They offered all kinds of arguments about how that advertising worked to improve these ratings without hurting the dandruff-control reputation of the brand.

Wondering what the business looked like, I asked to see the revenue and market share information. Both were down roughly 5 percent versus a year ago. When I probed into what was going on, they made a lot of excuses about the competition spending significantly more money on advertising. I then asked about promotion activity. Eventually, I uncovered the fact that they had blown the execution of two of their four key promotions over the last twelve months and that sales would probably tell me about the problems that they were having with the Head and Shoulders brand group. What I was seeing was typical of fiefdom-like activities. Our Italian subsidiary was almost incapable of being objective about what really had gone on with regard to their Head and Shoulders business.

I then went on to Germany and found they had done the opposite of what I experienced in Italy. They started out discussing their market share information—they had achieved marvelous gains compared to the prior year. The basic business numbers were terrific. Then I probed deeper and asked them about their attribute ratings as well as their marketing costs. The brand image ratings seemed to be at the same levels as a year ago; the competition hadn't really made any significant progress against Head and Shoulders. On the other hand, when I got the German team to present the marketing-cost information, it became clear that they had essentially bought the business. They had increased the number of promotions over the last twelve months from four to six and increased their promotion spending by more than 40 percent.

After probing further, I began to better understand the health of the Head and Shoulders brand in this country. Basically, the Germans weren't satisfied with their advertising. It was only holding their ratings at the same level of the competition rather than improving them. But it took me a while to understand this. I learned that to get the business rolling, they had thrown a bunch of promotion dollars into the brand. Unfortunately, that's short-term thinking. Realizing this, I began a discussion of what they were doing to improve their advertising. Again, the brand group was acting like a typical fiefdom; they weren't really up front with me about what was going on. We should have spent all of our meeting time focused on the issue of how to improve their advertising. Instead, we wasted a lot of time unraveling all of the data that eventually got me to the core issue.

Next, I went to France. They started their Head and Shoulders review by showing me some new advertising and a lot of focus-group information that indicated the focus groups thought the new advertising was very provocative and persuasive. When I asked them how long this advertising had been on the air, they indicated that they hadn't begun to air it yet! They were just preparing the final production of the advertising. Then I asked to see their business results over the last twelve months. It showed that Head and Shoulders's market share was down about 8 percent; their revenue was down a similar percentage. Only then did I understand why they had been focusing so heavily on the new advertising. Rather than burying their declining revenue, they should have told me up front.

So I looked again at the advertising they were about to produce. The more we looked at it, the more I became concerned that it was a bit too focused on great-looking hair; it didn't provide enough of a reminder about the unsurpassed dandruff-control characteristics of Head and Shoulders. I asked to see some of the standard measures used within Procter & Gamble to measure the potential of advertising. They indicated that the creative folks at the ad agency looked down on that kind of testing; they strongly preferred to use focus groups to measure the potential impact of the ads. I had to remind them that time after time we had seen focus groups mislead us with regard to the impact of advertising. They finally, reluctantly, agreed that they would field the standard test battery for the new advertising before they went into final production.

This is yet another example of how organizations try to put their best foot forward and give the impression that they are running their businesses well. Our French subsidiary should have said up front, "Our business is sick; we know it's the advertising; we're developing new advertising, and we're trying to get it on the air as fast as possible." Then we could have immediately begun a discussion of how effective we believed the new advertising would be, and what kind of changes could be implemented to strengthen it. Unfortunately, fiefdoms try to cut off that kind of productive dialogue.

Let me point out that centralizing the management of these consumer brands was not the answer. On the other hand, it is important to understand whether the organization is making progress with its business. To gauge whether there is progress, core data such as market share, revenue, profitability, and brand-attribute ratings need to be measured in a standard way from country to country. Only by making these measures available to top management—while realizing that the brand group's job in a particular region or country is to come up with creative marketing and solid product initiatives—can the right balance of corporate control and individual responsibility be achieved.

PERSONAL FIEFDOM

This tendency to control data can also occur at the managerial level, at the department level, and even at the executive level. In a pharmaceuticals company I consulted with (which I'll call Skylark), a high-level employee in research and development (whom I will call John Doe) controlled the negotiations for all research partnerships at the company. He handled the dialogue with the business unit that was championing the partnership, as well as the dialogue with the outside companies or universities that were the potential partners. John created an incredible personal fiefdom based on his control of key data and relationships.

How did this happen? First, he was perceived as absolutely superb in negotiating these arrangements. He had a great track record within the company, and some of the deals were extremely complex from a patent and future-revenue-sharing standpoint. Most of Skylark's business units quickly concluded that they needed him to do the negotiations because they weren't skilled enough with the nuances of the law and finance required to make such deals.

Unfortunately, John made things far more complex than he needed to. One of the ingredients of success in such a partnership is simplicity and clarity with regard to what is going to occur and why. This applies not only to keeping the research scientists abreast of what will happen to them after the agreement is made but also to clarifying the legal and financial aspects of the arrangement.

John was extremely skilled at negotiating and prided himself on knowing how to handle complex deals. But he used this complexity as a negotiating tool, creating the perception on the part of the R&D folks working with him that they couldn't handle it alone.

There was one particular partnership that demonstrated what an impenetrable fiefdom John Doe had created. One division of Skylark was striving to set up a joint research effort with a particular university and a small biotech firm. Skylark wanted to get access to three university researchers who were leading the basic research; the biotechnology company had patents that were important to Skylark if it planned to launch a product in this area.

Though John Doe held meeting after meeting with the other parties, it eventually emerged that he had not addressed one of the key issues—the need for a long-term contract with the university regarding the three researchers. Instead, he got the university to promise a level of spending for a lengthy period of time. But clauses in the agreement clearly permitted the university to swap the three key researchers with replacements after two years. John Doe had not vetted the language with top management in Skylark. It caused a huge problem, given that Skylark was virtually committed to the partnership. In addition, at a very late stage of discussion, it became clear that John had agreed to give the biotechnology company a royalty rate far higher than what Skylark's top management was prepared for.

The basic problem was that John was far too confident in his abilities; he prided himself on being knowledgeable about every aspect of Skylark. He was a classic one-person fiefdom with a very large ego. He took over the negotiations in such an independent, self-sufficient, overconfident manner that he would often agree to terms far beyond his authority. In some cases, he misrepresented what Skylark wanted to do—not deliberately, but because he wasn't as knowledgeable as he believed he was. Yet John blamed top management as well as the particular division handling the deal for any miscommunication, indicating they were doing a lousy job in prepping him with regard to what they wanted.

It was obvious that John had built up a level of independence and autonomy in putting together these partnership deals that was not in the best interest of the company. He controlled all of the data and information in all of the negotiations. While John seemed like a terrific asset to Skylark, it became obvious to management that in some of the transactions, the business unit had far more background and ability to understand the nuances of what was being discussed than John did. Unfortunately, they were being blocked from the dialogue because John didn't want others to evaluate the quality of his negotiations, or the quality of the eventual deal.

In later chapters I talk about how companies and managers can deal with such a tough situation as well as how to avoid putting yourself in the situation in the first place.

FIEFDOMS AT THE DIVISIONAL LEVEL

When divisions emerge as strong fiefdoms, they can make it very difficult for the company to coordinate its activities and function at a high level. At one university I know of, the fund-raising and development efforts were in chaos. The individual colleges or departments had gained control of the fund-raising activities, and each worked independently, minimizing its interaction with the university's central office.

The problem with these fiefdoms was the fact that each maintained the alumni database for its particular college, and the colleges were highly possessive of them.

Each of the colleges ran up unnecessary expenses with respect to its computer systems, development staff, and mailings to alumni, because each did everything independently. Moreover, each of the colleges occasionally launched its own fund-raising campaign, utterly uncoordinated with the university's efforts to increase the size of its endowment.

This situation began to spin out of control. The university's development office decided to launch a large-scale campaign to raise money for the university's general endowment fund—funds that would not be earmarked for a particular college or scholarship program.

The engineering school got wind of the program and beat the university to the punch. It sent materials to its alumni stating that the university would be launching a major fund-raising campaign. It encouraged all the engineering graduates to earmark their funds for the engineering college, and, if they wished, to designate a particular department to receive funding—such as chemical engineering, or even a particular professor and his or her research efforts. The way the letter was worded, it sounded as if the engineering school's solicitation were blessed by the university and that the upcoming campaign was an effort to help the individual colleges be successful in their own campaigns.

The medical school also found out about the upcoming university campaign. Four months prior to its launch, the medical school persuaded the university to turn over its alumni list without saying what it was to be used for. It was, in fact, used to launch a major solicitation to every graduate of the university (not just of the medical school). It explained to the alumni that the national ranking of the medical school was improving, and that the university's upcoming campaign was an opportunity to push the medical program into the top ten nationally by giving it the financial capability to hire several world-class researchers. It suggested that the alumni designate their funds for whichever medical programs interested them.

Alumni of the university, and in particular alumni of the engineering college, received several solicitations: one from the university, one from the engineering college, and a third from the medical school.

As is the case with a lot of development efforts, when the people solicited sense that an institution's efforts are uncoordinated and out of control, they tend to take the envelopes and throw them in the garbage.

That's apparently what happened here. After the first twelve months, the university achieved only 40 percent of its goal.

Weak management within the university development office and the absence of an overall fund-raising plan by the chancellor of the university allowed the individual colleges to form powerful fiefdoms. The answer, again, is not to centralize everything but, rather, to achieve the right balance between control and flexibility. For example, basic data on individual alumni, such as history of giving, and the university's prior contacts with an individual should be "owned" by the university but made available to the individual colleges and the central development office. A database on the various initiatives and special campaigns should be available to all the colleges in the university. Strong leadership in the university's development office would have coordinated such campaigns so that they did not overlap or collide.

Given the absence of such leadership, the fiefdoms went off on their own and did things as they pleased.

FIEFDOMS IN GOVERNMENT

The government is a prime example of an organization filled with fiefdoms. Following the events of September 11, 2001, the public discovered that unwillingness among government departments to share information relating to national security had been going on for years. The Immigration and Naturalization Service (INS), the CIA, and the FBI all had pieces of information about terrorists and terrorist activity, but each of them worked separately. A sophisticated biometric fingerprint identification system exists at INS, and a completely different one is used by the FBI, yet the two systems are in no way coordinated. Who is the loser here? The American people. Their tax money is being wasted, and their security is compromised as a result.

As the media has reported, organizations such as the FBI aggressively defend their need to maintain their own databases and not share them with other government agencies. Because of these fiefdoms, Congress passed the Homeland Security Act. The new department that resulted faces a major challenge in breaking these fiefdoms up so that security information can be shared.

Such fiefdoms can be potentially devastating to the U.S.—an agency could miss an opportunity to stop a terrorist act because key information is never shared.

BEHAVIOR # 2: INDEPENDENCE

The second human tendency that I've found leads to fiefdoms is our desire to be as independent as possible and to run our own affairs. The positive aspect of this tendency is that it means people assume responsibility. The downside occurs when people act in a completely independent fashion—separate from the best interests of the organization—instead of playing a cooperative and coordinated role.

This human tendency toward independence causes companies and organizations to become fragmented as they evolve and grow. Foreign or regional subsidiaries, business divisions, and even small departments become more and more independent.

As companies grow, it is natural for leaders to want to delegate responsibility to others. And therein lies the problem. What often happens is that delegation becomes so complete that there are very few links back to the management of the organization.

These two factors—people wanting autonomy and leaders delegating responsibility—can lead to organizational fragmentation and the emergence of fiefdoms. Without management's knowledge of the fundamentals of its subsidiaries or business units, large and diversified companies can end up as nothing more than a disparate, loosely knit group of independent fiefdoms barely held together by a bureaucratic and inefficient structure. When managers running business divisions or subsidiaries start to see themselves as "top dogs" in their own small worlds, they begin adding resources to become as self-sufficient as possible, and to increase distance from the "head office."

In such situations, costs soar. Perplexed managers may have trouble tracking the problem to its root causes because the "lord" of the fiefdom controls the data that would allow the head office to understand what behaviors must stop. As executives find themselves with less and less control over these fiefdoms, a management headache can become a management migraine.

Because employees wish to be as independent as possible, they often decide they need their own IT resources, HR department, and manufacturing arm, and unique marketing approaches to address their particular business problems. This can lead to an explosion of staffing as the management of the fiefdom duplicates efforts that should be handled by the company's headquarters.

Remember, I'm not arguing for total centralization of business. I believe it is important to delegate responsibilities and it is appropriate to split the organization into reasonably sized business units and subsidiaries. However, companies need to exercise overall control so that top management can achieve revenue and profit goals, contain costs, manage headcount, establish common policies for developing staff, and create common performance-appraisal processes. For example, it is simply not effective for salespeople in a subsidiary to run their own HR department or IT center. These functions should be executed in a disciplined manner across the organization, while allowing the business units and departments enough flexibility to do what they need to do to win customers and meet their goals in their areas.

Once again, it is a question of balance. Pieces of a larger organization should not become so independent that they begin to look like stand-alone companies.

WHERE CHAOS RULES

I recently consulted with a major food and beverage corporation that I will call Good Foods. Each of its five separate business units marketed separate kinds of products, but the products in all of the business units carried the same Good Foods trademark.

Some companies, such as Procter & Gamble, have decided not to use their corporate name on products marketed by individual business units. Sure is marketed as Sure, not Sure from Procter & Gamble. Other companies, such as Microsoft, carry the company name on a majority of their products, while also using a product name (such as Windows or

Office). When the corporate trademark is used on all of the company's products, there is a risk of the trademark brand being diluted if the individual brands take their marketing in different directions.

At Good Foods, there was no strong corporate marketing effort to provide guidelines on what that trademark should stand for. For example, at Microsoft in the mid-'90s, we were very specific with the individual product groups as to what the Microsoft trademark stood for. We developed a brand strategy statement much like P&G had for its brands. This is the brand strategy statement Microsoft utilized:

Microsoft software leads the way in providing access to new ways of thinking and communicating.

In addition, we created a character statement that isolated the character elements that we wanted the world to attach to the Microsoft name. Those character elements were:

Innovative, intelligent, positive, honest/honorable, and interested in who you are and what you do.

There were specific corporate-wide guidelines for how the name Microsoft would appear (color, font, and placement on the package), as well as which background colors were acceptable.

What all of this meant to the typical Microsoft marketing person was that his or her advertising, if it used the Microsoft name, had to be consistent with the above strategy and character statement. The strategy made it clear that Microsoft should stand for leadership in software and the providing of new and exciting ways to get work done and communicate with others. This character statement set the overall tone of the advertising.

Good Foods, on the other hand, had no overall strategy statement or character statement for their trademark. Therefore, the five divisions were completely on their own in terms of how they utilized that trademark. The result was chaos.

In one of its divisions, there were several food products that used a health strategy. The advertising focused on good nutrition, responsibility, and taking care of yourself. The tone was professional and emphasized the importance of making good choices and doing what is right for your overall health. The corporate trademark was used both at the beginning and the end of this advertising.

Startlingly, another division marketed a set of beverage products that focused on fun. It had all kinds of unusual flavors, and it used animated characters to represent each of them. The advertising was whimsical and upbeat and intended to challenge the viewer to try something new. Yet it, too, used the Good Foods trademark in its advertising. It was a confusing message when taken in context with the company's health products.

To make matters worse, Good Foods had another set of food products that focused on great taste, urging consumers to treat themselves to something special. Although Good Foods didn't overtly acknowledge it, these products were high in fat and calories; the advertising focused on making exceptions to your diet and treating yourself to a great-tasting, well-deserved reward. Again, the same corporate trademark was used in the advertising.

Each of these products used its own advertising agency. There was no coordination between creative personnel regarding the trademark. As a result, there was an incredibly broad and confusing set of images associated with the same Good Foods trademark.

The corporation should have decided, as Procter & Gamble did, that none of these products should use the corporate trademark, but there was no central marketing conscience to drive such a decision.

Good Foods also had no guidelines regarding market research to gauge the success of its advertising. There was no clearance process regarding the overall strategy of each of these products. Marketing organizations in each of these five divisions operated as completely separate fiefdoms. The fiefdoms were in total control.

FIEFDOMS WITHIN THE MEDICAL WORLD

Hospitals are another hotbed (no pun intended) for the creation of fiefdoms. Within a hospital, there typically are a number of very different groups of employees who don't necessarily see themselves as connected to the hospital as a whole.

In my interaction with one hospital, the physicians had outstanding credentials but as a group worked completely independently. Little data about their work was available. Yet they were constantly pushing for better facilities and asking management to bring on additional physicians. While they had some allegiance to the hospital, they operated as a unified group independent from the hospital itself.

The nursing group also was impressive, talented, and dedicated. However, when administrative or operational issues emerged that might change their world, they quickly banded together to form an impenetrable fiefdom. Like the physicians, they were always seeking better facilities and additional staff to take the pressure off their excessive workloads. As with the physicians, they could provide no data to demonstrate how severe their needs were with respect to their workload.

The hospital's individual department staffs, such as the operating room technicians, the in-house pharmacy, the information-technology staff, and the administration of the hospital itself, all operated with incredible independence. That's why the top management team's job was so difficult: They had to manage all of the individual fiefdoms. Ironically, that group operated independently as well, striving to launch marketing efforts to improve the perception of the overall service levels and reputation of the hospital but without working with the other departments to achieve those goals.

By themselves, none of the positions taken by the various groups was bad. However, when taken collectively, each was going off on its own, and the hospital management team had to face the nearly impossible task of getting all of these independent fiefdoms to collaborate in a way that could help the hospital be effective in its mission.

The community in which this hospital resided had a huge excess of beds. Consequently, some hospitals were going out of business, and it was clear that more mergers would take place. For this hospital, the idea of a merger was incredibly ugly. Most members of the board had been in place for well over ten years, and the hospital had a large endowment that the board thought cushioned them from the need for participation in any merger activities.

Before long, one of the larger hospitals in the community decided to go after them, suggesting a merger. This brought out the absolute worst in all of the fiefdoms. The physicians had their reasons for not participating, as did the emergency room group, the operating room group, the nurses, etc. The administration of the hospital knew that it was only a matter of time before consolidation occurred in the community, because there was so much excess capacity. They tried to get the various fiefdoms to pull together and seriously consider the merger, since it would be with one of the larger hospitals in the community, which happened to have a very strong reputation.

The board would have none of it. They heard from all the fiefdoms, who wanted no part of it. The board themselves had become a fiefdom of sorts, comforted by their large endowment and their inflated sense of the importance of the hospital. They had gotten quite comfortable with the hospital just cruising along.

So they fought off the merger and remained independent. Unfortunately, they held on to their independence too long and in the end had no alternative but to merge with one of the less reputable hospitals in the community because their business had degenerated so much.

It is the unique and narrow charter of each of the groups in a hospital—the operating room crew, the emergency room crew, the physicians, and the nurses—that makes fiefdoms such a natural entity within hospitals. To some extent, this problem is characteristic of the problem in the healthcare industry in general. It could easily be argued that the health insurance industry, the physicians, the nurses, and the hospitals each represents very strong fiefdoms, making it difficult for the U.S. healthcare system to work in a unified manner. There is no top management that can institute a structure across all those fiefdoms, allowing them to participate on the broad issues that affect the entire industry while still permitting them to execute their local responsibilities with excellence. Consequently, the fiefdoms get stronger and stronger, and healthcare staggers on as a rather out-of-control industry.

FIEFDOMS IN THE AIRLINE INDUSTRY

One could select almost any major U.S.-based carrier and see that its groups (pilots, flight attendants, and maintenance) operate as fiefdoms playing incredibly independent roles. It has proved to be a major heartache for the carriers and the industry.

In the spring of 2003, *The Wall Street Journal* reported that data disclosed in bankruptcy filings showed that American Airlines pilots flew an average of only thirty-nine hours per month in 2001. United Airlines held the record for the lowest number of pilot hours flown during that period. Its pilots flew an average of only thirty-six hours a month. The number of hours flown by pilots for the major airlines had been decreasing for years. The pilot fiefdoms have become more and more independent, pushing the airlines to add more resources to reduce their workload. These strong fiefdoms put tremendous pressure on airline management to increase salaries and retirement benefits, further pressuring the individual airlines and their ultimate sustainability.

Southwest Airlines has often been highlighted as a highly disciplined company in the industry and the only major carrier that was making significant profit. During this time, the profitability of Southwest actually exceeded the profitability of all the other major airlines combined. How did Southwest do it? They had a system that prevented the formation of the kind of fiefdoms I've discussed. They had solid direction from the top on what was going to be allowed and what was not. For example, their pilots averaged sixty-two hours a month, compared to the thirty-six hours for United and thirty-nine hours for American. Southwest simply explained to the team that they couldn't make any money flying the number of hours American, United, and the other airlines did. They explained why the pilots and the flight attendants and the mechanics should want the company to make a significant profit and be a healthy organization.

What did it take to break up the incredible fiefdoms at these major airlines? The risk of going bankrupt. At the height of American Airlines's problems in mid-2003, management made it clear that they simply could not continue to operate with the costs they were saddled with because of the pilots, flight attendants, and mechanics. Without major concessions, the airline would face financial disaster. At last, the fiefdoms woke up, realizing they were all part of a common company called American Airlines, and if they wanted the company to continue, they had to change their ways. Huge concessions were made (over 20 percent reduction in costs) by the three fiefdoms in their last-ditch attempt to help save the airline. And they have been successful, at least for the time being.

The sad part about these fiefdoms is that they lose any sense of belonging to the overall organization in which they reside. It's up to top management to make sure the right checks and balances are in place to fight off that kind of situation.

BEHAVIOR # 3: INFLATED SENSE OF SELF-WORTH

As a general rule, people tend to become complacent about their performance over time, focusing more on their strengths than on improving their weaknesses. Why is this? Humans naturally advocate for themselves. They want to succeed and they want to have others perceive that they are succeeding. It's just basic human nature. The fact is that it's hard for individuals to be objective about their work. They tend to be biased in a positive direction.

If you look at this tendency among a group of people isolated from the rest of their organization, you'll notice these people tend to form an inflated sense of self-worth. They blame any problems they are having on external forces, over which the group or individual claims to have no control.

In addition, the individuals within the fiefdom become blind to what is happening outside the walls of their "castle"; they don't see new competitive threats emerging. They lose their sense of paranoia and become smug about the future. They lack the necessary degree of motivation needed to watch what competitors are doing and what the future holds.

INFLATED SELF-WORTH AND DEC

Digital Equipment Corporation (DEC) was on top of the technology world in the late '70s and early '80s with its VAX minicomputer system, an immensely popular system ideal for departmental computing.

While the mainframe computer dominated the '60s and '70s, it was DEC's uniquely designed mini-mainframe with its small central processing unit that captured the attention of the corporate world. The system allowed numerous terminals to be wired to it and placed in the hands of people in various offices around a department. The central processing unit could be put in a closet and serve as the hub of that department's computing configuration. Individuals on one terminal could send messages and information to another person in the department who was wired to the central processing unit. Large files could be kept on the central processing unit and accessed by numerous members of the department. This design was wildly successful. This tool also became an ideal fiefdom configuration, enabling departments to separate themselves from the corporate mainframe and become totally independent.

DEC had the architectural win of the decade, catapulting it to the top of the technology industry in the '80s, driving its market cap from $5 billion in the late '70s to $25 billion in the mid-'80s. That was an astounding company valuation at the time, and DEC management became not just technology industry heroes but heroes to all of industry.

The management team was deservedly proud of its achievements. By the mid-1980s, the press portrayed DEC as the king of the industry, and management began to believe the hype. This blinded DEC from seeing a world where the minicomputer architecture could be knocked off by another computer architecture. This is an example of inflated self-assessment at its worst; it became evident when the personal computer gained momentum, as businesspeople networked their PCs together to talk to one another and access data sitting on servers. The networked personal-computer architecture trumped the minicomputer architecture. It was no longer necessary to think in the context of a departmental configuration. Personal computers could sprout throughout the entire organization, across all departments, with databases in numerous different servers around the company, allowing all the PCs access to that data for a fraction of the cost.

Meanwhile, DEC management was so caught up in the success of its VAX system that they couldn't conceive of anything surpassing it. DEC founder and CEO Ken Olson was the leader of this top-tier fiefdom. He made derogatory public statements about the personal computer, predicting that it would never amount to much. Those statements were a clear example of an inflated self-assessment. This is understandable considering that at the time Olson had been lauded as the hero of the industry after launching one of the most successful computer architectures in the history of the industry.

Given the length of time it took DEC to acknowledge the role of the personal computer, and the fact that the networked personal computers offered a better solution than minicomputers, DEC's business got very soft very fast. The company's market value plummeted from $25 billion back down to the $5-billion level where it started. By 1990 the organization was struggling to find a role in an industry that had passed it by. Eventually, DEC began to market its own personal computer, but it was no longer a major player in the information-technology industry.

Because of its inflated self-assessment of the VAX minicomputer, DEC didn't keep its competitive antenna up to look for the next big wave of change in the rapidly moving technology sector. DEC, which later on became known as Digital, ultimately was purchased by Compaq, a personal-computer maker, and Compaq was subsequently purchased by Hewlett-Packard.

A COLLEGE BOARD OF TRUSTEES THAT DID ITSELF IN

A good friend of mine is an incredibly loyal alumnus of the small private college he attended. He has kept me aware over several years of a problem at his school that was caused by its board of trustees. The college's executive committee of the board was very powerful, dominated by three individuals who had been on the board from ten to fifteen years. This was essentially an old boys' club that had outlived its usefulness.

The executive committee was a perfect example of a fiefdom that had suffered from a bad case of inflated self-worth. Over the years, the members had lost touch with students and faculty, and the overall quality of the college had badly atrophied. The president, who also had been there for well over ten years, was blocked on many issues by the fiefdom. And the president's motivation to tackle the fiefdom was low, since he was on a path to retirement in a few years.

The executive committee kept reminding itself of the greatness of the college and the strength of its programs, reliving the good old days even as they were losing relevance.

This handful of trustees tackled every issue that surfaced with an outdated value system and such an inflated sense of self-worth that they did not realize they had lost their vigor to raise the excellence level of the school.

Let me give you an example of just how bad it had gotten. For years, the head of the chemistry department was the chair of a group called the science steering committee, which included the heads of the departments of chemistry, physics, biology, and mathematics. This individual was going to retire within the next twelve months. The provost of the university argued that the replacement should come from outside the college—a strong performer who could revitalize the chemistry department and also potentially set the tone for the other science departments at the college. Clearly, the provost wanted to use this opportunity to move the college to another level.

Unfortunately, the head of the physics department had been around for more than two decades and had become quite friendly with several members of the college's executive committee of the board. He made it clear to the "old boys" that he should be made the head of the science steering committee and that a good friend of his on the chemistry faculty should be made the head of the chemistry department.

The president of the college had such a poor relationship with the executive committee of the board that he decided to avoid taking a position on the issue. He decided to simply go along with the head of the physics department and his suggested candidate to run the chemistry department, but he also saw the clear advantages of going outside and doing what the provost suggested. He told the executive committee that they had two great choices and that since he was retiring, they should make the decision.

As a result of its friendship with the head of physics, the executive committee did exactly as he suggested. The loser was the college, which ended up with a journeyman head of the science steering committee and an insider to run chemistry. Essentially, the executive committee fiefdom continued its shortsighted ways.

Rather than dealing with the growing problem, the president decided to move his retirement up one year. The problem came to a head when the board of trustees found it difficult to get quality candidates to interview for the upcoming presidential vacancy. As candidates emerged and came to the campus to meet with various members of the executive committee, they became disenchanted and lost interest. Informed alumni heard about the large number of candidates who had been put through the system; a group of highly involved alumni began to bind together and question the board about what was going on. The group of alumni eventually confronted the president just prior to his retirement. It became clear to him and the head of the alumni association that the executive committee had outlived its usefulness. Their fiefdom was badly damaging the college, and their inflated assessment of the college's reputation blocked their ability to find a leader who could take them to new heights. After all, they believed they had already reached those heights.

Eventually, the lame-duck president and the head of the alumni association confronted the fiefdom, got the chairman of the board to retire, and involved the remaining members of the board in restructuring the executive committee. As new players eager to massively overhaul the college jumped into the game, the fiefdom was beaten.

The three basic human tendencies that lead to fiefdoms will come into play in most organizations if you let them. However, with disciplined behavior, an organization can make sure such tendencies are identified, modified, and corrected before they damage the company.

PART II

DISCIPLINE AND CREATIVITY

3 THE SEVEN DISCIPLINES OF THE WELL-RUN CORPORATION

AT ITS HEART, a fiefdom lacks discipline. It can be corrected only if management adopts new behaviors that make discipline a priority.

There are seven key disciplines that must be instilled to eliminate fiefdoms. The first three are process-related and require an organization to institute precise ways to do things. The other four relate to behaviors—how activities are approached by groups and individuals. Taken together, these seven disciplines provide strong and efficient functional practices in the core areas of an organization.

THE PROCESS DISCIPLINES

1. THE DISCIPLINE OF CREATING LEAN GLOBAL PROCESSES AND ACCESSIBLE DATA COMPANY-WIDE

Fiefdoms tend to hoard and hide their data. They often try to create their own information systems to reflect how "unique" their territory or turf is and show how well they are doing, making it difficult for top management to determine the health of the fiefdom, and leading to significantly increased costs.

To fight this human tendency to control information, companies need to institute systems that disseminate all crucial data to the entire organization. Such systems should reach across every part of the organization and be extremely easy to access and use.

CLEANING UP A FINANCIAL MESS

Earlier I discussed how frustrated Bill Gates became when he had to wait several weeks at the end of each quarter to see how Microsoft's business was doing. Microsoft found that its subsidiaries overseas had become fiefdoms that controlled key financial data for their businesses and, in some cases, redefined the data or created new ways to measure performance—ways they claimed were superior to those in Redmond.

To tackle the problem, the finance organization assigned two employees to the task of developing an architecture for finance that would provide key financial data for the subsidiaries to run their business.

Microsoft decided that it needed to move fast and focus only on the basics, using this as an opportunity to eliminate complexity. The two people selected to lead the effort were strong, proven leaders with a thorough understanding of Microsoft's financials. They understood the issues and could quickly identify solutions.

One of these individuals was a highly talented finance veteran in his late thirties. The other was an eight-year veteran with Microsoft—a consistently strong performer from the information technology group with years of experience dealing with finance problems from an information systems perspective. The two understood Microsoft's challenge and its goal but from a different perspective.

What Microsoft lacked was a rich database that provided a variety of reports on revenue and cost. The revenue knowledge was extremely important to sales and the business units, as they gauged their progress in the marketplace. The information on costs was vital to all departments and groups. Naturally, both revenue and costs were critical to finance when it came time to close out a month or pull together a quarterly summary of the company's financials.

The two individuals developed a "global chart of accounts" and carefully defined all the cost "buckets" involved in executing the business. Next, they refined the personal computer user interface to make it easy for managers to retrieve the data needed to judge progress against a department's or business's goal.

But the duo and their small team would have failed without top management support. Steve Ballmer, who was an executive vice president at the time running worldwide sales and support, was a strong driver of a unified system across Microsoft's global sales organizations. Steve's strong involvement in defining the system, along with Bill's backing, created the required mandate for change. The large database that contained all of Microsoft's products and revenues by region and country enabled top management and the business units and subsidiaries to analyze revenue for any product for a given time period for a particular country. The database also made key cost data instantly available, accessible via Web-based menus.

In creating this design and implementation process, the two leaders didn't resort to committees or task forces. Because they knew the financial aspects of Microsoft, they knew how they wanted to create the systems. They were not interested in trying to find out what everybody wanted; instead, their goal was to build a system that met the minimum needs of the company and was extremely easy to use and quick to put in place.

Was there serious pushback on this approach? Yes. For example, our Italian general manager just couldn't understand why he had to give up some of his treasured methods of reporting on the business. My key role as the COO was to deal cordially with such questions while making it absolutely clear that we wanted to drive this system across the entire organization. We emphasized that while the individual business units and countries would have an opportunity to craft a few things on their own, the goal was to make this a company-wide system that *everyone* would use.

We also made it clear that we didn't want people in sales or in the product groups dreaming up new financial reporting schemes. We made it clear we were leaving that up to the finance organization, and to the small team we put in charge. We also made it clear that our goal was to reduce redundancies in the finance and IT areas that the subsidiaries and the business units had created. Too many of the units were duplicating functions that rightfully belonged in Redmond.

Sometimes you need a crisis in order to be able to implement the kind of radical change we implemented at Microsoft. The crisis I immediately focused on when we initiated this project was that we needed to demonstrate to our customers how our technologies could be used productively and how they could be implemented in a simple and effective manner. They also improved profitability—headcount decreased in staff areas such as IT, manufacturing, procurement, etc., for several years, even as the company's business was exploding.

The lean global process that provided easy access to key financial information had a significant impact on Microsoft's subsidiaries, providing them with up-to-date, clearly defined information at their fingertips. While the subsidiaries preferred to control the information themselves, they were impressed at how easy it was to get to and at how it simplified their lives. And the company could now close its books in a few days, with all the key data regularly collected and sitting in a database on a server in Microsoft's Redmond data center. That was in stark contrast to the ugly process of obtaining spreadsheets from each of the subsidiaries and then attempting to piece them together and figure out all the variables from those fiefdoms.

REDUCING IT SYSTEMS PROLIFERATION

An aerospace/defense firm I consulted for, which I'll call Zoom, found itself with more than 4,200 information systems supporting its business. This mess was choking the IT department, driving IT costs to 9 percent of net revenue (the industry average was about 3.5 percent). Each business unit became its own fiefdom; each developed a huge number of information systems that had minor impact on improving the company.

Zoom had fiefdoms within fiefdoms. To start, most of its business units acted as fiefdoms. They typically had their own procurement organization and their own manufacturing arm. Each of these departments within each business unit was doing its own thing: reporting its own data and creating expensive-to-maintain information systems that already existed in other business units.

One of the problems was that the company culture was very engineering-oriented. The employees loved to tinker with things like information technology. They built a lot of systems that they thought were clever and that affected the jobs of a few people around them. That was part of the reason for the explosion in systems. But the company's profit margins continued to sag year after year due to the incredible accumulating costs. And the company's stock price was getting clobbered due to its poor financial performance. This was the crisis that forced the company at long last to face the issue.

An individual I will call Sam worked in one of the product divisions. Sam was incredibly creative and managed a set of very successful aircraft navigation products with unique technology. Sam spent huge amounts of money on staffing because he believed he needed topflight technical expertise to continue to be competitive. Without good financial information on a product-by-product basis, he had no idea how big a problem he had regarding excess costs.

Sam prided himself on his independence and on the expertise of his people. But when executives brought up fiscal issues, he would immediately wash his hands of it, indicating that his job was to get great products out the door, and that he was confident that the uniqueness of the products would make them successful for the company. Given the absence of any kind of meaningful information that would counter his beliefs, management continued to support Sam and the many information systems he had accumulated to run his business.

Once management understood how out of control their costs were and felt a fair amount of pressure to fix their financial problems, they went to work on driving the percent of net revenue that was spent on information systems down to the industry standard of 3.5 percent.

As at Microsoft, the company created a small team led by an extremely talented information-technology professional whom I'll call Joe, who also knew the business well. Joe received full backing from the CEO and top management to create a technology architecture to lead them out of the mess.

Upon completion, Joe and the leaders of the IT organization introduced the business units to the new architecture over the next three months and prepared them for the changes that would occur as they instituted global procurement procedures and a global order/shipping/billing system. Unfortunately, as the IT staff began to make the rounds to these divisions, they faced a cold reception. After the chief information officer told the CEO about the problems that were slowing the company's effort, it became obvious that the CEO would have to intervene. He took the initiative and made it clear to the business units that he expected them to achieve specific IT expenditure targets, which would allow the total corporate IT effort to be cut significantly, down to the targeted 3.5 percent of revenue.

Had the CEO not intervened, or if the CIO had lacked the nerve to go to the CEO, the fiefdoms likely would have suffocated the effort.

In circumstances like this, the groups or divisions must understand why global systems are good for the company. Top management must make clear why the change is occurring and why employees have to incur the pain of change. This communication is absolutely vital in determining the success or failure of such an initiative.

2. THE DISCIPLINE OF STANDARD TEMPLATES AND DATA

Each department of the company, such as finance, human resources, manufacturing, product development, etc., should make its data available across the entire organization to employees authorized (via password) to have access to it.

Individuals should be able to pull up templates of key information on the screen of their personal computer that can answer 95 percent of the questions that come up. Having that ability is an incredibly powerful tool in every area of business.

With such databases and easy-to-use tools in place, it becomes extremely difficult for fiefdoms that try to hoard information to prosper. While business units and subsidiaries may need to have limited unique systems or data to help them run their business, such information should be kept to a minimum. The goal is to keep the business as simple and focused as possible. Such an approach yields the right kind of checks and balances that make it difficult for fiefdoms to form. When top management and the management of the individual business units have easy access to such data, they can better understand what is working and what isn't, while they delegate responsibility for generating the positive results to the individual groups within the division.

OBTAINING KEY INFORMATION ON KEY PEOPLE

One Fortune 100 company I consulted for was putting renewed emphasis on developing a strong "farm team" of up-and-coming candidates for key positions, as well as mounting a major campaign to weed out substandard performers. The CEO pushed hard in these areas, but he and his senior team could see it was very difficult to get the necessary information on some individuals. Each time such information was needed, executives would have to talk to their HR people, who would have to pull together information from different files. There was a lag of several days before the information could be gathered. Sometimes the executive would lose interest in the question or would get involved in a pressing problem, and the request would be forgotten.

Sometimes when management asked about key people, the fiefdom that the individuals worked in would intentionally slow the process or claim to be unable to provide key information. Fiefdoms love to "own" their personnel. As a result, they tend to make it difficult for management to learn more about them. This is especially true of "stars" within the departments. Unfortunately, everyone loses when this happens. The organization is prevented from developing a future star and from getting the individual's help in solving a tough problem, and the employee is buried in a department that doesn't afford him or her opportunity to grow.

In this particular company, there was a general manager, whom I will call Ralph, who was uncanny in hoarding people and persuading strong players to join his fiefdom. Ralph was notorious for mooching top people. His peers claimed he misused the salary structure, promoting people one or two levels higher than they should be in order to lure them to his group. Ralph came up with special titles to make comparisons across the company difficult.

Ralph's business was generally healthy. But some felt his real strength rested in telling management what they wanted to hear and keeping them off his turf. Employees liked working for Ralph, but they knew the risks, namely, that they could be stuck in his department for a long time, albeit with good short-term financial rewards.

When executives from other departments inquired about one of Ralph's people, or tried to understand some aspect of Ralph's business, Ralph personally deflected such inquiries.

To overcome Ralph's territorialism, the CEO decided to require standardized data and templates for all personnel in the organization. He charged a couple of HR professionals and an information technology architect with developing an easy-to-use database that contained everything he needed to know about every employee. The database contained the name, history of assignments, history of promotions, salary history, performance review scores, and even the benefit programs for each employee. The database served the needs of virtually every aspect of human resources while providing executives with a powerful tool to quickly obtain information on key employees. Standard templates were quickly developed to view the history of employment, compensation, and performance.

As you might guess, Ralph and a few other department heads and general managers fought this idea like crazy. But the CEO was insistent; he would not budge. There had been too many times when he and others were unable to get the necessary information to identify and place a strong candidate in an important job.

When the system was completed, it proved to be exactly the kind of powerful tool the CEO had anticipated. The CEO could access the information he needed from anywhere in the world. The system was configured with various masks, so that only approved personnel could see information on an individual. When an individual was first entered into the payroll system, HR created a record for him or her. All the other systems within HR, from compensation to performance appraisal, used this same database to store new information as well as call up existing information.

This was a great example of how standardized templates or data can cut through powerful fiefdoms.

FIGURING OUT THE SIZE OF THE STAFF

I'll never forget a funny incident at Microsoft in 2000 when Steve Ballmer, who had just become CEO, was holding an annual budget review of one of the business units. The business unit head, along with about twenty-five of his people, were sitting around a large table. They were plowing through a long and detailed PowerPoint presentation they had created, and Steve popped in regularly with questions. Steve is a big, tall, commanding figure and an incredibly quick study. He typically uncovers a few flaws or inconsistencies in whatever is being presented. What many Microsoft insiders soon realized is that Steve also has a great sense of humor.

I could see Steve beginning to fume when one of the business units couldn't tell him the exact number of people they were authorized to hire or the exact number of people actually on payroll. Various people from the business unit jumped in, indicating that they knew the answer, and provided yet another set of numbers. After this had occurred three or four times, Steve suggested that they suspend the meeting and have the business unit managers go back to their building and count heads quickly so that when they reconvened in forty-five minutes they would have hard data in planning the manpower needs of the future.

The entire room fell silent. One look around at the faces at the conference table showed that everyone was trying to decide if Steve was serious. After about ten seconds (an incredibly long time in such a situation), Steve couldn't hold back a boyish grin.

At the time, though Microsoft had systems that captured headcount, the information had become very fragmented as the company quickly grew. The systems could not keep up with:

▓ New recruits rapidly coming on board
▓ Part-time contractors being converted to full-time employees
▓ Additional contractors being hired
▓ Reorganizations
▓ Buffers put in budgets to anticipate future needs
▓ Transfers between the business units, departments, and subsidiaries

These complexities made it hard to know whether the data on the headcount of a particular unit was up-to-date or not. In addition, finance was interested in headcount for different reasons than HR or recruiting. Consequently, managers often were forced to use out-of-date data from various additional databases developed by divisions or groups within the company for other reasons.

Steve decided as a result of that meeting that Microsoft needed a straightforward database containing all the fundamental headcount information on every organization in the company—one that would be constantly updated.

The database became an important scorecard for all the managers at Microsoft. At Microsoft, it was very hard to get approval for additional employees because we tried to keep the budgets extremely lean. As a result of Steve's decision, however, when you did get approval for some new positions, you would make sure the database was updated to reflect that new manpower limit for your group.

Microsoft tackled the issue head-on by developing easy-to-use menus that allowed various standardized templates to be displayed on a manager's screen. Managers could see how many people were in the organization, their hiring authorization for the year, how many positions they were recruiting to fill, and their attrition rate—how many employees they were losing each year. The database also contained historical information on headcount. Furthermore, the on-screen organization chart eliminated the need for printed organization charts. With a few clicks, we could pull up the organizational chart of any group within the company.

The system became a great checks-and-balances tool to minimize the formation of fiefdoms.

REALLY UNDERSTANDING COSTS

I was continually impressed with the information made available to Procter & Gamble employees on the unit costs of products. For example, when I was working on the Crest brand, I could easily access per-unit costs on packaging, the cost of the chemicals used in the product, marketing costs, distribution costs, etc. While each of the business units at Procter & Gamble had its own manufacturing entities, the overall corporate manufacturing organization set the standards in maintaining manufacturing costs and factoring them into the overall unit cost of the products. This data were available both to the brand groups and top management.

When producing consumer products whose individual units generally sell for $3 to $8, the cost of the products is a significant portion of the company's revenue. We had to examine every penny as we worked to improve profits and find ways to put more marketing efforts behind our brand.

As the advertising manager of the packaged soap and detergent division at P&G, I fought hard, along with my team, to get more advertising muscle behind Tide. It was gaining share in response to some great new advertising. Having those detailed cost breakdowns on the product enabled us to realize that if we got purchasing to push hard on the suppliers for cost reductions of the key chemical ingredients and the packaging of Tide, we could save two or three cents per unit. That translated into millions of dollars of potential advertising funds. We could also look at sales and overhead costs and brainstorm ways to use these funds more efficiently.

The templates with the detailed cost information also helped us make better financial decisions. In the package soap and detergent division, we had three dishwashing detergents, Dawn, Ivory, and Joy, and they were battling to grow their businesses. Dawn was about 25 percent larger than the other two, and Joy was struggling.

The marketing folks managing the Joy brand argued vigorously with me for more marketing dollars. They pointed out that their business was soft and that the brand didn't have the level of spending necessary in the category to break through. Fortunately, because I had all the data at my fingertips, I could see that the Joy brand group was spending an excess amount of money on promotion costs. But the promotions weren't being executed very well—they weren't creating the typical short-term business increase needed to justify their efforts. Also, the Joy brand marketing people were spending more per unit for advertising than the other two dishwashing detergents. Their packaging costs were extremely high because they had so many special packs related to promotions, requiring manufacturing to modify standard packaging. To top it off, their commercial production costs for developing television advertising spots were much higher than for the other two brands.

When I discussed these things with the Joy brand group, I explained that they needed to do a heck of a lot better in managing the fundamentals of their brand. What they really needed, I said, was a great marketing idea—one that was distinctive enough to motivate customers to come to the brand. I sent them away to clean up their costs and to find a creative advertising approach to excite the consumer about their product.

You can fight off the formation of fiefdoms by having a detailed system of checks and balances like P&G's easy-to-use information systems that enable you to access cost information.

Another company that I got to know well, which I'll call Visionaire, had basically no data on how its procurement of raw materials was executed by different business units. There was no central repository of vendor information, nor was there any cost-per-unit data on the various components of their products. Visionaire was the opposite of Procter & Gamble when it came to making information readily available.

Fortunately, Visionaire lived in a fast-growing industry where it was possible to survive all kinds of inefficiencies in areas such as procurement and still make good money.

As is usually the case, when the industry eventually slowed down, Visionaire realized it had to understand its business a lot better. Without rapid growth, pricing became incredibly competitive. This put tremendous pressure on the players in the industry to have access to detailed information about their costs and to employ personnel who could efficiently manage vendors, drive down costs, and achieve real procurement efficiencies.

This company had no such information systems or personnel. Logistics within this company was a low priority; no one knew the state of raw material inventories, production rates, or finished product inventories. Visionaire operated on a crisis basis; their hordes of procurement personnel all operated in a firefighter mode, rushing orders on scarce components from various suppliers just to keep production rolling.

When it began to compile more detailed data, the company realized that in just one of its business units it had more than 600 procurement people, even though that business unit represented only about 12 percent of the overall revenue of this $12-billion company. Prior to the industry's cooldown, there was no data available on headcount, vendor count, or unit cost of the various components in individual products. While the organization had tons of information systems performing specialized tasks, none of the systems was pulling together the basic information in a well-defined manner across the entire company. By the time I stopped consulting with Visionaire, they understood the mess they were in but had yet to figure out how to tackle it. The reason? The company was ravaged by individual fiefdoms. They knew they had to drive the concept of standardized templates and data through their organization, but the strength of those fiefdoms was creating fragmentation on so many fronts. The fiefdoms were running wild, putting top management at a tremendous disadvantage.

3. THE DISCIPLINE OF INSPECTION

There is simply no substitute for the leaders of an organization to regularly schedule reviews to "inspect" key performance data of the various groups under each manager's responsibility. This is much diffrent from an audit, which is more of a checkup. "Inspection" implies a direct involvement in understanding what is going on. The intent of such an inspection is to ensure that key measures about the performance of a group, division, or company are being reviewed and that action plans are being put into place to generate improvement where it's needed.

In *Execution,* Larry Bossidy discusses what he calls "the importance of robust dialogue." What Larry is suggesting is that top management regularly meet with key groups in the organization to have a thorough discussion of the critical issues. Such discussions are open, candid, and informal. Larry points out that only when such dialogue occurs can real progress be made on key issues. This is the kind of interaction I suggest should occur during inspection. Inspection should not involve top management attempting to run a business unit or functional area. It means that top management is working to assist the groups in thoroughly understanding their business and creating action plans that will lead to significant improvement. The key thinking, execution, and creativity should be left to the group. But top management needs to create an environment where inspection is expected. Doing so will push the organization to reach new heights.

KEEPING THE BOARD UNINFORMED

Given the serious problems at companies like Enron, WorldCom, and Tyco, there has been a ton of publicity about boards of directors who lost touch with key areas of the company; the companies eventually imploded and caused huge problems. Often this occurs because top management itself exhibits the characteristics of a top-tier fiefdom. It instinctively works to keep the board happy, yet uninvolved.

I know of the board activities of another company (the CFO is a close friend), a large supplier to the automobile industry. I'll call it Car Parts. The board meetings are heavily orchestrated by the CEO, who pre-clears scripts of the presentations to be given to the board by members of the company. The agenda is crammed full of items about completed projects or promising new technologies. After each presentation, the CEO carefully reminds the board of the principles that the project represents and how they tie in to the overall culture of the company; he explains how good the board should feel about continuing the solid practices of the past. What's really fascinating, however, is that the same agenda seems to exist whether the company is doing well or not.

My friend, Car Parts's CFO, described to me what occurred when two new directors were appointed to the board within a six-month period. Each was strong-willed, and neither had been associated with a board as "orchestrated" as this one. One director, whom I will refer to as Jack, was interested in making sure he understood the business and probed when he didn't. It was a new concept for this board.

The CEO became unnerved on numerous instances when Jack drilled down into an issue to try to understand what the company was experiencing. For the first time, this gave a couple of other directors the nerve to ask their own probing questions. Some of the more traditional directors gave the impression that they thought such questioning was rather rude and time-consuming. But it was clear that Jack had created a turning point in the oversight conducted by the board. The discipline of inspection began to slowly break down the incredible fiefdom that the CEO had created.

When I am asked about my experiences at Microsoft, I often respond with a description of how the board meetings were run, because they were unique. During my tenure as COO, the CFO and I would present the state of the business for the first hour or so, and then we would discuss any legal issues for the next hour, as well as the committee reports. By late morning, we had covered all the items on the agenda. The remainder of the full-day meeting was put into the hands of board members to talk about things that needed to be tackled by the company to improve it. Bill Gates set the tone here, focusing exclusively on areas that needed improvement. He would constantly encourage us to think about how to strengthen a particular product in order to be preferred over its competitors. Sometimes a particular product discussion was preplanned, and a group of product developers was invited to discuss its efforts to gain leadership in a product category. The focus, however, was on continual improvement—moving the company to the number-one position in every one of its product areas. But plenty of time was allowed to take full advantage of the skills of the board members and to address the issues on the minds of the individuals of the group. It was about as healthy a board atmosphere as I have ever seen.

What does a member of a board of a public corporation or a non-profit do when the agenda is limited to positive items designed to give the board a positive perception? When there is no time for meaningful dialogue on areas that need to be addressed? It is that board member's responsibility to execute the discipline of inspection. That's the only way top-tier fiefdoms can be cut down to size so that a dialogue about the important measures that need to be addressed can begin.

THE BEHAVIOR DISCIPLINES

4. THE DISCIPLINE OF AVOIDING OVERCONFIDENCE

One reason fiefdoms occur is that people convince themselves that their work and their products/services are better than they actually are. Such overconfidence leads to disastrous results in just about any setting. One example is how Ken Olson's confidence in the ongoing success of the VAX minicomputer led to DEC's downfall. On the other hand, because

Andy Grove was famously paranoid about the competition and never took anything for granted, he helped to keep Intel on its toes. Microsoft's methods are much closer to the Andy Grove model. Bill Gates constantly looks for problems. He looks at everything that happens on a day-to-day basis and asks what Microsoft needs to improve upon.

This willingness to ignore your successes is critical—it's the only way to get serious about preparing for the future.

THE PITFALLS OF OVERCONFIDENCE

A company that I consulted with, Vibrant, had been purchasing marketing data services from a supplier, Market-Track, for many years and had thoroughly integrated that data into the decision-making process of their company. Market-Track had placed inside Vibrant people who were well trained in the workings of the industry and could give valuable insights regarding performance of competitors and the overall industry trends.

Over time, as Vibrant found itself facing serious financial difficulties, the company needed to quickly get itself back on track and pursue ways to improve profitability.

In the marketing data services industry, there was more than one vendor to choose from. The company's five-year contract with Market-Track was about to expire, offering an opportunity for Vibrant to find a less expensive vendor and reduce costs. Vibrant's top management decided to place one of its purchasing wizards, Peter, on the task, much to the chagrin of the market research organization within the company, who were the purchasers of the data services for use by all marketing personnel. This purchasing wizard set up a competitive bidding system between the current vendor and two competitors.

Bringing Peter into the situation caused a huge blowup in the company. A marketing director in one of the divisions, Mark, fired off an e-mail to the CEO opposing the action. He copied the other marketing directors and most of the people in procurement. He pointed out that whoever invited procurement to this party didn't know a thing about the role of a vendor in providing marketing data services. Mark felt that procurement was too focused on cost and ignored some of the real value the current data vendor, Market-Track, provided—the talented individuals who assisted Vibrant's employees in interpreting the direction of the industry and the performance of the competitors. He pointed out that Market-Track brought in expensive talent to work with the company, which consequently caused its bids to be a bit higher than those of the other two competitors. On the other hand, these talented analysts were extremely valuable.

As you would expect, the procurement folks became very defensive. Peter fired off his own e-mail to the CEO, pointing out the deep expertise that purchasing had in such vendor situations. He claimed marketing was showing a reaction typical of a department unschooled in the nuances of procurement. That sent the marketing people through the roof.

The CEO brought together a few of the marketing directors and the head of market research, as well as Peter and a few other procurement folks. Marketing stated their case eloquently—procurement should not be focused only on the numbers; they should not recommend a supplier just because of a lowball estimate. They explained the importance of the quality of the people who would be assigned to the account, and their experience in the industry. Peter, in response, claimed that the marketing folks were personally attacking him. The CEO, he said, had asked him to do a job based on his experience in procurement, and that's what he was doing. While Peter's comments didn't make the marketing people feel any better, they did remind the CEO that he had made a commitment to procurement to let them handle some of the more complicated procurement tasks. The CEO indicated to Peter that he needed to take into account what marketing was saying, but he authorized him to move ahead. The most important thing was to achieve significant savings. The marketing folks were furious, but the decision had been made.

So the company went with the cheapest vendor. Twelve months later, there was such anger among the business units about the poor quality of the vendor's analysis that the decision needed to be reversed.

Peter's purchasing fiefdom had taken over a problem that it lacked the skill to deal with. But its overconfidence did not permit it to acknowledge its lack of expertise.

The financial pressures on the CEO, and the overconfidence of the purchasing fiefdom, resulted in a poor decision that took a year to fix.

A MACHO MANUFACTURING MENTALITY

Back in 1994, Microsoft owned its manufacturing facilities. It was light manufacturing—loading floppy disks and CD-ROMs with software, packaging the floppy disks and CDs in boxes with an instruction booklet, and shipping these products to retail outlets or warehouses. The goal was to perform these services with great efficiency so that Microsoft's costs were lower than their competitors', especially as market share—and the total number of units manufactured and shipped—grew.

Because Microsoft hires really smart people throughout the corporation, these folks in the manufacturing area were confident that they had become world class in efficiency.

When I became the COO in 1994, I immediately asked why manufacturing was done in-house at all. Bill Gates had been raising this question for a couple of years, but in the wake of the company's explosive growth, it had fallen off the priority list. But I agreed with Bill. Why not outsource our manufacturing and shipping to people who make a living putting bits on CD-ROMs? There were vendors doing this in the music and software industries. Why not take advantage of their incredible scale and expertise in this area?

When I raised this issue, the manufacturing fiefdom at Microsoft pushed back hard. As mentioned earlier, they had come to believe they were best in class in this area. And in fact, they *were* very good. The employees who had been hired had extensive expertise in manufacturing, and they seemed to be executing well in an environment where products changed rapidly and the number of new products increased all the time.

Several individuals from manufacturing came to talk to me individually about Microsoft's exploration into outsourcing our manufacturing. They gave impassioned pleas that I not overlook their deep expertise. They showed me data demonstrating how well they had reacted to crisis and had their costs under control. It was a very emotional issue for these folks. Nevertheless, I sensed the overconfidence oozing out of them. One particular manager looked me in the eye and told me that their performance was outstanding and would continue to be outstanding. He said he just couldn't understand why the company would want to turn its back on such committed and talented people. In fact, I knew how committed and talented they were, so these were tough conversations!

I pressed on, looking at the trends in the information technology industry. I saw a world in the not-too-distant future where people would download software over the Internet instead of purchasing CD-ROMs. This caused me to pursue the outsourcing of manufacturing with a real sense of urgency.

In the end, we decided to sell the manufacturing facilities in 1995. We were very eager to get hard data on whether using outside vendors would result in a lower unit cost, as we confidently predicted. Eventually, we'd find out.

The launch of Windows 95 in mid-1995 proved to be one of our best benchmarking opportunities. At the time, we were still making some products at our large U.S. manufacturing facility, while outsourcing others. The unit cost for outsourcing each package of Windows 95 was 13 percent lower than our costs for producing them in-house. Microsoft's "world-class" manufacturing team couldn't believe it.

The lesson here? Human beings tend to become overconfident of their capabilities over time. Rather than assuming you are already good enough at your job, assume instead that there are competitors out there who are learning to do things differently and better. Follow Andy Grove's wise advice: Only the paranoid survive.

5. THE DISCIPLINE OF AVOIDING FRAGMENTATION

In finance, human resources, manufacturing, procurement, information technology, and public relations, business units tend to want to develop their own departments in order to make their group as independent as possible. The behavior stems from the basic territorial tendencies I discussed in Chapter 2.

For example, people often push to eliminate centralized procurement departments and to disperse procurement throughout the organization.

Why? Each business group wants to do its own thing and respond to its own unique needs. People hate feeling controlled by procurement experts who sit at corporate headquarters, far removed from the fray.

Unfortunately, this leads to enormous increased costs and potentially massive duplication.

EVERY EMPLOYEE AS A PURCHASING AGENT

When I arrived at Microsoft in 1994, it seemed that every employee had become a purchasing agent. Each employee had a phone, the Yellow Pages, and the power to call the vendor of his choice when he needed supplies. There was no real procurement department or expertise within the company and no system or guidelines for handling procurement on an ongoing basis.

The bad news was that there was no way to capture the data on how much business we were doing with each vendor. As a result, we missed opportunities to negotiate volume discounts. Company-wide, we literally didn't know who our vendors were, since the materials usually were ordered independently.

How bad did it get? One day, after about four months at Microsoft, I was sitting in my office when Bill Gates came charging out of his office next door with a letter from a vendor. Although he was amused by the clever writing style of the author, you could almost see the steam coming out of Bill's ears. As he handed the letter to me, he said: "We've reached a new low, Bob. Here's a vendor who thinks we may be going under." While Bill calmed himself down, I read the letter. It basically said, "I'm one of your key vendors and I've been sending you bills for six months without getting paid. I thought you guys were doing OK financially, but maybe not. How come you can't pay your bills?" I couldn't stop myself from laughing. I quickly promised Bill we would handle the situation immediately with the vendor. More important, I assured him we would get the procurement situation fixed quickly.

The reason for Microsoft's procurement mess was that all of the business units had decided to go it alone and had gotten away with it. When they needed something—from personal computers to hard drives to servers for testing new software—employees would simply go out and buy it.

My first step in tackling the problem was to pull together the various personnel dealing with procurement. This included people from finance, manufacturing, and a few from each of the business units. With these people as a core, I formed a corporate procurement group and put a talented rising star in charge. Next, the newly appointed leader took two seasoned individuals who were extremely knowledgeable about procurement and IT and put them in charge of designing the architecture to solve the problem.

As we pulled together the procurement organization, the biggest task we faced was matching invoices with purchase orders. It was in a complete state of chaos. The newly formed procurement team established some basic principles:

1. Invoices would be generated by the system at the same time as purchase orders, and both would reside in the system together. Never again could a situation arise where we had an invoice but no purchase order (we eliminated a lot of "re-work" by doing this).
2. All vendors would be asked to interface with our newly launched Web-based system so that we had a unified way to get data into the system from outside the company.
3. One common set of Web-based menus would be used by all employees.
4. We would significantly limit the number of vendors employees could use to order supplies, printers, personal computers, etc.

Our two-person design team didn't resort to committees or task forces. They were already experts in the field and knew we expected them to come up with a system that would both work well and keep all employees happy. Given that responsibility, they knew they were expected to deliver. There was no backstop.

That kind of delegation, as I've pointed out before, brings out the best in employees, causing them to grow significantly.

Within six months, the design team, working with some additional information systems personnel, developed a Web-based system that all Microsoft employees could use to order materials they needed. The simple Web pages were extremely easy to understand; they enabled employees to access a series of menus that described the various products and services that could be ordered. At the same time, we cut off all other procedures for ordering supplies, indicating to all employees via e-mail that if they went out on their own and placed an order with a vendor, Microsoft would not pay for it.

Basically, we instilled some discipline in the procurement process through a new easy-to-use system. The system, called MS Market, quickly became extremely popular among employees. Not only was it simple to use, it had a wide selection of supplies that employees might need to help them do their job and was tied directly to the suppliers, resulting in fast delivery of whatever was ordered. The Web sheets were tied in to our SAP financial systems as well as to our key vendors. Our central procurement group selected the vendors and negotiated volume discounts. The employees got their orders filled much more quickly and could more easily track the status of their order before it arrived.

Twelve months later, 99.8 percent of all purchases by U.S. employees were made through our new system. Two years after its inauguration, MS Market was being used in forty-nine countries where Microsoft had employees and required only two people to support it. The system ran on one database server and one Web server sitting in Redmond, Washington. The initial development effort of the system took five months and involved five people.

The financial impact was huge:

▓ The average cost of processing a typical purchase order went from $60 to $17, a 72 percent reduction.

▓ The average cost of an invoice went from $30 to $5, an 83 percent reduction.

▓ The corporate procurement group that was first formed by pulling together everyone who had been executing some kind of procurement task was eventually decreased by 70 percent.

▧ Microsoft began to receive more than $250 million in supplier discounts that it had been leaving on the table.

This is a great example of how fragmentation—in this case, of the procurement function—had been costing the company immensely.

MANUFACTURING CHAOS

A close friend of mine works for a company that makes electronic components for the consumer appliance industry. Unfortunately, the company's manufacturing was completely fragmented across its product lines.

The fragmentation was so severe that even though the majority of the products sold in the different business units had many common parts, there was no central manufacturing headquarters to notice this and gain volume leverage by standardizing certain parts throughout the company. Of the tens of thousands of parts the company used, thousands were practically identical to one another, with only modest changes. But because each part was designed and developed by independent fiefdoms within the company, none of the parts was standardized.

The company was so fragmented that even within a single division, each of its products had its own manufacturing department. The company was tremendously inefficient, to say the least.

One reason there were so many fiefdoms was that the executives prided themselves in promoting independence throughout the organization. One group vice president in charge of several of the business units, Sam, constantly spoke about the importance of protecting the company's culture, hiring strong people, and letting each group operate independently. Anytime someone suggested centralizing anything, Sam would discourage the CEO from doing so.

As a result, the company treated areas such as raw-material procurement, raw-material inventory, and finished-product inventory as unimportant and trivial. Sloppy procurement and inventory practices can lead to tying up large amounts of cash. But there were no strong financial directives in these areas, and the financial data the company had were extremely weak. The fiefdoms couldn't even see the consequences of their sloppy procurement and inventory practices.

The fragmentation in manufacturing led to small usage rates of individual component parts and huge inventories of parts, given that many of their suppliers required them to place bulk orders. For example, if you were using 20 units per week of a particular part, and your supplier had a minimum order of 5,000, that order represented a 250-week supply (that's five years!). Your supply on hand for that particular part was going to be huge.

There was absolutely no effort at the top to improve manufacturing excellence or to contain manufacturing costs. Because the fiefdoms controlled all the data on costs, management had little insight into how bad things had gotten.

The out-of-control costs were somewhat camouflaged by the solid growth of the company's business in the '90s. When their business softened in 2001, however, the cost excesses related to manufacturing began to catch management's attention. Eventually, the company had to instill a stiff dose of discipline, which resulted in thousands of employees being let go. Manufacturing received a major overhaul. Sadly, innocent, hardworking individual employees got caught up in these fiefdoms—and the fallout.

6. THE DISCIPLINE OF CONSTANTLY LEARNING NEW SKILLS

Another characteristic of fiefdoms is that they tend to freeze the skill level of the people caught inside them. When people are protected and are not challenged to continually improve or to offer new ideas, their motivation for change evaporates. They assume they have already mastered their job and often doubt that anyone outside the fiefdom has anything to teach them—especially competitors.

TOO MUCH EXPERIENCE CAN SUFFOCATE INNOVATION

I vividly recall an experience with a heavy-manufacturing company that required its enormous machines to be extremely reliable. The machines were very expensive, and it took a while to fine-tune them. But once running well, they were productive and profitable.

The individuals assigned to run these machines got to know them very well and achieved impressive levels of productivity that left competitors in the dust. When that happens, however, pride can take over, compromising one's ability to innovate and squeeze more out of the machinery. Over time, the machine operators' ability to ensure their machine's consistent performance became viewed as almost magical.

As in most industries, the technology utilized in manufacturing was evolving. New capabilities were being developed. In this industry, some fabulous new process-control technology had emerged; the company decided to invest in the new equipment and place it in one of the facilities manned by some of its top-rated machine operators. What occurred surprised me, but maybe it shouldn't have. The machine operators experienced with the traditional equipment felt a certain degree of fear over the equipment changes, although they wouldn't acknowledge it.

The engineering folks selected a machine operator named Willy, a veteran of twenty years, to test this new technology. Willy had always done a superb job of running the existing equipment; he had one of the best records in the company.

At the start of the testing, Willy was introduced to a young electrical engineer named Ken who was to assist Willy in becoming familiar with the new technology.

The combination of a sophisticated new piece of equipment and a talented young engineer made Willy very uncomfortable. For twenty years he had been considered the expert at using his experience and trial and error to get the most out of the machines. When someone asked Willy what he did to achieve such high performance, he joked that it was black magic. But it was more than that. Willy had gained enough battle scars to know what to try and what not to try, and he was very good at applying his experience to the problem.

It was embarrassing to Willy to confront a new, complex piece of equipment and be instructed on its use by a much younger, university-trained electrical engineer.

While it certainly wasn't Willy's intention, his attitude was distrustful and even slightly defiant about the huge performance improvements the company expected from this new technology. Worse, Willy didn't have a clue about what to do to maximize the new technology's use. And Ken wasn't much better—even he had no idea how to make these big machines run reliably. The two of them could not admit their weaknesses to each other, and as a consequence, the test was a disaster.

Although the test results were disappointing, the machine operators were secretly gleeful at seeing the technology fail. But instead of giving up, the company moved the equipment to a different facility and assigned a fresh crew who had no experience with the existing technology to run it.

You can probably guess what happened. This time the results with the new equipment were sensational. The machinery resulted in a 20 percent gain in productivity, and the young engineers had a ball tweaking and improving upon the new machines.

My point? If you leave people in the same job for too long and allow them to become too comfortable, without encouraging them to grow and learn, they lose the capability to renew themselves and think about alternative ways to get the work done. They become a liability for the company rather than an asset.

Fiefdoms encourage employees to believe that they are better than they really are. As a result, they cease to learn and grow and add to their skills. They atrophy. The company I mentioned above eventually moved entirely to the new technology, achieving even higher levels of productivity gain. They did this by hiring new, highly talented engineers to run the new equipment. The real losers were the employees who clung to the past and lost their curiosity, blocking them from expanding their skills and causing them to be stuck in the past.

UNDERSTAND WHAT BUSINESS YOU ARE IN

One ad agency I've worked with had a group of creative individuals who were incredibly talented in developing television advertising for a fashion-related industry. For a period of twenty years, they were absolutely revered for being able to consistently drive up the revenue of fashion-related products.

Over time, however, other forms of marketing were becoming important to the industry, yet they held no interest to these individuals. Because they were experts in developing TV ads, they ignored direct marketing, public relations, and the multifaceted skills needed for creating buzz around a product. They had forgotten what business they were in. Their job was not to develop *television* advertising; it was to create marketing that drives the revenue of the products they worked on.

Here's a perfect example of what I'm talking about. A very good friend of mine was a top developer of television advertising. Norm had twenty-five years of experience; he consistently came up with TV advertising that drove business ahead and had tons of plaques and awards on his wall (the ad business is great at giving awards). Over time, Norm began to worry that top management no longer liked his work—they were asking him to do all kinds of strange things he knew nothing about.

While extremely talented in television advertising, Norm was incredibly insecure. He took it as an affront that his management was suggesting he branch out and take advantage of new marketing approaches; he assumed they no longer believed he had the right skills to grow his brands. When he was asked to work with teams of marketing people, including Internet marketing and public relations folks, he winced. He never had to do that in the past. He didn't understand these various marketing approaches and consequently claimed he shouldn't be in the meeting.

Norm was exhibiting all the characteristics of skill atrophy. He'd lost his sense of curiosity. He knew he was good at television, and he became so focused on that medium that anything else threatened him. The ad agency had several people in their creative department like Norm.

They would have been far more valuable to the agency and their clients if they had become students of the new approaches in marketing—looking for ways they could complement some of the techniques that were successful in the past. These TV advertising experts should have been focused on continually acquiring new skills and testing their creativity in new areas.

There are incredibly important lessons here for any individual. The pride you justifiably have in the skills you have developed can become a liability as the world evolves. Like it or not, you have to deal with change.

7. THE DISCIPLINE OF AVOIDING BOTTLENECKS

Sometimes in finance, human resources, manufacturing, or procurement, you will find individuals who are in very important jobs with respect to their expertise but are not strategic to the corporation; they are important executionally. This alone shouldn't be viewed as a negative. However, because such people often have difficulty accepting this fact, they set up procedures to exercise veto power over aspects of the company's business and create processes that elevate their importance.

These kinds of fiefdoms emerge when people with key executional roles understand that if the process changes, their role might be eliminated. As a result, they build their responsibilities in such a way that they remain critical to the company.

This kind of defensiveness is extremely destructive to the organization and can kill a career.

At one company I consulted with, the marketing people had been charged with taking the lead in getting new products and product improvements into the marketplace. Much like the brand groups at Procter & Gamble, their job was to help product development to develop a new or improved product and then work with manufacturing to make sure it could be made. A couple of manufacturing managers set up a procedure requiring the marketing team to submit a production request detailing what they wanted manufacturing to make, how much of it they wanted, and the timetable they wanted manufacturing to follow. This was often done in preparation for a test market launch to see how well consumers responded to a product improvement.

In manufacturing, a production coordinator whom I'll call Jerry was assigned to review and reject or approve all production requests from marketing before manufacturing could begin production. Jerry was a powerful person who could make or break a marketing team initiative by determining its cost, schedule, and even feasibility. Jerry prided himself that during his fifteen years there, manufacturing had never dropped the ball or made a major mistake.

Of course, Jerry achieved that track record by never taking risks and by being extremely tough on the marketing teams when they wanted to try new things that generated any challenges for manufacturing. Furthermore, Jerry padded the timetables in such a way that he could ensure manufacturing would always meet them.

Naturally, the manufacturing fiefdom greatly admired Jerry. He protected them from risk and helped them establish an unblemished track record. But from a marketing standpoint, manufacturing was considered the wet blanket that inhibited new-product innovations.

Eventually, an incident broke open the production coordinator's fiefdom. R&D was working on a hot new product, and top management was extremely enthusiastic about its potential impact in the marketplace. They formed a brand group to manage the product and placed it in the marketing organization. They assigned Carl, who had a lot of experience within the company, including some in manufacturing, to head the group.

As the brand group assembled marketing plans and prepared packaging, Jerry constantly warned them of the need to prepare their formal production request.

At a meeting with Jerry concerning the brand group's initial production request, it became clear to Carl that the schedule was being padded to protect manufacturing. But this time Jerry was dealing with somebody who was stubborn and knew the ropes. Carl asked why some unorthodox things couldn't be done to move the schedule up by three months. Jerry balked and got very defensive. The two started shouting at each other; eventually, Carl stomped out of the room.

Almost immediately after that meeting, the manager of manufacturing called the group vice president responsible for the business unit and explained that an obnoxious person leading the brand group, named Carl, had to be dealt with—his people were being treated poorly. The group VP got involved and called the brand group and Carl up to his office. Carl was as forthright with the group VP as he had been with Jerry. He presented detailed charts showing how the schedule could be moved up and claimed that manufacturing wasn't coming back with good reasons why his schedule wouldn't work.

The group VP loved the idea of moving up the schedule because he knew the impact in the marketplace could be quite significant. When the group VP confronted manufacturing, they couldn't refute Carl's claims.

The company at last realized that Jerry's fiefdom was causing the organization to be less competitive than it could be. After the launch of the hot new product, Jerry was transferred to a production management job, and his fiefdom was broken up.

SLEIGHT OF HAND

A manufacturing division of a computer-hardware maker recently decided to sell off its manufacturing facilities and move to an outsource model. Within the division, however, there was a great deal of dissension over the agreement, which involved selling the facilities and transferring employees to the outsource vendor.

So, without top management's knowledge, the manufacturing unit set up an agreement with the vendor whereby the only thing outsourced would be the final assembly of the product. Manufacturing still made all decisions pertaining to product production schedules, raw material inventory purchasing, and raw material inventory management. The vendor loved this, because most of the risk in the business of outsourcing manufacturing is the cost associated with managing raw material inventories.

Why did this happen? The head of production planning, whom I'll call Corey, felt extremely threatened; at the same time, he genuinely believed that he was so important to the organization that it could not operate without him. He had crafted a process for utilizing the vendor that included himself as a key decision-maker on an ongoing basis in ordering raw materials and managing inventories. The head of manufacturing, Will, who had relied heavily on Corey, had no reason to doubt him. Since top management's only concern was that things were being outsourced, Will agreed to Corey's model.

It took about four months for the division's management to realize that their costs were even *higher* than they had been before they moved to the outsource model. The finance people looked into it and found that manufacturing was outsourcing only the assembly of the product.

The division quickly brought in new personnel to oversee its outsourcing, going to a full "turnkey" model, where the only thing that the outside vendor was told was the production schedule that the division wanted to achieve. The decisions on how to accomplish that were left to the vendor. Finally, the division began to see the cost efficiencies that they had expected.

Functional dictatorships are hard to break up. These fiefdoms can be incredibly strong, and management is usually somewhat reluctant to challenge the people controlling the fiefdom because of their expertise. Only when top management can get the detailed data on the company's performance can it hope to understand what is working and what is not working and confront those areas of the business that aren't performing the way they should.

Following these seven disciplines will allow you to begin to tear down fiefdoms and put more effective processes in place. However, it is important to keep in mind that to revolutionize processes, the people performing those processes may have to change as well. Just as process disciplines are needed to break the fiefdom syndrome, so, too, are people disciplines.

4 THE SIX PEOPLE DISCIPLINES

IT TAKES MORE than strong process and behavior disciplines to control the fiefdom syndrome within organizations; it also takes *people* disciplines—the ways people are developed, managed, evaluated, and compensated.

Some of these issues can be addressed through stronger coordination across the human resources groups in various divisions and subsidiaries. Strategically, however, the people disciplines have to be addressed by the leaders of the organization, whatever size the organization happens to be.

Fiefdom heads tend to try to keep the territory or group under his or her control and as independent as possible with regard to headcount, salary practices, performance-appraisal procedures, and communications to those under them. Larger fiefdoms sometimes try to hire their own HR experts and even establish their own culture, often at odds with the values of the organization. The costs of this are enormous. Not only do such units become overstaffed, but they also tend to hoard IT and finance resources to run their fiefdoms as independently as possible. In order to streamline costs and make the company more competitive, the organization must find ways to break such fiefdoms' grip.

1. THE DISCIPLINE OF A STANDARDIZED PERFORMANCE-APPRAISAL SYSTEM

Just as there is a natural tendency in fiefdoms to hoard data, there also is a tendency to hoard people. Rather than confronting poor performance, fiefdoms tend to offer protection in exchange for blind loyalty. This creates a safe and familiar environment for the members of the fiefdom. Such an environment tends to discourage a sense of urgency to accomplish great things. People feel as if they are already good enough, and there is very little effort to weed out weak performers. Add to this the basic human reluctance on the part of supervisors and subordinates to conduct performance appraisals, and it is not surprising that overall performance lags.

Such fiefdoms rarely lead to a performance-driven environment. The overall tone the leaders of fiefdoms tend to establish is that we are a well-run, cordial group that gets along very well with everyone. It's the kind of environment where mediocre managers and employees say their company is "a great company to work for," while actually accomplishing very little. Basically, they have all tacitly agreed to be mediocre.

A strong performance-appraisal system driven from the top of the organization can break through such a fiefdom. In fact, it is one of the major tools for breaking up fiefdoms and tackling some of the leadership issues that cause fiefdoms to arise in the first place.

THE NONAPPRAISAL

It is incredibly difficult for most supervisors and subordinates to talk performance. Supervisors constantly water down what they say because they feel uncomfortable pointing out negatives. The subordinate hears any feedback through a very positive filter, and even some of the most negative statements register in his or her mind as points for improvement rather than as major problems. The basic dialogue degrades to the point where either the evaluation gets put off or it takes place in the most superficial manner. This is human nature, and it happens all the time in organizations. Because of this, when performance-appraisal processes are put in place in an organization, they tend to atrophy. And that is all the more reason for top management and the human resources department to pay close attention to it.

One company I consulted with went from about the worst performance-appraisal system I have ever seen to the best. The new system proved to be a major tool in breaking up some of its toughest fiefdoms and streamlining the organization.

The company's performance-appraisal system had deteriorated to the point where the company had no set time period during the year when performance appraisals took place. The write-ups were not collected by HR, and the company offered no training for managers on the proper way to execute a performance appraisal.

When I started working with the company, each person's performance was supposed to be categorized as outstanding, strong, solid, or needs improvement. The thing about these categories is that generally the perception of the individual receiving such an evaluation is that the evaluation is neutral to positive the overwhelming majority of the time. Typically, less than 1 percent of personnel received the "needs improvement" label. The bottom line: Many people were turning in below-average or average performances and were being called "solid." That term was consciously selected so that it would not be offensive to employees, which was a huge mistake.

When I asked Fred, the head of human resources, how the company got into this mess, he was fairly objective about the situation. He'd been in human resources for only twelve months, so he really didn't have a vested interest in defending the status quo. Fred explained that in most cases, the company's expectation when it hired an employee was that he or she would work at the company for their entire career. Of course, they believed they always hired top-notch people, even though Fred admitted and I could see that that was not the case.

The culture in the company was one of harmony as opposed to a culture of excellence. People were hesitant to discuss negatives about anything. That alone would lead to the demise of a realistic performance-appraisal system unless driven very hard by top management. The company thought it already had very strong people and didn't see a need for the kind of hard-charging performance-appraisal system that would isolate weak performers. This is a managerial disease that I see in most companies at one level or another.

During the annual employee survey, only 24 percent of the employees indicated they had received a performance appraisal during the past twelve months. A larger percentage had a performance discussion with their supervisor, but in many cases the meetings lacked substance, were not recorded, and were quickly forgotten, because both parties feared the exercise. The supervisors were reluctant to discuss performance, and the subordinates so badly wanted to avoid a potentially painful confrontation that neither worked to make it happen in a worthwhile manner.

Again, this situation is typical of many companies. This is particularly true inside fiefdoms, where there is no strong reason for a crisp performance-appraisal system when managers' and employees' primary goals are not driving the business forward but maintaining a safe and protected haven.

Fred saw an opportunity to change that in the wake of the relatively soft business results the company had turned in over the prior eighteen months. He convinced the CEO and top management that there was a lot of deadwood in the company, and that he could play a part in streamlining the company and kick-starting it out of its lethargy. While top management was defensive at first, it agreed with Fred's assessment and decided to look at what other companies were doing in the performance-appraisal area. Perhaps it *was* time to consider replacing some business unit leaders who weren't performing. It took an extraordinary amount of courage and leadership on Fred's part to bring this to a head. It underscores how crucial it is to have extremely strong leaders in key roles within the company, including human resources, finance, and information technology. They need to be incredibly thick-skinned, talented, and forward-thinking.

As a result of its extensive benchmarking of other companies, management realized something had to be done. It was clear to the CEO that the performance-appraisal system was in shambles. The company wasn't developing the leaders it needed; it needed to get the "deadwood" out of the organization.

The company moved performance evaluations to a five-point system. For managers responsible for 100 or more employees, the distribution of ratings was required to fit a slightly positively skewed bell-shaped curve. This put tremendous pressure on managers to sort out the very strong performers and the very weak performers.

Managers were required to sort employee performance into the following groupings:

* 10 percent of employees would receive a grade of 5 (outstanding)
* 25 percent of employees would receive a grade of 4 (strong)
* 40 percent of employees would receive a rating of 3 (satisfactory)
* 20 percent of employees would receive a rating of 2 (needs improvement)
* 5 percent of employees would receive a rating of 1 (unsatisfactory)

The company decided to create an annual performance-appraisal system where all individuals were rated during a specific four-week period during the year. The performance-appraisal form was standardized throughout the company. Upon completion of the appraisal discussion with the employee, supervisor and subordinates each signed the form and turned it over to human resources.

Managers at the department level and above, which typically had responsibility for more than 100 employees, had to ensure that they achieved the percentage targets for each of the five rating groups, give or take a percentage point or two.

Salary increases were given at the time of the performance appraisals, and the amount of the increase was directly tied to the numerical value of the performance rating for each employee. Moreover, there was a big difference in the amount an employee's salary increased depending upon the performance rating he or she received.

Salary increases within a department were not put into place by payroll until HR signaled that all of the signed performance-appraisal sheets for that department had been turned in. There was no way for a supervisor to get out of giving a performance appraisal to every one of his or her employees, since it would hold up salary increases for the entire department.

How does such discipline help in breaking up fiefdoms? First, the most talented achievers are identified and rewarded, and the weakest ones are identified and, if their behavior persists, terminated. Employees can no longer be "protected" in exchange for their blind loyalty. They have to perform. By identifying top performers, management plays a key role in making sure the strong people are given opportunities and assignments that will develop their talents and advance their careers. Much to the chagrin of someone who runs a fiefdom, this kind of system eliminates a fiefdom's ability to control an employee's career. Many of the best people are moved out, and some sharp people from outside are inserted into the fiefdom. That usually does a great job of breaking up the fiefdom.

I have to emphasize that it is critical for top management to drive the performance-appraisal system each and every year. This is a great tool for advancing the careers of the most talented employees in the company and weeding out the underperformers. And it helps to create a culture of excellence. It is effective not only in the for-profit world but in government organizations and nonprofits as well.

FAILURE OF SUPPORT BY TOP MANAGEMENT

I feel very good about my experience with the company described above. But I had an experience with another company where the results were very disappointing. Why? Because top management did not stand tall.

This company, which was roughly the same size as the previous one, wanted to revitalize its performance-appraisal system and implement it across the company. The effort was being led by corporate HR. But it wasn't facing up to the fact that huge, powerful fiefdoms were at work within the company.

The CFO worked hard with human resources to create the new performance-appraisal process. HR had gotten an informal agreement from the CEO that the finance people would be the first department to implement the new process before rolling it out across the company.

HR developed a four-point rating system with a forced bell-shaped curve roughly similar to that of the company I discussed earlier and began training the finance people at headquarters in the new procedure. Next, they began to roll the system out throughout the finance department across the company, which meant dealing with the finance people who worked within the major business units where the fiefdoms were incredibly strong. Those fiefdoms tended to hoard their finance people, training them in the way they wanted and paying and evaluating them by a completely different protocol from that being advocated by the CFO. And they weren't about to change.

Two business-unit general managers hit the roof when they heard that the finance department was "sticking their nose into how our finance people were being evaluated." The two sat down with the head of HR and the CFO, and the meeting didn't go well. They screamed for fifteen minutes about the fact that they didn't need any help in evaluating their people, making it clear that they viewed the finance people in their business units as their people, not finance's people. They were really hot. One of them screamed to the CFO, "My world is complicated enough; I don't need any 'help' from people like you in trying to run my business." The meeting broke up with no real steps being taken. The GMs of the business units clearly expected the subject to simply go away. It was clear to the head of HR and to the CFO that they needed to regroup about what to do next.

One of the GMs in the meeting fired off a blistering e-mail to his group vice president, strongly criticizing the fact that HR and finance were "meddling with his people." The group vice president forwarded the e-mail on to the CEO, asking what this performance-appraisal "stuff" was all about that was causing such a major disruption. He wanted to get the CEO to make it all go away. In the past, he had been successful in helping his general managers protect their turf, and he was confident that he'd be able to do so again.

At this point, the CEO needed to play a strong role in making it clear he wanted a new uniform performance-appraisal system instituted across the organization. Without that kind of strong stand by the CEO, the CFO and head of HR would not be able to succeed in getting the business units to comply.

The CFO and the head of HR confronted the CEO next, making it clear they weren't getting the strong backing and clear communication from him they needed in order to make the new appraisal process stick. The CEO responded by making all the appropriate remarks—that he would talk to all the business units so they understood what was expected. But that never happened. The CFO ended up being completely unsuccessful in implementing the new procedure within the business unit fiefdoms.

As a result, the finance organization was further fragmented; the fiefdoms continued to do what they wanted to do, with few checks and balances. The head of HR was so frustrated that he resigned.

Business units need to be independent in developing creative products and creative ways to work with their customers. However, the efficiencies and excellence of execution that can be gained with standard functional (HR, finance, IT, etc.) procedures company-wide are something that really should be seized.

2. THE DISCIPLINE OF UNIFIED FUNCTIONAL DEPARTMENTS

The formation of fiefdoms results in the fragmentation of departments such as human resources, finance, R&D, manufacturing, marketing, and information technology.

This breakdown of these departments leads to a lack of a unified point of view from them and also a lack of leadership from them to drive significant improvement in these areas. For example, when divisions or groups control their own HR personnel, the result can be bloated HR staffing for the company and varying quality and performance of HR in different areas of the company. It can also result in a lack of opportunity for individuals who work in the HR talent pool.

Ideally, you want to get the balance right. You want company-wide discipline from the corporate group while giving the right amount of latitude to the individual divisions and regions. I believe the head of each major department or functional unit must have responsibility for all of the employees in the department regardless of which division or subsidiary or group they work for. That is the only way employees from these departments will get treated fairly from a career standpoint. Without that, companies tend to experience high turnover in those areas, and when that happens, it is often the strongest players who leave the company because of the lack of attention and opportunities they receive.

HR RUNS AMUCK

In one $21-billion industrial products company I know of, there was an almost complete breakdown of the HR organization. Each division had its own team of HR specialists; the corporate HR group at the company's world headquarters had degenerated to the point where no one paid much attention to it. For years, no one within the company knew how large human resources was. It was only when the company began to experience serious financial problems that it began to investigate its general and administrative budget, especially as a percent of net revenue (in comparison to its competitors).

Top management asked for a chart that pulled together all the employee information for each of the departments, including human resources. The chart showed there were 1,125 HR personnel within the company (and it took more than two months to get that information).

The CEO could hardly believe the numbers. Not only was HR bloated, but the IT budget for the company, once he could see it pulled together, was out of sight. This was true for finance, manufacturing, and others as well. The divisions had become very fat indeed. After several more quarters of weak results, the CEO finally got up the nerve to do something. It was clear to him that the head of HR was making unacceptably slow progress on the cost problem. The CEO reached down to the second in command in finance, whom I will call Dave, and put him in charge of HR. Dave had spent the first ten years of his career in manufacturing and the last five in finance; as a result, he had a broader view of the company than most of the managers. He was also a top development prospect for the company, and this would be a great stretch assignment for him.

Dave had the perfect personality for taking on this task. Everyone knew he was a common-sense guy who had a great sense of humor but that he was also quite tough. As Dave began in the new job, he constantly talked about the crisis the company was experiencing with respect to costs. All of the business areas were going to have to contribute, he told them, and that included human resources.

Dave constantly went around asking questions, getting oriented on how HR had been run. He spent a lot of time accumulating information before he made any decisions, and that was very comforting to those who worked under him. On the other hand, they also sensed the urgency he conveyed, based on the company's problems.

Two months later, Dave published a new charter for the human resources organization, focusing on making the group as lean as possible and making its work as simple as possible. He introduced his plans with his usual dose of thoroughness and humor, which made it acceptable to the troops. Dave was able to play back to them a lot of the information he had learned from his immersion in how human resources worked, and those in the department knew he was on target with respect to his assessment.

The thing that surprised folks a bit was the speed and decisiveness with which he acted. Within three months of issuing his new charter, he was ready to reorganize the department, and he had a plan for eliminating about 60 percent of all the information systems used to run HR. He already had a couple of information technology people working on the creation of a single global database of employee information that would be used by all of HR.

He launched a major plan to reduce the HR generalists within the business units by about 70 percent. His homespun logic for this move was that the company simply couldn't afford a lot of HR people out there holding the hands of employees to make them feel better. It was a luxury that Dave knew the company could no longer afford, and Dave was determined to fix it quickly.

He formed a benefits group that administered all of the plans throughout the company, resulting in an enormous cost savings for the company (previously, the benefits personnel in each of the business units would have helped people with questions). He launched an HR Web site that contained all the information on the benefits, and also contained all the necessary HR forms employees might need to file, allowing them to cut back on the number of employees needed to field calls and answer questions.

The company had clearly picked the right person to run HR. Dave understood the goal, was determined to achieve it, and was great at working with people. He also understood the power of a unified HR across the company.

Within 8 months, the HR department was cut from 1,125 people to 310, and, while a few HR personnel did remain in each of the business units to carry out the company-wide HR programs, they were also charged with making sure that unit performed well from an HR perspective.

This kind of dual responsibility is key to driving the efficiency of global centralized systems and processes while providing the flexibility needed in regional plants or divisions.

In this case, information systems played a key role in helping to systemize and clean up the HR mess. Old systems were discarded and new software and databases were created that were light-years ahead of the capability the company previously had. A new performance-appraisal system was also installed across the units, and for the first time, a process to help develop key personnel was put in place to ensure a steady stream of future leaders within the company.

The company had paid a huge price for its lack of unified leadership in human resources and other areas. There is no substitute for having strong centralized departments able to implement company-wide standards and processes, led by individuals who are not afraid to blow the whistle when things start going off track.

SPOTTING KEY TALENT

One company I consulted with decided to launch a process to identify talented prospects within the company and make sure they were being appropriately challenged so they could develop their skills and have the chance to become part of top management in the years ahead.

In the first meeting to establish that process, every department, plant, and subsidiary had to sit down with the CEO and go over their assessment of their top fifty personnel prospects. The people they identified had to be distributed across the various organization levels so that management didn't pick just mature people who were already in the higher-level jobs.

It was hilarious to me at this first meeting how hard the different business units fought to hide their strongest employees. In some cases, the strongest performers were not on the "top 50" list. If someone else brought their names up, the head of the division or department would downplay their roles in order to retain them. As the meeting progressed, an executive whom I will call Jack, the head of one of the strongest fiefdoms in the company, claimed that a particular employee he knew from another division was a strong performer, but that employee wasn't on that division's list. The room went silent. You could tell from the looks passed back and forth that a sacred code of the fiefdoms had been broken. Jack had violated the golden rule—If you leave my fiefdom alone, I'll leave yours alone.

Jack continued to ask about the individual he was interested in, and finally the business unit that "owned" her had to confess she had very strong performance-appraisal ratings and had been in her current job for well over three years. It was clear she needed to be moved into a challenging, new assignment.

When the general manager of that business unit realized he was going to lose this person, he started to go after some of Jack's people. Before long, it was a free-for-all. Jack had opened the floodgates. Pretty soon, the business unit heads were jumping all over one another, criticizing one another's lists, claiming they were filled with weak performers while they hid their strongest performers. It was like a bunch of kids fighting over baseball cards. All kinds of deals were being proposed, and the meeting had gotten out of hand.

The CEO finally called the meeting back to order and, smiling, indicated that huge progress had been made. He asked to see revised "top 50" sheets within two weeks, after which they would schedule another session.

This "key people" process was repeated by the CEO every six months. The presenters had to first comment on their exhibit from the previous six months, explaining what happened to the individuals who dropped off the list. This was a great exercise. If a business unit consistently lost its strong contributors, that became clear as the process got stronger. If the overall caliber of personnel in one area wasn't as strong as in the other areas, that also got discussed and the recruiting practices questioned.

This was an incredibly healthy process, driven by the CEO. Without strong leadership from the top, there is no way the groups would have shared information on their best people.

This process of developing key personnel reinforces the need for strong and unified departments within the company, so that top talent isn't bottled up within a particular department, business, or subsidiary. The process requires a lot of openness on the part of the business heads, which is why the CEO has to drive it.

3. THE DISCIPLINE OF PERSONNEL ROTATION

In areas such as finance and IT, a company can end up being held hostage by individuals who build their own fiefdoms around their expertise. The same holds true for project managers and other managerial positions where, because an individual has been left in place for many years, the company perceives a risk in moving the individual. Such expertise or seniority-oriented fiefdoms can lead to missed opportunities and antiquated approaches as the skills and motivation of these individuals atrophy.

Moving personnel in and out of an organization is an important tool for breaking up potential fiefdoms and prohibiting their formation in the first place.

FIEFDOMS IN THE FINANCE DEPARTMENT

In one Fortune 500 company I know of, the finance organization had become an incredible fiefdom, constantly protecting the methodology it used to record and analyze the business. When the corporation decided to move to SAP software in sales, finance, and manufacturing to achieve greater efficiencies, the finance department appealed to the CEO. It did not want the IT people to implement SAP in "its" domain. As far as it was concerned, it was in charge of the finance systems; the company could build its information technology architecture around them. It argued strongly that it should be exempt from SAP because it already had top-notch systems that had been proven over the last fifteen years (which should give you some sense of how antiquated things were).

After continued pressure by IT to roll out SAP broadly within the company in order to achieve significant savings through the reduction of legacy systems and staffing, the finance organization suggested that the IT organization build bridges from the new SAP modules to its traditional finance systems. But the effort would extend the SAP project by eighteen months and increase its cost by 60 percent.

The reality was that the finance organization was incredibly insular and had antiquated information systems. But the CFO was comfortable with the way finance was running and didn't want to make any changes. He believed it made good sense not to change the system in order to ensure the continued reliability of finance's performance. Such reliability, he felt, was worth whatever the company had to pay to work around finance's systems.

This was a classic example of a company-wide project that was about to get much more expensive than people thought. I often hear companies complain about the high costs or cost overruns on SAP implementation. But I've seen SAP implemented in a very streamlined manner with very reasonable costs and a short timetable. What happens too often is what I discussed above. Departments or divisions within companies are unwilling to change and consequently build a lot of bridges between SAP and their old systems. In this way they adopt SAP but keep the interfaces with the antiquated systems that they are accustomed to using.

At this particular company, the CFO, whom I will call Ken, constantly took swipes at the IT organization, claiming that from what he heard from his fellow CFOs at other companies, IT was wrong about SAP.

In fact, Ken wanted IT to report to him and had been arguing unsuccessfully to make that happen for the last four years. IT reported to a group vice president whose business units under his control represented about 70 percent of the company's revenue. That group vice president took pride in the fact that he had gotten the IT organization to the point where it could tackle this SAP project and achieve some major efficiency for the company. All of this only angered the CFO.

The IT organization took its case to the CEO, insisting that finance not be allowed to drag the SAP effort down. The CEO had grown up in the sales arm of the company and did not have a strong relationship with the CFO. In fact, the CFO and his finance group operated like a large fiefdom, one that would work with the CEO when required to, but it otherwise kept him as uninvolved as possible.

IT scheduled three different meetings with the CEO to get this resolved. In the last meeting, the CEO finally admitted that he was reluctant to force the finance organization to adopt SAP as proposed by IT. After making excuses for finance, he told the IT organization to spend the extra money and to take the extra time. This devastated morale within IT, and several key people on the SAP project quit. As it turned out, the changes added about eighteen months to the effort, and it almost doubled the cost. And believe it or not, the CIO lost his job because of the cost overruns.

So what's the lesson here? Clearly, the CEO needed to take on the finance fiefdom early on, when he saw that they refused to participate with the rest of the company. He should have moved some key personnel out of finance and moved in strong performers from other departments who had financial expertise. It would have taken courage, but that's exactly what a CEO is expected to do.

LEGACY PEOPLE PROTECT LEGACY SYSTEMS

When people are left in their jobs too long, they tend to form territorial fiefdoms. They fear that if they are moved out of their jobs, they won't be able to do anything else. I saw this vividly displayed with the implementation of an order/shipping/billing system at a major corporation.

At Corporation A, as I'll call it, I found an incredible group of legacy people and antiquated systems in the order/shipping/billing system area of the company. The leader of the department, whom I will call Rick, had worked in order/shipping/billing for more than fifteen years. He was considered the "owner" of the current system, and he directed the IT efforts on an ongoing basis to make sure this system served the company's needs. Rick had two people reporting to him who had worked with him for more than ten years. One was an expert in the order/shipping/billing process, and the other was in charge of the hardware and software used in the process.

Rick took great pride in his team and in its excellent track record of reliability. The bad news was they spent a ton of money to maintain the antiquated system. The system ran on hardware that was outlandishly expensive compared to new server technology. Based on cost pressures, the company launched a major order/shipping/billing overhaul.

Rick and his people fashioned the changes in such a way that they were able to move in some of the new hardware, saving a lot of money, but they did very little with the software except to port it over to the new hardware. Basically, the group couldn't contemplate any way to do order/shipping/billing other than with its current legacy approach.

The changes it made to take advantage of the hardware were written in the same old programming language it had used for fifteen years. It incurred huge conversion costs to move the databases onto the new hardware, while continuing to have those databases interface with the old software. This approach enabled it to hold on to its established roles in the company as the experts in those systems, while claiming significant savings due to the new hardware.

To my mind, this was a group of people who had been in their jobs for too long. They were essentially building a moat around their old systems in such a way that the company had no way to penetrate them.

In contrast, another organization I consulted with—Corporation B—overhauled its order/shipping/billing system but in a remarkably fresh way. It asked: What is the best, cleanest, simplest, most up-to-date way to handle the basics of order/shipping/billing? It put a highly regarded thirty-two-year-old information technology wizard named Curt in charge of the project to develop and implement a completely new approach. He formed a small team to develop a new architecture around new, off-the-shelf software. Curt was a dynamo. The group designed a new order/shipping/billing approach built around key databases that would contain all the input and output data. When implemented, these databases would enable an entire organization to keep up with orders, their status, and when and where the order was shipped and billed.

Because it used off-the-shelf software with easy-to-use Web-based menus as the user interface, it took only months to get the system up and running. It then designed a lengthy period where the current order/shipping/billing system ran parallel to the new system to make sure the new approach operated smoothly and achieved the results generated by the old system. Once the parallel testing was complete, it rolled the system out, first in Europe, then in the Americas, and finally Asia.

Corporation B had one-sixth of the personnel engaged in overhauling order/shipping/billing compared to Corporation A. Yet Corporation B developed a completely new, up-to-date order/shipping/billing system in a cost-effective, timely manner, while Corporation A used significantly more resources and took significantly more time to overhaul its legacy system.

The new approach used at Corporation B yielded a new, up-to-date system that was incredibly easy to maintain.

What made the difference for Corporation B was the steadfast leadership of the organization and the top talent selected to tackle the task. These folks, because they had not been stuck in their jobs for a long time, were not wedded to the company's old approach. After revitalizing order/shipping/billing, they expected to move on and take on greater responsibilities within the company. In Corporation A, the protectionist mentality of the legacy personnel, and a lack of top management involvement to crack through the shield of the fiefdom, cost the company time and money. More important, it still uses an antiquated order/shipping/billing process. Rotating key personnel can have a huge positive impact for the company in terms of time, responsiveness, and cost.

THE FAVORITE SUPPLIER FIEFDOM

Another company I worked with had a hardware development group led by an individual I will call Bill, who was viewed as a talented technologist. He had been in his job for well over ten years and was generally viewed as someone who kept up with the latest trends. On the other hand, he was a control freak. He made sure that he and his organization played a key role in any of the business unit's decisions with regard to hardware. He was always recommending hardware from the same manufacturer. In fact, many claimed that the company, because of Bill, was far too close to its hardware supplier, to the point where cheaper equipment opportunities were being missed.

When Bill was confronted about being wedded to this vendor, he would lose his temper and start tossing technology jargon around to convince the skeptics that he knew what he was doing and that his supplier decisions were wise decisions.

The worrisome part of this was the total dependence on the quality of the vendor regarding improvements and innovation. And the company's buddy-buddy relationship with the vendor made it impossible to confront the vendor on costs and creativity.

One time the sales organization pursued some ingenious new desktop workstations for some of the accounting offices. They formed a small team within sales and told the systems people nothing about it. They ordered several of these new desktop systems, tested them thoroughly, and then ordered more than one hundred of the units to be used throughout their accounting offices. Bill and his hardware-development folks found out about it after the large order had already been placed, and he went absolutely through the roof. He harassed the CIO whom he reported to about going to the CEO and getting the order blocked. The CIO did the wise thing and called the head of sales and asked him what was going on. The senior VP of sales explained that they had simply had enough of Bill and his favorite supplier, and they weren't satisfied with the alternatives. So they went off on their own. At last, the CIO started to get the picture.

To break up the fiefdom, the CIO began to move personnel into the group from other units, to challenge whether better opportunities existed with other vendors, and to explore whether the existing vendor could improve its terms. Over the years, the fiefdom members had lost their aggressiveness and entrepreneurial thinking, convinced that they were doing superb work with their current vendor, who they assured their management was state of the art.

It's sometimes tough to penetrate technological jargon to see what else could be done. But management should never underestimate the value of a set of fresh eyes to question established procedures. Rotating personnel is a way to continually develop people and bring in fresh thinking.

4. THE DISCIPLINE OF PERSONNEL DEVELOPMENT

The combination of strong fiefdoms and weak performance-appraisal systems is deadly in terms of developing strong leaders. Fiefdoms trap and limit people; they don't tend to differentiate between strong employees and weaker ones. As a result, strong leaders get frustrated and leave.

Well-run companies focus on earmarking future leaders within the company early on and putting development plans in place to put these people on a fast track, exposing them to many different responsibilities in order to prepare them for increasingly bigger assignments.

This is counter to what typically goes on with a fiefdom. What is seductive about fiefdoms is the protection they offer against change. Also, people working in a protected fiefdom usually believe they are doing a good job and employees tend to be satisfied with their performance and their work. This can lull them into a sense of complacency. Underperformers are treated much better than they should be, and strong performers are not challenged to crank up their overall effort.

MEASURING ATTRITION

One company I consulted with instituted a creative new approach emerging in the HR profession to measure attrition, which can help to drive out weak performers and ensure that proper attention is paid to the strongest performers. The company defined "good" attrition as the departure of an employee whom they wanted to leave the company. Such employees tended to receive substandard performance-appraisal ratings for several appraisal periods, and it was clear they weren't going to play a strong role in the overall direction of the company. The company defined "bad" attrition as losing someone whom they didn't want to leave the company, an individual with strong performance ratings and a clear ability to tackle new assignments well.

The head of HR at this company, whom I will call Andy, had heard about this approach while benchmarking other companies on how they weeded out poor performers. He brought some of these ideas back and reviewed them with the CEO. The CEO liked them but feared incredible pushback from the troops. Their company had not done a good job over the years in confronting poor performance, and this would be a huge intervention. In the end, the CEO decided to have Andy explain good attrition and bad attrition to his direct reports. At that meeting, two of the business unit heads balked strongly. They became very defensive, claiming that they knew their people well, and they knew when to fire someone and when not to. They also claimed that they hired extremely competent people and that this kind of system was unnecessary for an organization such as theirs. Neither the CEO nor Andy was surprised by these reactions. Fortunately, the CEO had a fair amount of guts. In the meeting, he went after the most vocal of the business unit heads and candidly told him the company needed a culture change. People were too comfortable, and the level of performance needed to be raised.

Andy then described what he had learned through his benchmarking efforts at other organizations; he admitted that what he had in mind with regard to attrition was a huge change for their culture but that something had to be done to confront poor performance in the company. Andy also pointed out that this would work only if the top team supported his approach 100 percent. The CEO underscored this and came down particularly hard on those who had pushed back. He announced that he had asked Andy to implement the program, and he wanted their full support. And that if he didn't get it, he would be incredibly disappointed and would take subsequent action. That was about as clear a signal from a CEO as you'll get in a team meeting of that nature. So Andy began implementing the new approach.

Each department learned each quarter what their good and bad attrition numbers were, as a percent of their total employees. Management looked at the figures carefully. They made it clear that on an annualized basis, they expected a good attrition rate of about 3 to 5 percent. This meant they should be moving out 3 to 5 percent of employees who were the weakest performers to make room for fresh talent.

This may sound a bit cold, but in reality it was fairer to the employees than letting them falsely believe they were performing adequately and then suddenly having the rug pulled out from them years later, when it might be too late for them to change their ways and get another job.

This constant upgrading of the talent pool at a company sends a powerful message throughout the company that strong performance is rewarded and that the company has no patience for mediocrity. Strong performers love to work in that kind of an environment.

Management also looked carefully at the bad attrition figures for every department. The ideal bad attrition rate is zero. If it is too high or increasing, management needs to understand what's going on in that department. Why are valued employees leaving? This is a powerful tool to ensure that each group in the company works to keep their strong performers motivated and excited about what they are doing and about their future with the company. *That* is great personnel development.

This combination of good and bad attrition is a powerful management tool for dealing with fiefdoms. When bad attrition starts to grow, the fiefdom needs to be scrutinized by top management. If the good attrition is too low, the fiefdom is not adequately dealing with poor performance. Top management needs to address these issues quickly.

In the company discussed above, the system sent clear signals to every employee that the company was determined to create a performance-focused culture, where strong talent was promoted and where individuals who weren't making the grade were weeded out.

THE TOTAL EMPLOYEE REVIEW

As I've made clear, fiefdoms like to keep their personnel information to themselves and control their own pool of employees. The sales organization in one large company I consulted with tackled all of these issues with a terrific tool called the "total employee review." The VP of sales met once a year with the head of sales for each division and the heads of each of the staff sales groups. He developed detailed templates to be filled out prior to the review, requiring each group to come up with an immense amount of personnel data in addition to internal benchmarking by human resources.

The templates showed the headcount within each unit, by job type (i.e., marketing, sales, IT, etc.), and by level, and showed the trends over three years. There were compensation charts by job type and by job level as well as benchmarks versus other units within the company and, where possible, benchmarks versus competitors. Additional templates pulled together average performance ratings by job level, by job type, and by department. Still other templates captured the development of key personnel within the company and the jobs each of those individuals had had over the past five years.

The vice president of sales, Allen, drove hard to institute this total employee review because he knew what a powerful impact a strong salesperson could have. In their industry, two salespeople with basically the same job might have a huge difference in the revenue they brought in based on their sales abilities. The difference could be as much as 30 or 40 percent. Allen had been frustrated that he had no way to learn more about his people and to identify the strong and the weak performers. Before the total employee review, he was totally dependent on his trips into the field, where he was able to meet with only a few of his people. He would try to pick up tips on who was unusually strong or weak, and he would try to get summaries of performance appraisals, but it was always spotty. He never knew what people's underlying agendas might be when they talked about the performance of specific employees under them. In some cases, it turned out they were trying to pawn off weak performers by dressing them up more positively than they should, asking him to assist in getting them a "good opportunity" in another group.

When HR brought the total employee review idea to Allen, he was incredibly supportive. He knew his sales results were dependent on having great people. And he knew he wasn't doing a very good job of identifying the folks who were strongest—and weakest—and treating them accordingly.

So Allen and the head of HR within the sales department held half-day meetings with each of Allen's direct reports to go over in detail all the aspects of their personnel.

The exercise proved to be a fiefdom killer. One group that was especially protective of its personnel was easily spotted. It was very obvious if a fiefdom was hoarding great talent or inappropriately putting up with weak performers.

HR can play a key role in making this total enrollment review a success. To do so, it needs to be unified across the entire organization.

5. THE DISCIPLINE OF PERFORMANCE IMPROVEMENT

A strong human resources organization must drive discipline in improving the performance of individuals across the entire organization. This is particularly important at the middle and top levels. Without such discipline, change never happens, and the organization does not develop strong future leaders.

To drive such improvement on an ongoing basis requires support from top management, to give credibility to the programs that human resources launches.

There are several tools to help individuals understand where they need to improve, and to do this in as quantitative a manner as possible, so that employees can measure their growth.

ACHIEVING A PERFORMANCE-BASED CULTURE

One company I worked with sent shock waves throughout the organization by launching a major initiative to generate in-depth data on how individuals could improve. It was based on a "360 assessment." Many major companies, including IBM, Procter & Gamble, and Microsoft, have used this for years. It's an exercise where standard questions are given to the peers of an individual, a second set of questions is given to the subordinates of an individual, and a third set of questions is given to a variety of stakeholders in the organization (including the person's boss) who are affected by the individual's performance. Each fills out the questionnaire anonymously. This really helps get objective feedback from individuals who might be reluctant to give it if they had to be identified.

This organization required a 360 assessment for each individual at a department-head level and above once a year.

Often a 360 assessment is used when the individual knows there is a particular area they need to improve in, and the 360 assessment serves as a tool for getting feedback. Rarely does an organization put the kind of effort into performance improvement that doing a 360 assessment of all department-head-level personnel and above would involve.

Some amazing results occurred as a result of this annual, compulsory 360-assessment program. The head of one business unit, whom I will call Bruce, was an incredibly obnoxious guy who was consistently rude to his people. Many claimed that Bruce was not truthful with top management in regard to what was going on in his area. He constantly blamed others for any bad news. With his own people, he would throw tantrums when something didn't go his way. Fortunately for him, he ran a business that was fairly healthy (through no fault of his own). The products he was marketing and the part of the industry in which he participated was quite hot. Three weeks after it was announced that everyone at the department-head level and above would be going through one of these 360s, Bruce quit the company. He knew exactly what kind of feedback he would get and was furious. In essence, the 360-assessment approach had cracked one of the major fiefdoms within the company.

The general manager who scored second highest of all his peers was an incredibly quiet guy who didn't have any aspiration to move farther within the company. He simply rolled up his sleeves every day and did a great job. What the 360-assessment tool uncovered was that his people greatly appreciated his clear and aggressive goals, his overall positive attitude of encouraging them to do better, the confidence he showed in them, and how he managed the top management.

This guy, whom I will refer to as Frank, was incredibly encouraged by these results. In fact, he was totally shocked. Frank had always seen himself as a hard worker who would do the best job he could, but he had no sense of how far he could go in the company. He just never worried about that. These results gave Frank a ton of confidence, and, as a result, he became a rising star in the company.

There was a female department head, whom I will call Liz, who ran a strong organization but had a terrible temper. She just couldn't handle bad news, and she went off like a rocket whenever she encountered it. People feared her because of this, and her organization did not perform as well as it should have because she never got the bad news until the very last moment, when it was too late to alter course. Liz took the results from the 360 assessment and went to HR and *demanded* help in improving this aspect of her performance. She could see how it was holding her, and the company, back. They sent her to several management sessions outside the company, and she quickly became an incredible student of why she behaved the way she did. Her improvement was equally incredible. The next year when they did the 360 assessment, her overall ranking among department heads went from the bottom quartile to the second-highest quartile. It's inspiring to see improvement like that, because it really is hard for people to change.

This 360 assessment acts as a real fiefdom-crusher, because when used properly, there are no hiding places.

PUTTING EMPLOYEE SURVEYS TO WORK

Several years ago, a number of companies began to experiment with taking their employee surveys and adding questions that would be relevant in assessing the overall health of a particular department, as well as questions that would be indicative of the overall health of the company and its top management. They also added questions that would indicate how well an employee's vice president was doing.

The human resources departments then organized the results so that management really did have a measure of the overall health of a particular department and could compare departments across the company. Here are the kinds of attributes to which employees were asked to assign a 1 to 5 rating (1 = strongly disagree, 2 = disagree, 3 = neutral, 4 = agree, 5 = strongly agree):

- The way decisions are made in my department enables me to perform effectively.
- My department has a clear understanding of the company's external customers' needs.
- I can see a clear link between my work and the company's objectives.
- My manager considers the broader impact of his or her decisions.
- I feel encouraged to come up with new and better ways of doing things.

- My manager makes good use of my skills and abilities.
- My manager encourages me to take on big challenges in my work.
- The people in my department speak openly and honestly even when the news is bad.

These attributes gave each department head and their top management an overall sense of how well their group was doing compared to other groups in the company. The department heads also could see individual ratings of specific attributes, in order to isolate problems.

A separate set of attributes focused on the overall strategy of the organization and whether top management was driving in the right direction. Among the attributes were:

- I believe we are heading in the right direction as an organization.
- People are rewarded according to their job performance.
- I would recommend this organization as a good place to work.

These kinds of attributes gave top management insights into whether they were making clear the overall objectives of the organization as well as feedback on the type of environment they created for employees.

Several of these companies isolated attributes that gave individual vice presidents insight about how well they led, such as:

- I have confidence in the leadership of the VP of our group.
- The vice president responsible for my group demonstrates fiscal responsibility.
- In this group, decision making includes gathering feedback from other impacted groups.
- I have enough information about the company's overall strategy to make good decisions in our group.
- The VP of our group takes a global perspective when making decisions.
- The VP of our group takes on big challenges.

Each vice president was given the overall average of the scores and the data on each attribute. They also saw the scores of the other vice presidents (without being identified by name) so they could benchmark themselves against their peers. Given the usual competitive nature of these vice presidents, this data was incredibly powerful in motivating them to improve.

At one company I consulted with, when they instituted this approach, one vice president, whom I will call John, was devastated by the results. John had the reputation of never acknowledging anything positive in others. He was totally focused on what they did wrong. He also had a tough time delegating. He would charge the organization to fix a mess, but he couldn't keep himself out of diving into the details, often embarrassing the people who were supposed to have the responsibility to fix it.

The first time the company did the survey and summarized scores, the vice president ended up in the bottom quartile versus his peers. He was angry. It took HR a couple of days to settle the guy down and explain to him that the rating was based on the employee survey. They finally got him to understand that he was looking at input from his own people with regard to how he was carrying out his job. Naturally, his people nailed him for his consistently negative attitude, his lack of appreciation, and his inability to delegate, particularly in problem situations.

After about three days, he came into the office and had HR set up one-on-one interviews with each of his direct reports. Believe it or not, he sat there and listened carefully. He had an HR person join in the meetings so that they could explain the survey and people could comment on why they thought he got the scores that he did. Everyone was totally surprised at how aggressively he tackled the problem.

He next talked to two vice presidents who were suggested by HR because they scored high in their ability to communicate their division's strategy and to delegate. He asked them tons of questions about the kinds of meetings they had with their employees, the kind of communications they sent out, etc. He also asked them how they communicated their strategy to their organization. In general, he soaked up everything he could get from these meetings to find ways to improve.

No one was more surprised than the HR expert at how the VP took the exercise to heart. This doesn't happen very often, but when it does, it can result in transformational change.

The ability to develop individuals' skills and help them to become genuine leaders is enhanced significantly by this kind of data. It's also a great tool to break up fiefdoms or prevent them from forming.

6. THE DISCIPLINE OF COMPENSATION

It's important that individuals be paid a fair wage. But that fairness must be placed in the context of performance both in the organization as a whole and in the department in which they work. For example, in some industries, the pay scales for marketing people are far different from the pay scales for manufacturing people. Those differences should be reflected both in the marketing compensation and manufacturing compensation.

The head of each department must conduct surveys within the industry so that competitive pay scales can be established and strong performers rewarded for their performance. Weak performers should be identified. Overcompensating underachieving employees can undermine an entire department's motivation and morale.

AVOID "ONE-SIZE-FITS-ALL" COMPENSATION

In consumer products, an industry sector in which I lived during my twenty-six years at Procter & Gamble, there are significant differences in salary structures for various departments. Marketing personnel are the highest-paid individuals, and in most consumer-products companies, top management emerges from the marketing group. The remaining departments are paid well but not as well as you see in other industries, where that department is strategic. Someone in information technology at P&G, for example, would not be paid as much as an IT person in the software industry, or financial services, where IT is often at the heart of a company's products. The same is true of finance. Finance people are typically not involved in the strategic core of a consumer products company. That would be far different in a financial services company, where a finance person might play a very strategic role.

Procter & Gamble did an excellent job of making sure the head of each department did extensive benchmarking within the consumer-products industry to make sure that his people were paid appropriately. Human resources played a key role in monitoring this, making sure that the surveys were done correctly and that the compensation systems for each functional area were appropriate.

At a chemicals company I know that has grown over the past ten years from $300 million in revenue to about $2 billion, the compensation system was originally very simple. There was one pay scale and one set of titles for all employees within the company, whether they were in finance, R&D, manufacturing, etc. In the view of the founder of the company, it was one group of people launching one company, and he saw no need to make compensation complex.

This may have been the right approach when the company was small. But the company grew rapidly, and ten years later it had a sizable finance organization, manufacturing unit, etc. The compensation system that was in place was still the original plan the founder had established in the early days of the company. As a result, some departments, such as finance, were overpaid (finance was nonstrategic), while the chemists and engineers in R&D and product development were significantly underpaid (these were critical skills in the industry). In fact, the attrition rate of the chemists and chemical engineers began to be a major problem.

Two R&D chemists who had worked for the company since its inception confronted the CEO, showing him the offers they had gotten from competitors. It was clear that the salary system was out of whack. It was a wake-up call to the CEO to have two trusted employees approach him with hard evidence that some of his most trusted employees were about to walk out the door over salary. The head of R&D should have been screaming that his people were being short-changed, but he didn't. It took the two R&D chemists to bring the issue to the CEO's attention.

The CEO found that turnover had increased significantly in areas where salaries were lower than those in similar positions in other companies. He realized the problem needed to be addressed promptly.

In most fiefdoms, a single compensation system for every employee tends to be the rule, regardless of what functional area (marketing, finance, etc.) they are in. But what often happens is that some individuals complain, and exceptions are made, and the "squeaky wheel" process takes over. The complaining employee often receives special treatment to shut him or her up and make the issues go away. The result is a patchwork compensation system with no real established principles.

THE PRO FORMA SALARY INCREASE

Another company I consulted with just couldn't understand why it continued to lose top people. When I looked at the salary plan, I saw the company gave plenty of latitude to reward strong performers and to penalize weak performers. However, the individual turfs were so strong that there was no information available to see how well the system rewarded strong performers or penalized weak performers.

After working the issue with the CEO, he finally got up enough nerve to ask for the data. At first he was told that it wasn't available. He pressed on, and eventually the systems people, who were fragmented among different departments, and HR, which was equally fragmented, started to deliver a trickle of the information needed.

The CEO soon found out why it was taking so long to get this information. The head of R&D—let's call him Ken—had 80 percent of his people getting the same-size increase, the recommended five percent. That was the mandated average across all employees for that particular year. Ken's group had about 10 percent who were viewed as strong performers. They got a 6 to 7 percent increase. The remaining 10 percent of employees, the weak performers, got 3 to 4 percent. Clearly, the top performers weren't being compensated enough, and the bottom performers were getting too much—they shouldn't have received a raise at all. And not having any differentiation among the middle 80 percent was a mistake.

When confronted with this embarrassing data, Ken explained that his people argued strongly that they didn't have any weak performers. As a result, while they could isolate 10 percent of the people who were not as strong as they should have been, they insisted those people get a

3 to 4 percent increase. Because Ken had to average 5 percent across the board, that left him with little latitude in rewarding the strong performers.

In essence, Ken had just leveled the playing field, in effect penalizing his top performers, and potentially squashing their motivation. The CEO realized that fiefdoms such as this don't deal with poor performance because they don't want to upset the troops. Because their primary goal is to make all employees relatively happy, they find themselves saddled with mediocrity.

After he found what was occurring in Ken's organization, the CEO kept pounding away to get the data from the other groups. And that's the kind of leadership it takes to deal with fiefdoms.

Department heads must constantly make sure their salary system significantly rewards outstanding and above-average performers and holds back on the below-average and unsatisfactory performers. This kind of salary differentiation leads to a high-performance organization.

The six people disciplines I've outlined in this chapter, combined with the seven process and behavior disciplines discussed in Chapter 3, set the stage for fostering the creativity and innovation needed to better serve customers, as we'll see in the next chapter.

5 CREATIVITY AND FIEFDOMS

A COMPANY MOST visibly touches its customers and consumers at an area I call "the edge." These are the points of contact in a company where maximum creativity is needed. In my experience, there are three areas, or departments, in organizations in which creativity is at a premium: sales, marketing, and research and development. Sales organizations must be highly creative in interacting with customers in order to make them aware of the advantages of the company's products and services. Marketing departments require creativity and innovation to assemble persuasive materials to describe those products and services. And R&D, by its very nature, must be highly creative and innovative to create new products and features superior to the competition's and preferred by consumers.

1. MINIMIZE TIME SPENT ON NONCREATIVE ACTIVITIES

The most important contribution a sales organization can make is to establish a successful relationship with its customers. That requires innovation, creativity, and focus. In order to accomplish this, people in sales cannot waste time on non-customer-focused activities such as developing marginally useful databases, stockpiling IT resources, developing systems that generate an excessive number of reports and measures, or holding too many unnecessary meetings.

The same is true for marketing and for research and development. Each must guard its time carefully, spending as much time as possible on strategic thinking and creativity.

That is why sales, marketing, and R&D, whenever possible, should use standard measures and processes generated by company headquarters rather than by individual departments in their organizations, to gauge market progress and quantitatively capture the interaction with customers. Doing so will free sales, marketing, and R&D from the time-consuming efforts of reinventing such measures and processes and building resources to duplicate measures that should be driven across the entire organization.

SALES SHOULD WORK AT ACHIEVING, NOT DEFINING, KEY MEASURES

Shortly after I joined Microsoft in 1994, Steve Ballmer, who was heading up Microsoft sales at the time, invited me to sit in on some midyear reviews. Steve had developed carefully defined templates that he asked all of the subsidiaries to have filled out when he visited for their reviews. This was great discipline from the top, letting the subsidiaries know what was important to the organization from a sales perspective and what was important in order to understand the performance of a particular sales subsidiary. Steve and a small sales group in Redmond put a lot of energy into defining those templates.

One Asian subsidiary decided to modify some of the templates, adding a series of measures they considered valuable in order to understand how successful their sales efforts were. This meeting began at the end of the second day of midyear reviews. The first day turned into an eighteen-hour marathon; the second day also went late into the evening. The management team from this subsidiary had fifteen people huddled around a conference table littered with the leftovers of a buffet dinner. They began their presentation to Steve by pointing out that the retail trade was dramatically different in their country compared to other countries. They strongly argued that some of the standard measures in Steve's templates didn't do justice to the nuances of their market.

Steve started fidgeting as they attempted to defend the ways they had modified his standard templates. They passed out two exhibits designed to show the unusually large marketing efforts being launched by two major competitors, which clearly hurt their business. The first one detailed how much money these competitors had spent in the previous two fiscal years versus their estimate of the enormous increase they were seeing this fiscal year. They discussed how much of that marketing money was being used to fund discounts on pricing. The second exhibit focused on advertising funds the two competitors had used in the prior two fiscal years compared to substantial increases in marketing they'd spent this year. The head of the subsidiary went on to discuss how much revenue he believed these activities took away from his own business.

By this time, Steve's face was heading toward a brilliant red. Apparently, the general manager of the country missed that unmistakable signal, because he launched into a third exhibit that showed what two large customers had spent with the company the previous two years, and what they had bought so far this fiscal year. He explained that one of these accounts had significant personnel turnover in their information technology area and, consequently, all the decisions for new software and hardware were being put on hold until new people were in place. The second account was experiencing a severe downturn in revenue and profits; as a result, its marketing and information technology budgets had been cut significantly. He pulled out several newspaper clippings to try to substantiate his story.

The general manager then stepped back and summarized the competitive environment, reiterated that two large customers were pulling back in their spending on technology, and concluded that it was absolutely essential to look at his business via some additional measures intended to show how these detrimental factors in the marketplace were clouding the solid success of his basic business.

Steve finally lost it. He chastised the group for several long minutes (which probably seemed like an hour to the group) for not facing up to the fact that their business was soft. He forcefully told them to move on to the templates that would explain what they were going to do to revitalize it. The general manager tried to steer Steve back to the "additional measures," but Steve would not have any part of it. He finally stood up, resting his fists on the table, leaned forward toward the general manager, and said: "I'll define the key measures. It's your job to grow them." To soften the blow, and release some of the tension in the room, he then broke into one of his classic boyish grins before continuing.

What Steve was telling the general manager and his team was this: Don't waste my time coming up with a story that doesn't match the overall performance of the group or division. He made it clear that the group would be measured by the same data every subsidiary was measured by.

The subsidiary had wasted time and effort and had even hired additional staff to generate additional analyses on an ongoing basis to justify its actions and performance results. From Steve's perspective, it was an unacceptable diversion to try to distract management and make themselves feel better. More important, it diverted energy, intensity, and critical time needed to fix the business.

One key lesson here is the importance of top management deciding what tracking tools and measures are appropriate, making sure they are instituted uniformly and broadly so the organization runs in an efficient manner and making it clear that attempts to circumvent such standards will not be tolerated.

MEASURING YOUR MARKETING IMPACT

Marketing, like sales, must focus on its primary task: generating creativity and persuasiveness in its communications with consumers and customers. While its performance has to be measured, such measures should be standardized across the organization. Marketing personnel should spend minimal time generating new ways to measure their performance and trying to positively position results with top management.

This is not to belittle the role of measuring the effectiveness of marketing. Companies should use fairly standardized approaches that can be applied throughout the organization. For example, one company with which I consulted had a weak public image with respect to innovation. Their products were viewed as useful for households but not for business. The company knew business could benefit from their products, and in many cases that was happening. But their brand remained stuck in the past. So they created attitude surveys to track the progress they achieved as they tackled the problem.

For just about any product and related marketing, there should be measures in place that enable you to watch the change in the attitudes of the target audience toward that product or service. You need to be very clear and focused regarding the elements of the image, reputation, or brand you desire to change. Then create attitude studies so that over time these measures improve among members of the target audience. Such standard tools can be very easily implemented.

The bad news is that these tools are so obvious and responsive that marketing personnel often don't want them—they feel threatened when the marketing is not working. In the company mentioned earlier, the head of marketing, an individual whom I will call George, was relatively new in the job. He came from sales and, as a result, was a bit uptight about whether the people around him really viewed him as a marketing specialist. He was also overly eager to make an immediate impact. He knew his job was to drive up the company's attribute ratings with respect to "innovation" and "products for business." He wanted to make that happen quickly to establish his credentials.

George launched a crash project with the advertising agency and made some hasty decisions on advertising that he hoped would work. He quickly got the campaign produced and put it out into the marketplace. To justify his decision, he conducted focus groups and then took the tapes of those focus groups and spliced them in a way to show members of the focus group responding positively to the ads. He then presented these snippets to management and to the top sales folks to get their "buy in" (and to establish his credentials as an effective marketer). What was so strange was that for the first three months, George spent a minimum amount of time actually working with the ad agency to understand the typical users and come up with the creative idea. But he spent a huge amount of time coming up with "evidence" via focus groups to confirm his judgments that what he was putting on the air worked.

Six months later, after the campaign had been launched, management insisted that he do some of the standard market research studies on attitudes and attributes. He found that consumers' attitudes toward the company with regard to "innovation" and "useful to business" were not improving. George ranted and raved that the market research folks didn't do their studies correctly. In fact, he went so far as to hire another market research firm to do further studies and to word the questions the way he thought was appropriate (which biased the answers toward the results the company wanted). An enormous amount of energy was being spent defending what he was doing just to make himself look good, and not enough was going into real understanding and creativity that would excite consumers and customers.

When George's research came back, not surprisingly it showed some improvements in the company's branding effort as a result of the ads that he had fielded. But the group vice president in charge of the business unit in which George worked asked the internal market research folks to repeat their study in order to find out if their original assessment—that the campaign had no impact—was correct. Four weeks later, the repeat of the original study came back showing that the advertising campaign, indeed, was having no impact. It was a serious blow to George's reputation.

The confrontation around whether his campaign was working eventually caused him to quit. The organization had to appoint yet another marketing person to pump vitality into its branding efforts.

Standardized market research tools (i.e., conducting attitude surveys among the target audience; "usage" studies to see how members of the target audience rate the products when they use them; market share trends) will satisfy 95 percent of a company's needs in determining whether specific marketing is working. These standard measures should be put in place quickly so that the majority of the efforts of the marketing personnel can be focused on developing the advertising and marketing materials that can drive these measures to the levels desired.

In fiefdoms, marketing personnel may hunt for all kinds of measures to justify the success of their marketing efforts. Having standardized marketing measures that every marketing group must implement creates discipline and maximizes the amount of time marketing personnel spend on creating ads that excite customers.

2. AVOIDING LOOKING INWARD

Too often, fiefdoms worry more about internal assessments of their efforts than letting the consumer or the customer be the judge. They do this out of fear, believing that the results of their creative work may not come back as positive as they want. They worry more about seeking the approval of their bosses than winning over customers. While the results may dilute their creative efforts, on the other hand, they ensure that the boss is part of any failure.

There's no truer test of whether or not a marketing effort is working than exposing your creative and innovative ideas to the consumer and getting genuine feedback. Fiefdoms tend to hide behind internal feedback rather than the feedback that counts.

CUSTOMER SATISFACTION THE RIGHT WAY

One common way to assess the quality of the sales department's interaction with customers is to conduct customer-satisfaction studies. If done correctly, they create a kind of report card of how well the needs of the customers are being served.

One company I worked with had a sales organization charged with implementing a periodic customer-satisfaction study. But it asked the field sales representatives to come up with a list of the individuals who provide the feedback. The sales organization's fiefdom-like tendencies caused it to make sure that the "right people" were picked among their customers. (A better way would have been to select a representative number of customers through random selection.)

It gets even worse. Some of the individual sales representatives met with customers who were filling out the survey and urged them to score their performance in a particular way. I know one example where the sales representative took incredible pains to ensure that the survey put him in a positive light. This individual, whom I will call David, listed all of his customers and the key contacts at each of those customers. Next, he talked with the majority of those contacts about how they felt about the overall service they were getting from him and his peers. Basically, he did a verbal "pre-survey" in order to find out who was predisposed to be positive. They were the ones who were given the opportunity to fill out the customer-satisfaction survey. He also discussed the implications of this survey for him personally and urged them to make sure that they were as positive as possible. Doing so would enable him to demonstrate success with his customers to his company and, consequently, could enhance his ability to get more staffing to help that customer.

In one of these sessions, David, in talking to a fairly high-ranking individual, went too far. He basically pleaded with this woman to make sure her comments were positive. He outlined what it would mean to him from a salary perspective to get a good review and how the review was partially based on the customer-satisfaction survey. He even discussed the fact that he had three children and needed help in getting them into a particular school.

This customer became incensed that he was trying to tell her how to fill out the customer-satisfaction survey. She told him she wished he and his peers would put a whole lot more focus on providing bright ideas than on worrying about how well they were doing in their boss's eyes. She escorted David to the door and promptly called his vice president of sales. Angered at being pressured to fill out the questionnaire positively, she made it clear what she thought the company ought to do with David! She complained about how much time David was wasting on this survey, as opposed to bringing smart ideas that could help them run their business better.

This customer's feedback made David's VP of sales realize the customer-satisfaction data was fundamentally flawed. Not only was the sample of customers positively biased, but he realized his salespeople were putting pressure on their customers to provide positive ratings. Worse, his people were wasting huge amounts of time that should have been spent more productively.

Genuine customer-satisfaction data, on the other hand, when collected properly from the target audience in an unbiased way, can be a powerful tool for *minimizing* fiefdoms and measuring the degree of creativity and innovation between the sales organization and customers.

WHEN CREATIVITY OUTWEIGHS COMMON SENSE

When I was at Procter & Gamble in the early '80s, I worked for a time in the health and beauty aids brand management area. One product we test-marketed was Oasis, an antiperspirant and deodorant stick. What was unique about the product was that there was a central core of white antiperspirant material, encased in an outer layer of green gel, which provided the deodorant. When you looked at Oasis, you saw a green ring around a white core. It looked different, unique. But its uniqueness was limited to the way the product was put together. Other antiperspirant and deodorant stick products, while they weren't encased in green gel, also provided both an antiperspirant and a deodorant.

Nonetheless, our hope was that Oasis's unique green gel/white core would look distinctive enough to suggest that it was superior in delivering results. It was up to our marketing to create that perception.

The ad agency and the brand group became incredibly excited about a bizarre TV ad that featured a surreal, contemporary bathroom scene with a twenty-one-year-old male who had a dazed, admiring look on his face as he held up the Oasis and the camera slowly zoomed in on its unique white core/green gel. The background music was intended to create an aura of mystery and suspense. The only words uttered in the ad came at the end, when the announcer said, "Oasis, a feel like you have never felt before." How's that for a selling idea? It sounded like something Yogi Berra would say!

This situation was tricky in terms of the politics. The CEO of the agency had handpicked a creative team with a great track record in developing and producing brilliant advertising. This handpicked team, and the backing from the top management of the ad agency, meant that no one within the ad agency could question the direction of the creative work or the advertising it produced.

The agency made sure that everyone at Procter & Gamble knew they were putting their A team on the assignment. The P&G folks were elated.

Both the ad agency management and the creative team loved the advertising, and they convinced the P&G brand group that this was some of the most creative TV advertising they had ever produced. It was as if the creative and unusual nature of the advertising in and of itself trumped all normal evaluation guidelines. In fact, the ad agency convinced the brand group (and me!) that because it was so different, it wouldn't score well in the usual advertising testing. Consequently, the agency strongly recommended, and P&G agreed, that the usual market-research testing of the advertising be skipped and that the ad be accepted as the test-market advertising.

Oasis went into the test market with the unusual advertising. When consumers saw the ad, attitude research showed they didn't know what Oasis was all about.

What led the advertising to be put into the test market was the internal focus of the ad agency and of P&G. Because the ad didn't deliver a distinctive message about Oasis and what the product would do, the test market was a failure.

What did I learn? When it comes to innovation and creativity, it has to be grounded in the reaction of consumers. You can't rely solely on internal judgments within the organization. You need to avoid those strong fiefdoms (at the ad agency, at the client, or both) that will defend the work purely on its raw creativity rather than on any objective feedback on its impact in the marketplace.

3. DON'T COMPROMISE ON CREATIVITY

In my experience, innovation and creativity are primarily driven by individuals. It is rare that a group comes up with a truly creative idea. Consequently, it is vitally important to make sure to minimize any filtering or compromising of the creativity generated in the organization.

When someone in sales or marketing or R&D suggests a new idea, there are numerous opportunities within the organization to pressure the originator of the idea to make changes and compromises. Manufacturing can claim there are aspects of the idea that are infeasible, or based on an unrealistic timetable. Sales can throw up roadblocks with regard to customers. Lawyers can warn of legal risks, and the managers in charge may fail to realize that legal is giving advice, not issuing orders.

There has to be a value system in place in the company so that those charged with coming up with creative ideas are given permission to fight for their ideas and cut through fiefdoms that attempt to block them unfairly or modify them in such a way that they lose their zest.

SALUTING CONVENIENCE RATHER THAN CREATIVITY

I recently consulted with a large company that had a sales merchandising organization at headquarters that all of the marketing people interfaced with as they put together their retail promotion ideas. The role of the sales merchandising group was to take the initiatives from the different marketing groups, put them on a schedule, and develop the proper expectations for the field sales organization so the total program made sense. Basically, the sales merchandising organization acted as middleman between the marketing operations and the field sales force, who called on the retailers. As the business units developed more and more products and initiatives, sales merchandising became overly protective of sales. Once a month they would hold court with the marketing groups and allow each of them to argue for the implementation of the creative promotional ideas they had generated to grow their business.

The sales merchandising group originally was put together to make sure that sales did not have an unreasonable number of promotions to execute with retailers. To ensure that the sales force executed well, the sales merchandising group became more and more conservative in working with marketing. Often, the ideas the marketing groups came up with were cut back significantly or put on such crash timing that they couldn't be properly implemented. This hurt the overall revenue potential of the products and hurt the business. Creativity is all about distinctiveness; when other groups become involved in the decision making, the creative aspects of ideas often get eliminated.

In this particular company, the sales merchandising manager, whom I will call Sam, and his two assistants had been in their jobs for almost five years. His two assistants were former sales division managers, and the three of them together had a macho attitude that was really unhealthy. They viewed themselves as the "high court" of sales with respect to what promotions would be acceptable and took great delight in flexing their muscles.

One of the largest brands was being managed by a group relatively new to marketing, and when it was their turn to have a monthly arm-wrestling match with sales merchandising, Sam and his two henchmen really roughed them up. Sam's objective was to make sure the promotion offers that this brand wanted to field were simple, so that the field sales organization could execute them well. In essence, they were protecting their own turf.

In this particular meeting, Sam was at his worst. He quizzed the young marketing personnel about issues related to retailing that he was fairly confident they weren't aware of, simply to establish his authority. He coerced the marketing people to put more money behind rebates and to simplify the point-of-purchase materials so that it would be easy for sales to get the necessary displays in supermarkets.

The marketing group had a manager who, while he hadn't been assigned to the brand for very long, was a fairly seasoned veteran with the company. He was shocked at what his group went through with Sam; he went to the head of the business unit and complained bitterly. The head of the business unit went to the sales vice president and told him about the misbehavior of the sales merchandising organization. The sales vice president promised to look into it. The very next day he got back to the head of the business unit, indicating that all would be fine in the future. Part of the blame, he told the head of the business unit, was due to the naïveté of the marketing personnel. He explained that sales merchandising was just trying to do its job, teaching these youngsters what it's really like out there in the retail world. The business unit head let it drop, and he reported back to the brand group that the relationship between the two groups should improve.

Within the next two months, the marketing people had several more confrontations with Sam. It was clear that Sam and his people were confident that the sales vice president would patch up any hurt feelings that they generated. In several of these conflicts, they went too far. As a result, several of the marketing groups went to the heads of their business units to complain of the kangaroo court that they had to go through. With numerous marketing groups now up in arms over sales merchandising, the heads of the business units began to grasp the true nature of the problem.

They demanded a major housecleaning in the sales merchandising organization. The group was hurting the overall creativity of the organization and, consequently, their ability to excite customers. Several business unit heads brought the problem to the CEO, who did indeed order a "housecleaning." In the end, a lot of innocent employees in the sales merchandising organization were fired because of the actions of a few people determined to protect their fiefdom.

KILLING BY COMPROMISE

In my days in brand management at Procter & Gamble in the '80s, we were preparing to launch a new toothpaste called Pace. We wanted to get it into a test market as soon as possible. We believed that what was different about Pace was its incredible "cooling" taste. After you brushed with it, your mouth felt remarkably clean and refreshed as a result of a unique "freshening agent."

Our testing of the product with consumers indicated that they liked the unique feel and taste. Consequently, the marketing group pushed hard to have the advertising strategy focus on Pace's sensational refreshing, cooling feel.

The group that had developed Pace, on the other hand, wanted to focus primarily on the therapeutic aspects of dental products. In fact, they were absolutely world class in this area and had a long list of highly regarded scientists. In developing the Pace formula, this group had focused for the past four years on coming up with a toothpaste that cleaned your teeth better than anything on the market.

To be able to make the advertising claim that Pace cleaned teeth better, however, the product-development group needed clinical studies that showed a significant advantage over the competition with respect to cleaning. Their original technical work during the first two years gave them some very good leads on how to accomplish this difficult task. When their first set of clinicals came in, however, Pace had only a slight advantage over its competitors, not a statistically significant one. They had to do better. After tweaking the formula and testing it on small panels, they were confident they had achieved the cleaning efficacy they needed. They were ready to go with the final clinical. In fact, they were so confident they could achieve a statistically significant advantage that the

marketing group was changed to begin to prepare advertising and marketing plans to put Pace into a test market as soon as possible. We wanted
to move quickly before our competitors found out about our plans.

When the final clinical results came in, however, they were similar to
the prior clinicals. The formula had some cleaning advantages over the
competition but not advantages that were statistically significant. On the
other hand, the consumer data continued to flag the fact that consumers
responded to the uniqueness of Pace's fresh, cooling feel after brushing.

Everyone agreed that they needed to put Pace into a test market. The
dilemma was in the message to be conveyed. The product-development
personnel, based on their background in therapeutics, believed the
product's cleaning characteristics should be emphasized in the marketing. The marketing people (including me) felt that it was the coolant
that was unique, as was the refreshing mouth feel it gave users. We
wanted to orient the marketing in that direction.

The advertising agency sided with the marketing people. A compromise was engineered, and the two groups settled for an ad that said "so
clean you can feel it." In essence, we tried to focus on both the cleaning
and the great mouth feel. The way your mouth felt was supposed to be
evidence of Pace's unique cleaning capabilities.

Compromises kill great marketing. In this case, we should have made
a decision one way or the other: Either Pace had incredible cleaning capabilities or an incredibly refreshing and cooling mouth feel. To mix them
created confusion in the message and resulted in weak advertising. As a
result, the product failed in the test market, and it was taken no further.

What happened? Neither the product-development group nor the
marketing group budged from their fiefdom-like behavior. The compromise satisfied both groups but confused the consumer. Great marketing is about uniqueness and distinctiveness. When that is lost, the
power of the idea atrophies and dies.

4. FOCUS ONLY ON THE CONSUMER

When fiefdoms emerge, the focus typically is on internal issues within a
company rather than on evidence gleaned from the marketplace. Noth-

ing is more important in an organization, be it a for-profit company or a not-for-profit group, than staying close to the end user of the products or services you offer. What excites them? Knowing that is how progress gets made. Unfortunately, fiefdoms force issues to be decided for internal reasons rather than in response to customers.

A global health and beauty aids company I worked with that I'll call Vortek had a product-development organization that was extremely arrogant. It focused primarily on its own scientific skills, as opposed to its ability to "win" in the marketplace. Vortek was convinced that it was doing the best work on the planet in its particular areas of focus. Members of the product-development fiefdom cited their academic credentials as well as the involvement of key individuals in various professional associations and activities.

Vortek's largest brand, which I'll call Everest, was the market share leader in its category for well over two decades because of its great product innovation when the brand was launched. But that product-based lead occurred long, long ago. Since then, Everest had been riding the perception that it was superior to competition when, in fact, competition had caught up in recent years. It was clear to the marketing people that some new product-based ideas were needed to energize Everest, or competitors would take over category leadership.

The intensity around the issue skyrocketed when new market research studies showed for the first time that Everest's brand was judged about equal to the competition.

The head of marketing was a man named Frank. Frank observed that competitive products in the marketplace were coming up with all kinds of aesthetic improvements and getting small market share bumps each time they introduced them. That's exactly what Frank wanted to do. He knew he needed some of the same kind of product news to begin to gain some momentum with Everest, and he knew the sales organization would respond positively since they would finally have something to trumpet to the retail trade.

Frank was convinced this was the right direction to go in, since it was clear from the last five years of effort that there probably wouldn't be any significant technical improvements in the basic capabilities of the products. He made this point over and over again to the head of product development and to the VP of the business unit. He got the sales manager to join in the battle by having him point out how competition was stealing shelf space in retail outlets.

But the head of product development wasn't interested in wasting time on aesthetic improvements. His folks were scientists; they weren't interested in applying their world-class talent to insignificant modifications just to generate sales news and retail excitement. Their view was that such thinking was short term, that they shouldn't take their eye off the long-term task of generating significant technical improvements. They seemed to imply that it was beneath them to work on anything but the most significant improvements. Nonetheless, their batting average was pretty low, and people were desperate to pump some excitement into the brand.

Frank constantly went back to the head of the business unit and pounded the table, claiming that product development should not take such a narrow view. In his view, product development should be working on both the short term and the long term. He pointed out that recent market research studies showed that the competition had caught up with them, and he felt a real sense of urgency to gain back that leadership.

The problem was that the general manager of the business unit didn't hold product development responsible for generating growth. After several months of campaigning by the marketing group, the general manager finally moved into action and tackled the technology fiefdom of his product-development organization. He got them to reorganize around long-term research and short-term product news, so that marketing and sales would have a steady stream of initiatives behind their big-revenue brand Everest while the development group worked on the next technology breakthrough that could shake up the industry and put the product back in a leadership position.

As the above makes clear, the entire organization has to be focused on the fact that you exist to serve the consumer. Nothing else will do.

PART III

OVERCOMING THE FIEFDOM SYNDROME

6 BALANCING DISCIPLINE AND CREATIVITY

TOO MUCH OR too little discipline or creativity in a company can undermine its ability to achieve its potential. A lack of discipline can lead to chaos and breed fiefdoms; too much discipline can stifle creativity and suffocate innovation.

I believe that discipline is needed across an organization to carry out the basic responsibilities such as finance, human resources, manufacturing, and information technology. Executives need to manage the fundamentals in these areas with standardized methods. For example, in procurement, discipline is often at a premium. One set of procedures needs to be used by all divisions, business units, and subsidiaries, while allowing enough flexibility for a limited staff to reflect the special needs and nuances of their market.

In product development, on the other hand, creativity is at a premium. Individuals are charged with constantly improving products and services, and exploring new products and services to excite consumers.

In sales there is a premium on creativity as well, in interacting with customers. Salespeople need to be good listeners, able to match products and services of the company to the needs and desires of the customer.

Yet sales departments need discipline too—in obtaining product or cost information as well as information about customers. Such systems should be handled at the corporate level, with the ability to make minor additions at the business unit or subsidiary level to reflect the peculiarities of their businesses or region.

Marketing departments, too, require a balance of discipline and creativity. They need to be innovative and creative in the ads and promotional materials they develop in order to catch the attention of consumers and excite them. But they also need to be highly disciplined with regard to understanding market share data and consumer attitudes toward their products and services, and coming up with a crisp and well-defined marketing strategy.

The key to today's successful organization is to be disciplined and creative in the right areas.

HOW FIEFDOMS UNDERMINE DISCIPLINE AND CREATIVITY

The basic human tendency to want to control one's destiny or turf runs counter to discipline in an organization. If the CEO or the manager of a unit lets people act on their own, the company will soon fall into disarray. In the vacuum that results, fiefdoms will flourish. The sad fact is that a lack of discipline will lead to higher costs and a lack of communication and accountability. This can happen with organizations and individuals. Such groups or individuals become insular, developing their own set of procedures, data, and measures.

Of course, fiefdoms convince themselves that what they are doing is worthwhile and that their products are already competitive. As a result, there is less of a sense of urgency to create new and exciting products and services.

This attitude is true of individuals as well, as I pointed out in Chapter 3. When people are left in a job too long, they get complacent about the quality of their work. They lose the ability to step back and ask fundamental questions on how things could be done differently to generate improvement. They become fearful of any change in their current way of doing things or in their current responsibilities.

TOO MUCH CREATIVITY

When the balance of creativity and discipline is out of whack, the organization eventually becomes out of whack. But the problem is fixable.

In one case, the company I consulted with had a business unit that was incredibly creative with respect to just about everything it did. It was primarily driven by an individual whom I will call Jay, who was the head of marketing for the unit. I met several times with Jay, and he could absolutely drive you crazy. Everything he did had to be unusual and different.

In one session, the marketing team was working on the packaging for one of its products, and Jay was holding court. He had the art department develop a very creative package that had several complicated plastic parts included in it. Clearly, it was going to be very expensive, but Jay blithely blew by such details! An individual from manufacturing pushed back hard over the company's ability to make this package at a reasonable cost. Jay kept asking what the problem was.

The manufacturing guy finally told Jay he was going to assign a significant cost premium to the estimate of the package. Jay claimed that he would simply tell the general manager of the business unit that manufacturing wasn't trying hard enough to hold down costs. Jay could drive you nuts! He was 100 percent creativity, 0 percent discipline.

As a result of his lack of discipline, the business unit was out of control on many fronts, and much of it was due to the marketing department. For example, just before a special package for a promotion was sent off to the packaging supplier for production, Jay called his manufacturing contact, telling him the customer wanted to make changes. Jay said he was sending over a few mock-ups to show what he and the customer wanted. There is certainly nothing wrong with reflecting customer feedback, but doing it at the eleventh hour, when you are ready to go into full production, is not the time. Moreover, this was not the exception, but the rule. Manufacturing was constantly surprised by what the marketing folks requested. And Jay set the tone, allowing the marketing people to feel very comfortable in unleashing a blizzard of last-minute changes.

Thanks to my friend Jay, there was always a fair amount of financial chaos. His marketing operation was constantly moving dollars from one product to another and making last-minute additions to budgets. There were also constant changes to the media budget, and the ad agency was often beside itself as a result of the endless stream of changes requested by the marketing folks.

This lack of discipline and helter-skelter approach eventually led top management to reorganize the business unit. Before long, the general manager of the business unit was relieved of his duties. But Jay remained! A new individual was named general manager and was charged with cleaning up the mess. But you can imagine how far he got.

FIEFDOMS AND SIX SIGMA

In other fiefdoms, discipline is not the problem—rather, it's creativity that has been suffocated.

A health and beauty aids company I did some work with had an incredibly strong investment in Six Sigma. A guy named Dave was in charge of the Six Sigma effort within the company; he led several corporate-wide projects that were designed to instill more discipline in the way the company did their work.

On one project, Dave had two people creating a process for developing line extensions and new products for the retail market. The idea was that if the product-development and marketing arms of a particular business unit followed this process, they would increase their batting average in the marketplace.

This Six Sigma–driven process included all kinds of measuring systems in the early stages of development that would factor in consumer input as well as input from experts within the company. Armed with the results of that input, the businesspeople would involve the ad agency and the marketing department in generating lists of product ideas for potential development. The process included charts galore; hordes of people from different organizations were involved. Once they selected a few ideas, they used another intricate measuring system to decide the positioning of the product with the consumer.

I went to a meeting where the art department was unveiling their first attempts at the packaging for one of these new product ideas. An individual whom I will call Sam had done some very creative things in packaging the product, and it really caught your attention. Sam was hardly finished showing his ideas, when the engineering folks jumped in with their process for ensuring that packages were easy to produce and cost-effective. They pulled out all kinds of charts and ratios with regard to the size and shape of the package to demonstrate why Sam needed to make a number of changes to the package to make it more cost-effective to produce.

The product-development people went next. They came down hard on Sam because his package, they claimed, did not protect the contents adequately: It was too fragile. As Sam tried to explain that those were easy things to fix, product development had already moved on, explaining why Sam had to move to a more traditional package, the type they were used to dealing with, which would enable them to get to market conveniently and with minimal risk. The discussion was driving Sam absolutely nuts. He finally threw up his hands and said something along the lines of "Why didn't you tell me that we weren't interested in exciting the customer, that we're interested only in making this thing risk-free and cheap?"

While Six Sigma was very effective in some areas of the company, the business units were now applying it in areas where creativity, rather than efficiency and reliability, was key. Their processes had become so rigorous that they had eliminated any spark of creativity.

The vice president of the business unit became upset at the lack of innovation coming out of product development and marketing. He saw it leading to weaker and weaker business results. On the other hand, it was he who consistently talked up Six Sigma with the various departments, discussing how important it was to drive Six Sigma procedures into everything they did. The CEO was committed to driving Six Sigma throughout the company. It is clear he had read too many Six Sigma books!

The fundamental problem was that individuals, rather than groups of people, generate creativity. Seldom do groups of people come up with creative and innovative ideas; individuals do that very well. Unfortunately, with processes such as total quality and Six Sigma, innovative ideas typically are squeezed and shaped according to their feasibility from a manufacturing standpoint; then other Six Sigma–driven departments get involved in the implications the idea will have on their piece of the organization. Pretty soon, all kinds of changes are requested, and the idea gets beaten down into something that in no way resembles the original idea.

In other words, discipline and creativity at this company were wildly out of balance.

The mistake the CEO made is that he created the perception that the company's primary objective was excellence in Six Sigma as opposed to excellence with their customers. In essence, the CEO created a bunch of fiefdoms, all competing with one another around how well Six Sigma could be executed.

FROZEN IN FEAR

People who operate fiefdoms sometimes go to great lengths to avoid technology for fear of change. A food products company I worked with had a sales services staff that received orders on hard copy forms from the sales organization. Clerks in the office would then input the data into their information systems to process the orders and generate shipping papers and bills in paper format.

This sales services department had 12 facilities across the U.S. and employed roughly 30 people in each office, or about 360 people in all.

Many of the management team of this sales services department had been in place for over 10 years; they prided themselves in being very disciplined in the order-management process. Yet they refused to consider updating their systems and employing up-to-date technology that would do away with paper orders. The sales services fiefdom allowed them to continue doing things the old way, thereby protecting the jobs of all 360 people—and, more important, the jobs of the sales services management.

The leader of this fiefdom, whom I will call Roger, was a master at protecting the independence of his organization. In one instance a group vice president in charge of several business units went to the CEO and told him about an order-management system he had seen at a supplier where the entire order-processing sequence was completely automated. Sales personnel were trained to enter their orders via laptop computers and then download the accumulated orders from their laptop via the company's network whenever it was convenient, later in the day or in the evening. The orders were automatically processed, and a database allowed the salespeople to check the status of an order at any time. More important, the customer who placed the order could also check on its status, increasing customer satisfaction enormously.

The CEO was so intrigued by what the group vice president described that he asked Roger to follow up with the group vice president and to talk to the supplier about the system they had developed. Roger immediately flew into a frenzy at the CEO's suggestion, claiming the last thing he wanted to do was to move his organization to some kind of risky, unreliable technology with the potential to drop or delay hundreds of thousands of dollars of business each day. He then asked the CEO if he was unsatisfied with the way they were processing the business. He pointed out their incredible reliability over the years. He also pointed out that their headcount had been flat over the last several years, and he saw no need for a newfangled technology when what they were using was serving them so well. It was a speech that the CEO had heard many times before. This was just the latest instance of an executive suggesting Roger's group take advantage of the latest technology.

Roger told the CEO that he was fully aware of the kinds of systems that the group vice president was talking about and that the CEO could rest assured that he and his people were always on the lookout for smart ways to do things better. But the CEO should be pleased with the reliability of his organization—problems in sales services could bring the company to its knees from a cash-flow standpoint.

Roger left having made no promises to the CEO that he would talk to the group vice president or to the supplier. He did contact the sales vice president whom he reported to and alerted him that the group vice president and the CEO had this "harebrained" idea about automating order processing and pushing the company out on the bleeding edge of technology. He asked his boss to make sure those guys got off his back— they should be told how lucky they were that Roger's organization was so efficient and reliable.

What Roger's group avoided talking about was how massively expensive their approach was versus what information technology could do for them. Roger's role here was clear. He was extremely disciplined in keeping the current system going. He wasn't about to allow an ounce of creativity in his backyard.

Roger's group of 360 people had painted themselves into a box. They were protecting their turf in many areas besides technology. Newcomers in sales services were allowed in only at entry-level positions—no one was hired from other divisions or outside the company at the intermediate or upper levels. Promotions occurred only from within.

The losers here were the 360 people in sales services who found themselves boxed in from a career standpoint. But the company was also a big loser—they could accomplish the same work with about one-tenth of the number of people.

But a curious thing happened. The sales vice president to whom Roger and his group reported had a son who was in the information technology business. His son implemented a system for a large company that totally automated the order-processing task. He told his dad about the work he was doing and what a fabulous application it represented. He described the salespeople inputting the orders on their laptops; the whole system was paperless. In essence, it was the same kind of system that the group VP had seen when he visited the supplier.

The sales vice president learned more about the system from his son and then took a bold step. He visited the supplier the group vice president had mentioned. He came back with all kinds of facts and figures on its reliability as well as its incredibly low cost. It was about as people-less and paper-less a system as you would find. And its reliability was phenomenal. He confronted Roger with what he had learned. Roger had his usual reaction. So the vice president of sales met with the group vice president and the CEO. Together they agreed that it was time to make a change. Roger was given an early retirement package, and a thick-skinned outsider was put into Roger's position in sales services. The new sales services head decided on the appropriate new information-technology architecture within his first four months on the job. Nine months later the 360-person staff was replaced by a central group of 20 people, yielding enormous savings for the company and resulting in incredibly responsive new capabilities for their customers and sales personnel.

Unfortunately, many of the 360 people had to be let go since their skills had atrophied to such an extent that it made it almost impossible to place them in new jobs within the company.

The lesson for individuals: Try not to get caught in these kinds of situations. If you see you're in a dead-end position, isolated from the company, find another job. Neither companies nor people can ignore potential ways to do things better. To do so *always* leads to disaster.

OPERATING WITHOUT DISCIPLINE OR CREATIVITY

Not long ago I helped with a large company's acquisition of a successful family-run business in the same industry. The company being bought was about one quarter the size of the acquiring company.

The products being acquired fit nicely into the business units of the acquiring company. The companies looked like a natural fit.

When the deal was made, the CEO of the acquiring company, whom I will call Mark, told his management team that the family members running the acquired company were first-class people and would fit well with their culture. Mark was a dignified gent who had not done many acquisitions.

The acquiring company prided itself in having several leadership brands; it was highly ethical and very objective in reading consumer demand. Mark stressed to his management team that the family-run company they had acquired had those same values, and it was important to get off on the right foot with them.

He described the dinner he attended a few days before when visiting the newly acquired company. All of the members of its management team, as well as the founder of the company and several of the founder's relatives (who were significant shareholders), were at the event, as were some employees. The founder and his family members went out of their way to make sure everyone there knew Mark would not upset the dynamics of their firm. The founder even raised a toast to Mark for his respect for their culture, practices, and people.

To the members of Mark's own top management team, Mark's message was: "We should keep our hands off the new company." They assumed the usual disciplined steps to integrate the acquired company should not be taken until Mark told them.

As a result, the acquired company instantly became a protected fiefdom, sheltered unintentionally by Mark. Worse, it was run by family members who were smart enough to realize they had to join a stronger organization with a stronger financial base, while hoping to retain their own culture and remain as independent as possible. Their company had something of a country club feel to it (partially due to the fact that their headquarters and R&D facility were located in a quiet, dignified suburb). They wanted to maintain that "feel" as long as they could, and Mark was enabling them to do that.

As the months went by, the information technology people in the acquiring company were told to hold off trying to integrate the new company into their corporate systems. The somewhat brash CIO of the acquiring company openly asked questions like "When are we going to consummate this marriage?"

The same vague message of "Go slow so we don't mess up the great chemistry between the groups" was conveyed to the product-development folks in the acquiring company as well as human resources and other departments. Mark protected the new company for fear that the key players would be offended and leave. This led to little disciplined integration and little synergy between the two organizations from a marketing and product perspective.

After a year:

- No real progress had been made integrating the two organizations.
- Financials of the acquisition were not being met.

* None of the planned synergies were achieved.
* There was massive duplication in information systems, manufacturing, and product-development personnel.

The financial community began to recognize that the goals of the acquisition were being badly missed, although the acquiring company denied it. Six months later, there was little change; the acquiring company could no longer downplay the financial disappointment.

Fortunately, a strong vice president who ran one of the business units came forward, stating frankly that his financial projections for the next year would be another disaster, because he was not being given access to the brands and synergies that he thought would be placed under his unit more than a year earlier. A feisty Italian, he had run out of patience. He made it clear that unless he was allowed to get on with integrating the acquisition, his unit would continue to underperform vis-à-vis the financial targets. His willingness to come forward gave the other business unit heads the courage to join and collectively confront Mark.

Mark had no option but to finally make it clear to the managers of the acquired company that they had indeed been acquired and that the combined company had to eliminate duplication, including selling the country-club-like facility in New England. They adopted aggressive financial goals that everyone knew could be achieved. Finally, Mark had taken the lead.

So what is the lesson here? Fear of change, and other fiefdom-like tendencies, can cause people to "freeze up." They must instill the discipline to make things run better and create a sense of urgency around innovation.

WHEN INDIVIDUALS ARE OUT OF BALANCE

Individuals, too, can find themselves out of balance with respect to discipline and creativity.

I once consulted with a company that was a major supplier to the automobile industry. The company employed an individual whom I will call Alan, a terrific engineer. He was highly innovative in tackling tough mechanical-engineering-design problems related to manufacturing.

Unfortunately, Alan did not have an ounce of discipline in his body. He never became a student of how an engineering organization worked with manufacturing. Instead, he focused on his latest idea or theory, which often represented a solution without a problem. He constantly lectured the company on how manufacturing should be done versus how it is done. While he was helpful in assisting with specific problems, people began to get tired of all of his posturing and lecturing.

At the beginning of Alan's career, top management rated him very highly because of his ability to solve some tough engineering problems.

Over time, however, he developed into an individual fiefdom. He became extremely protective of his skills and ranted and raved when other people got involved in solving problems that he thought he alone could solve. Given his strong skills, top management protected him to some extent.

But Alan became more and more obnoxious and harder to work with. He was called in by a group of mechanical engineers who were attempting to isolate some engineering design problems in a complicated manufacturing line; they were intent on improving its overall productivity. The problem was tailor-made for Alan, and the group was eager to get his insights on what they could do to collect data, make changes, and achieve results. Their first meeting with Alan lasted two hours, and it was a nightmare. Alan kept asking how they had things set up and then would criticize the earlier decisions they had made. Alan never got around to making any concrete suggestions as to what they could do to achieve improvement. All the group wanted was some key tips. They knew they had an antiquated process—that's why they were calling him in. They wanted his help. But all he did was embarrass them.

This kind of thing happened again and again. But nobody wanted to deal with Alan's declining performance and disruptiveness. Eventually, Alan's boss was replaced by a man whom I'll call Fred. Fred had fifteen years with the company, most of them in manufacturing. He was a no-nonsense guy who rarely smiled and had a reputation for being tough as nails. He knew he had the confidence of management because he always tackled problems using the basics and got solid results.

Fred had heard about Alan's encounter with the mechanical engineers, so he asked him about it. Alan was extremely condescending, treating Fred as if he weren't able to understand the kinds of approaches Alan used to assist in the engineering redesign process. He asked Alan for a list of five or six individuals within the company whom Alan had worked with over the last six months. Fred then called these individuals to get their reactions about Alan. He found out that Alan really hadn't helped to solve any major problems, and his arrogance was intolerable. When Fred relayed this to Alan, Alan became extremely defensive and quite angry. Fred simply told Alan to continue to apply his skills to the best of his ability and keep him aware of whom he was working with. For three months, Fred collected feedback on Alan. None of it was very encouraging. Finally, Fred gave Alan three months to shape up or he would be fired. Fred had alerted the management chain of command of his actions, and they were totally supportive. Basically, everyone was fed up with Alan.

Alan was so incensed that he complained to top management: Rather than shaping up, he made life difficult for a lot of people with his thrashing around. Three months later, Alan was let go.

The lesson? No individual, no matter how unique his skills, is irreplaceable. Employees need to remind themselves of that constantly.

I believe employees should be as "paranoid" about their skills as the company is about its business, in terms of meeting the needs of a changing marketplace and capitalizing on new capabilities that emerge every day.

In another company I consulted with, a large industrial chemicals firm, I worked with an attorney who had been with the company for more than fifteen years. She was a specialist in developing contracts for their large customers, someone who could cut through the thorny details that can hang up large contracts.

Known within the organization as the expert whom everyone relied upon in difficult contract negotiations, she began to be convinced of her own good press, always a sign of trouble.

In the chemicals business, the products evolve over time, as do the services offered to help utilize the products. For example, while the company may be providing a consumer product company 250,000 pounds per month of a particular chemical, what was becoming more important was the help the chemicals company could provide in pointing out how to improve the efficiency and yield of the process involving the chemical. Service contracts to include various services were complex, covering things such as the number of "expert" personnel who would be available for consulting, how many chemical engineers would reside full-time at the consumer-product company to troubleshoot problems, the location and availability of an extra supply of the chemical in case of a surge in demand, and a variety of other service-level issues.

To some extent, the attorney felt threatened by the additional services being offered, since they did not involve legal issues but, instead, business issues with a lot of give-and-take between departments within the company and the customer. What the agreements needed was creativity in working with the customer to hash out compromises to the service agreements while staying true to the company's contractual obligations.

Unfortunately, the attorney was all discipline and no creativity. For years, she made her reputation by being a hard-nosed attorney who served things up in black-and-white terms. She was often the reason that various clauses in the contract were never modified even when the customers insisted on such modifications with good rationale.

The attorney performed extremely well as long as it didn't matter that she offered little give-and-take with regard to the formal terms of the sales/customer interaction. But when the offerings of the company broadened beyond products to services, which required far more flexibility and innovation in the company's agreements, she began to be a serious bottleneck.

Her prior successes fanned her fiefdom instincts, making her even less flexible as she protected her autonomy and power. She was openly critical of the direction sales was going in, as well as top management's priorities. She couldn't tolerate the loose service agreements that sales seemed to come up with, modifying them from customer to customer, based on customer need. Of course, that was exactly what the company *should* have been doing. But she had become such a fierce fiefdom that she didn't see the evolution in the industry. Unfortunately, her intransigence led to her management eventually realizing they had to move her out of her position, which she found so embarrassing that she quit.

When individuals become blocked in their ability to see the obvious because of their determination to protect their turf, they can hurt their companies—and undermine their careers.

INDIVIDUALS WHO HAVE LITTLE DISCIPLINE OR CREATIVITY

An information technology architect I knew in a large automotive company—I'll call him Joe—had an important job that could have had an incredible impact on the operating costs and efficiency of the corporation. But because of his shortcomings, he generated extra costs and complications instead.

Information architects are vitally important within large organizations, given the speed with which new IT capabilities emerge. This person suggests which technologies the company should use and how to piece them together in a disciplined manner to make the organization efficient and effective. The IT architect needs to be highly disciplined, able to say no to most new technologies and vendors that want to compete with the technology already in place in the company. Yet he or she needs to be highly innovative, knowing when it is time to jump on a new technology and to work it into the overall architecture.

Joe was short on both discipline and innovation. First, he just didn't have enough backbone. Whenever proposals from another hardware or software vendor came in, he didn't have enough nerve to say no. As a result, there was an incredible lack of discipline with regard to the hardware and software approaches utilized within the company. For example, the software vendor that supplied all the financial software for the company also had a terrific set of human resources systems that meshed well with the financial systems. But the human resources organization wanted to lease software for its basic systems from a different vendor. Joe knew he had to back one or the other. The differences between the two vendors and their HR offerings were quite minor; the company should have decided to use the same vendor for both finance and human resources. It would have saved a significant amount of money in support costs and in avoiding the need to build bridges between the databases and software of the two different suppliers. But Joe just couldn't take a strong stand on the issue. He let human resources do what they wanted, and he put up with the resulting complexity and cost.

Joe also had trouble dealing with innovation. He was very risk-averse. When new, exciting technologies came along that should have been tested and potentially moved into the architecture, if they offered significant opportunities to lower costs or improve effectiveness, Joe dragged things out, complicating the lives of those driving the new efforts.

In one instance the sales organization spotted a new customer relationship management (CRM) software package that was extremely simple to use, fairly easy to implement, and would have a huge impact in sales. Sales wanted to jump all over this opportunity. Joe realized that they were very interested in this new approach and that he couldn't simply push it aside. So he formed a task force consisting of people in sales and information technology and outlined a complicated set of steps that involved an incredible amount of due diligence. It was completely out of line in terms of the fairly simple piece of software that sales wanted to bring on board. But that was the way Joe avoided taking risks. He came up with all kinds of ways to delay decisions and diffuse responsibility so that if any new program backfired, he would not be held responsible. As a result, the due diligence was complex and time-consuming, and only the safest alternatives emerged.

The organization had the worst of both worlds. It didn't get the discipline needed to drive efficiency and excellence, and it didn't get the innovation it needed to significantly improve its effectiveness and lower its costs.

Joe held this key architect job for a long time, primarily because the CIO had characteristics that were similar to Joe's. The CIO could be pushed around by the heads of business units and would eventually agree to just about anything. The CEO was completely uninterested in technology issues. If the company had not been doing well in overall revenue and profitability, the CIO would have been in real trouble over the company's excess costs and lack of effectiveness. The CEO missed huge opportunities to reduce costs and seize the new capabilities that the technology offered.

Joe's fiefdom came to a screaming halt when the business conditions toughened up and top management could no longer accept the excessive percentage of net revenue that was being drained away by information technology. So they got themselves a hard-nosed CIO. As you might guess, Joe's fiefdom was one of the first casualties.

As an employee or manager, you need to be clear-eyed in assessing exactly where you add value in the company. Every employee needs to face that question because it's the question that is most on the minds of upper management, or should be. It's easy to come up with arguments defending how well things are going and describing how talented you are at your job. But only by regularly addressing the question of where you add value, and discussing it with your management, can you ensure that you don't fall into the fiefdom trap.

7

ACHIEVING DISCIPLINE

BY NOW YOU can see why organizations and individuals need to pay attention to the process, behavior, and people disciplines necessary to avoid the pitfalls of fiefdoms. But how do you make those disciplines a reality?

There are three tools I believe are critical to achieve the discipline necessary. But top management must play a strong leadership role in all three areas. Without such leadership, fiefdoms can take over and flourish.

1. CREATE A CULTURE WHERE WORK AND PERFORMANCE ARE INSPECTED REGULARLY AND OBJECTIVELY

It is vitally important that the top management of the company as well as its managers and executives make it common practice to regularly inspect the work of the company. I'm talking about creating an environment where everyone understands that top management is highly interested in the detailed data that describes the performance of the various groups within the organization. Each manager should probe to understand how things are going in their group, area, or division and ask what they can do to assist in the company's overall efforts.

It is essential that performance be objectively evaluated. With top management setting the tone and objectively surveying the company's goals and achievements, implementing the various disciplines should be easy.

MICROSOFT'S MIDYEAR REVIEW

The midyear review at Microsoft was a process designed to do exactly what its name suggests. Each business unit and functional area would meet with Bill Gates halfway through the fiscal year to thoroughly review their performance versus the company's expectations at the beginning of the fiscal year. Each regional or country sales subsidiary had a similar meeting with Steve Ballmer, who was in charge of sales at the time.

Prior to those sessions, top management developed standardized charts or templates so that all the geographical units prepared the same exhibits and showed the data in precisely the same way. There were separate templates for the business unit reviews and the department reviews. Having standard formats greatly enhances the way top management can inspect what is going on, and it enables a ton of benchmarking of business and product performance and encourages measurement of progress against competitors.

There were many kinds of information used in these midyear reviews. For example, several exhibits provided data on the market for a particular country. They would include size of the personal computer industry, size of the server market in that area, the database market, the messaging software market, etc. Studying the trends that show which markets are growing, and at what speed, is critical in deciding where to put scarce resources to grow the business as quickly as possible.

There would also be several detailed exhibits about competitors in that geographical area, providing data such as the estimated revenue and profit growth (or lack of it) for each competitor, detailed market share information on all of the company's key products and their competitors, and an analysis of which competitors have strong product offerings. There were also exhibits on the performance of Microsoft products, including not only an analysis of market share trends but also revenue, profitability, cost of goods sold and marketing costs, and a set of templates on key issues within the subsidiary. Those templates might include a discussion of a competitor gaining share or an analysis of challenging customers. There were exhibits on the top customers and the progress, or lack of it, that the unit had achieved with them during the first six months of the fiscal year, compared to prior years. Individual accounts would be discussed, focusing on what things were not going well and what could be done to improve a situation or turn it around.

These sessions resulted in great insights into how to grow the business faster, as well as the sharing of knowledge from top management's experiences in similar situations. The dialogue was open and constructive. These kinds of sessions help prevent fiefdoms. All the cards are on the table regarding operations and what kind of progress each group or subsidiary is making.

The midyear reviews for the business units were similar, only there was a lot more focus on the performance of individual products versus competition, and on the business and technology trends of those competitors that were improving. We would also discuss what to do about competitive threats, or how to take advantage of new products being introduced in the market to counter a strong competitor. With the departmental reviews, we focused more on cost as well as on key processes that were being put in place across the entire organization. For example, in the case of information technology, a key dialogue would take place around containing cost while continuing to equip the organization with up-to-date technologies that enabled business and regional units to operate more efficiently and effectively.

The midyear review meeting with a group might take two to six hours, depending on the number of issues being discussed and the complexity of a particular organization.

All was driven from the top down in a standardized manner, exposing any fiefdoms or inefficiencies that might be emerging. While the individual business unit could craft some performance measures they thought relevant, they had to have some good thinking behind them. And they could not substitute or eliminate any of the standard information requested by the company.

The midyear review helps avoid the formation of fiefdoms because it gets top management involved in an active dialogue on how things are going with the individual groups early on and creates a culture of partnership in growing the business. The dialogue should be detailed, and at times it will be contentious. But the contention is around how to improve the business, not to chastise individual people. Creating this kind of culture of inspection and objectivity is critical in ensuring fiefdoms do not emerge.

THE WAY TO GET THINGS DONE

In his book *Execution*, Larry Bossidy urges top management of an organization to make sure they are involved in the people process, the strategy process, and the operations process.

General managers left to their own instincts will inherently find reasons to avoid such involvement by top management. It generates a lot of preparation work; it makes you feel like you are not running your group or unit.

Of course, the task of top management should be to make sure the responsibility continues to lie with the managers and general managers, while making it clear that those in management will be thoroughly and objectively "inspected" on a regular basis. That's what a strong top management is all about.

As we pointed out in Chapter 3 when we discussed the discipline of inspection, Bossidy refers to this kind of regular inspection by top management as "robust dialogue." In discussing budgeting, he cites three typical problems that crop up at many companies. First, there often is not a robust dialogue concerning the budget plan's assumptions. Second, the budget is built on what top management seems to want versus actual marketplace trends, and product performance versus competitors. Third, the lack of robust dialogue prohibits opportunities for coaching.

"Budgets often have little to do with the reality of execution because they are numbers and gaming exercises, where people spend months figuring out how to protect their interests instead of focusing on the business's critical issues," says Bossidy. "The financial targets are often no more than the increases from the previous year's results that top management think security analysts expect. Down at the lower levels, people put out minimum bids for what they can do to beat those results. Often they will sandbag, proposing numbers lower than those they think they can achieve."

What Larry is describing here are the basic fiefdom tendencies in a world lacking top management inspection and objectivity.

In essence what Larry is talking about is the notion that through the inspection process, dealing with people, strategy, and operations, top management makes it clear what the expectations are of the various groups throughout the company. One thing that is remarkably consistent among people is that when you make it very clear what is expected, and offer measures to gauge progress, things get done. In *Who Says Elephants Can't Dance?*, Lou Gerstner notes that "people do what you inspect, not what you expect." Said another way, the way to make sure the organization gets things done is to make sure that they know what you are interested in and that they hear from you regularly in regard to your interest in their progress. The habit of management regularly "inspecting" what is happening, with a clear objective value system, goes a long way to make sure things get done, and that fiefdoms are prevented.

THE DIFFICULTY IN BEING OBJECTIVE

One of the jobs I held at Procter & Gamble was manager of the market research department. We reported to the CEO outside the chain of command of the business units in order to ensure that the market research department was completely objective.

What Procter & Gamble was protecting against was the basic human tendency to inflate one's assessment of one's work. It can be a serious vulnerability when you are trying to discover whether a product excites a consumer.

The brand personnel and product-development personnel at P&G usually tested their products against the competition by placing their product and the competitor's product in the hands of a representative group of users and asking them to use one product for two weeks and then the other for two weeks. This is referred to as a blind paired-comparison test. The participants have no idea what product they are using, since they are labeled only as Product A and Product B.

When the tests come back, the brand and product-development personnel frantically look for a statistically significant win for their product. Unfortunately, even when you achieved a statistically significant win (at a 95 percent confidence level), often the differences were only marginally noticeable on the part of consumers. We've all seen "improved" detergents in the marketplace that offer marginal cleaning improvement. Yet I can guarantee you that all of those were statistically significant wins versus their key competitor.

Here's where objectivity is needed. The business units often wanted to run to the marketplace with these minor "statistical" improvements, even though the real impact of the change was, at best, marginal.

This issue of striving for major breakthroughs from a product standpoint was of major interest to Charlie Bolek. Charlie was a real market research professional. He had spent his entire career at Procter & Gamble in market research. He was a pro at market research methodology and in the proper use of market research by the business units in qualifying initiatives for the marketplace.

Charlie and I struck it off very well. We both had a strong interest in increasing Procter & Gamble's batting average in the marketplace with respect to its product initiatives. We had both seen too many line extensions and small product improvements that had minimal impact despite the millions of dollars spent on these efforts.

There was one brand that Charlie was particularly passionate about. In this case, the brand group that managed that product generated a new set of line extensions, aesthetic variations of their basic product. Charlie was in charge of the market research personnel who helped this brand group. In Charlie's estimation, the brand group had pulled one over management's eyes in getting the money to place these aesthetic variations into a test market. They violated two of Charlie's rules of thumb: 1) the product test results of these new items were only average versus competition—they matched the overall performance of their competitors, but they really didn't show any strengths; and 2) in attitude studies where consumers were asked about the new items, nobody responded with anything distinctive.

The sales organization was the real driver in this initiative. When sales have new items for a brand, they go to the retail outlets and argue for more shelf space so that these products can be properly displayed. Hence, sales was extremely bullish about these new items and strongly encouraged the brand group to ignore the test market results, which were flat after an initial revenue bump, and convince top management to get funds to expand nationally. This was the kind of situation where Charlie really earned his pay. He made a pest of himself with the management of the division in which this brand group worked, arguing how average the whole proposition was from a consumer standpoint. The vice president of that division constantly got phone calls and memos from Charlie reminding him that the only winner here was the sales organization, who could sell in a bunch of this product and generate additional short-term revenue. Charlie pointed out that once all that flurry was over, the consumer would not buy any more of the overall brand than they were already buying.

Nevertheless, under pressure from the brand group and sales, the vice president of the division went ahead and recommended that the line extensions be expanded nationally. Charlie was furious. He went directly to the group vice president and made his views clear on the subject. The group VP promised to get everyone together to review the subject and told Charlie he appreciated his input.

A week later, the group vice president held court, and Charlie explained his objections. Fortunately for Charlie, he found a very receptive audience. The group vice president pored over the test market results and product test scores, which were both relatively weak. Sales responded by pointing out some new ideas they had to achieve ongoing excitement at store level, based on what they learned from the test market. In the end, the group vice president agreed with Charlie. He chastised the group for pushing new line extensions that really didn't offer anything new or distinctive. They had fallen into the trap of simply coercing the retail trade to stock additional items, generating short-term revenue.

But the folks in the brand group didn't get angry at Charlie. In fact, they respected him. He was simply doing what he was hired to do. They were upset that the expansion didn't take place, but they realized they should have listened to Charlie much earlier—it would have saved them a lot of grief.

In terms of ensuring objectivity, one advantage I had as the head of market research was my earlier experience as the head of marketing for the package soap and detergent division at P&G in 1983 and 1984. I had been involved in numerous discussions with P&G's CEO at the time, John Smale, about whether the company should launch a liquid version of Tide detergent. Tide had always been a powder detergent. In 1983 Procter & Gamble scientists invented a new liquid detergent formula that, for the first time in detergent history, matched the cleaning power of powders. The Tide brand group and its chain of command, including myself, argued hard that, at last, there was a liquid formula that was strong enough and powerful enough to carry the Tide name.

John Smale pushed back quite strongly on this. Tide was a treasured brand at Procter & Gamble and a huge success in the marketplace. And consumers knew Tide as a powder. On the other hand, John was struck by the incredible test results of the liquid version of Tide. The liquid formula solidly beat the leading liquid detergent in our product tests and tied the performance of Tide powder in cleaning capabilities. John was surprised at these results. Tide powder had always been the leader among powder detergents, but up until that point, Procter & Gamble did not have the leading brand in liquid detergents. John and all of the folks involved in the detergent business at Procter & Gamble were extremely eager to gain leadership in that sector of the detergent business as well. Based on the strong product test results, John finally agreed to test-market a liquid form of Tide.

When Tide liquid was placed in a test market, it was a huge success and was quickly expanded nationally. It's a great story of holding out for truly significant improvements and being very objective in turning down marginal improvements because they wouldn't have had much impact. John Smale waited to put the Tide name on a liquid until he knew that he had a huge win against the leading liquid detergent— and until he had a liquid formula that was every bit as good in cleaning as the Tide powder formula. His discipline and objectivity paid huge dividends.

Confronting problems and dealing with them objectively is hard to pull off. People's natural tendencies are to hold a more positive perception of their work than is true. As a result, it is up to top management to set the tone with respect to objectivity and realism.

Bossidy makes the same point in *Execution*: "It is shocking to see how many people don't want to confront issues realistically," he says. "They are not comfortable doing it. When I took over at Allied Signal, for example, I got two different pictures from our people and our customers. While our people were saying that we were delivering an order-fill rate of 98 percent, our customers thought we were at 60 percent. The irony was, instead of trying to address the customers' complaints, we seemed to think we had to show that we were right and they were wrong."

DELIVERING ON YOUR PROMISES

In my years in brand management at Procter & Gamble, there were very good checks and balances that forced employees to quickly learn the importance of objectivity and delivering what you had promised.

When I was the advertising manager of the package soap and detergent division, I was responsible not only for the marketing efforts behind the individual brands but also for the profitability of those brands. The brand managers reporting to me were not held responsible for profit; their job was primarily to grow market share and revenue and improve their products to outperform competition. If a brand manager was not objective about revenue potential and estimated too optimistically, securing precious marketing money to launch an initiative behind that inflated promise, he or she would eventually disappoint me from a profitability standpoint. It was up to me to make sure that what they promised was realistic.

This disease of overpromising the revenue potential of an initiative was often found in young brand managers who were eager to make a quick impact. They wanted to demonstrate that they were rising stars. I remember one particularly enthusiastic young brand manager, whom I will call Sara, who was very aggressive, energetic, and extremely persuasive. She was the new brand manager on one of the detergent brands we marketed at P&G. She was extremely bullish on placing in a test market an improved formula that had a fragrance our consumer testing suggested improved the perception of its cleaning power. But while the product test showed that the consumer noticed the new fragrance, and that there were small improvements in its cleaning rating, they weren't statistically significant. Sara argued that paired-comparison blind tests were too blunt a tool to be able to pick up the cleaning perception advantage. She wanted the company to spend a fairly large amount of money to launch a test market in 7 percent of the United States (that's a large piece of real estate for a test market).

As the marketing manager, I was lukewarm about this. It seemed to me that we would be spending too much money on a relatively marginal improvement of the product. Sara fought hard to convince sales that they would be able to capitalize on this improvement at the retail level in a big way.

Because Sara was so aggressive and enthusiastic and had engaged the sales organization so thoroughly, we went ahead with the test market but in a smaller territory, to hold down the test costs. Twelve months later, the results were disappointing. We saw a revenue bump during the first six months, when the majority of the advertising money and the additional promotion money were spent, but six months later, the numbers had returned to the previous levels.

In retrospect, Sara was simply overenthusiastic. She hadn't gone back to study the numerous other fragrance initiatives of other detergents that Procter & Gamble marketed and gauged the impact similar initiatives had achieved. That data was available, but Sara was too eager to do a thorough study of it. On the other hand, Sara gained valuable experience from her failed effort. She learned the value at Procter & Gamble of objectivity in estimating marketplace impact and on delivering on your promises.

The kind of experience Sara had would be reflected on her performance review. Everyone knew that was how the system worked. The individual brand managers were charged with growing revenue and market share. They were well aware that delivering on their promises determined whether their advertising manager would achieve his or her profitability goals.

These important checks and balances, put in place at a level where it could make a difference, was key to establishing a culture of objectivity at Procter & Gamble.

The point here is that systems were set up to evaluate a brand manager's objectivity in as quantitative a manner as possible and ensure that it got reflected in performance reviews. Without keeping score in some way, the fiefdom instincts of individuals take over, inflating their assessment of their work.

2. CONTINUALLY STRENGTHEN THE TALENT POOL

It is crucial that top management ensures that the human resources department owns and executes a uniform and effective performance-evaluation system and a meaningful employee-development program within the organization.

Without strong discipline from the top, these two areas can atrophy badly. Human resources cannot do this alone. Top management must be behind them 110 percent. Then it is up to HR to execute crisply.

HOW TO DO IT WRONG

At a chemicals company I briefly consulted with, the human resources organization had allowed the performance-appraisal process to fall into a terrible state of disarray. There was no prescribed time during the year when everyone's performance was evaluated. There was no process for collecting performance appraisals and sharing them with management to ensure that the performance appraisals were actually happening.

The grading system had atrophied badly. It consisted of vague adjectives that tended to be positively skewed so as not to disappoint anyone.

One of the key reasons the performance-appraisal system was so weak was that this company's business had been relatively stable for over ten years. Revenue and profits had grown by small percentage points each year, and that seemed quite satisfactory to top management and to the shareholders. Its stock price had grown at a relatively slow but steady pace.

A strong executive in one of the subsidiaries that was suffering from fairly weak performance had recruited several employees from within the company who, he had been told, were outstanding, based on their prior performance. Within a couple of years, he realized these individuals were actually quite weak, and that he had been fooled by the system.

As a result, he created a proposal to implement a disciplined and quantitative personnel review process across the entire company, one that would have generated significant improvement. He didn't want to be burned by the system again. The head of HR, whom I will call David, bought into the proposal and began to push it hard with top management, recommending that it be implemented throughout the company.

David had realized over the years just how weak human resources was and how deficient it was in the performance-appraisal area. But before now he seemed unable to get anyone's attention to make significant change. He looked at the proposal coming out of the subsidiary as a way to get top management's attention.

The CEO of this company, whom I will call John, had a somewhat lukewarm reaction to David's proposal. John worried about the impact on the company's culture, since this results-oriented performance-appraisal process and grading system would isolate the lowest-performing employees so that they could be retrained into a position that was a better fit, or be moved out of the company.

The core problem was a lack of sense of urgency around improving the results of the company. It was clear John himself didn't have a sense of urgency. He seemed to be satisfied with the results of the past ten years.

Before long, some of the fiefdoms within the company began to whisper to John that this new performance-appraisal approach that David was pushing ran counter to the culture, an initial concern that John had. They urged John to simply ignore it. This led to incredible debates within the company; it became a very divisive issue.

The debate seemed to go on and on. David continued to push it, and John would simply direct David to the latest general manager in the company who complained about making the change. He had David running all over the company, talking to various department heads, collecting their viewpoints. John's mistake was that he let the debate go on and on, hoping the issue would just go away. The mistake that David made was in not confronting John and making him agree to be the champion of this cause or to kill it. Instead, after six months of infighting, John decided to leave things alone and asked David to stop work on the new approach.

Strong leadership would have either killed the idea at the outset or put it on a timetable so that it could be resolved quickly and in an orderly manner so that it didn't become so divisive.

Fiefdoms can be extremely effective in killing ideas that don't have a strong backing at the top. The leader of the organization must set the tone in areas where change is to be pursued, and where it is not, and make this clear to the troops.

DEVELOPING KEY PEOPLE

Another company I consulted with was just shy of being twenty years old and was led by a top management team that had been with the company since its inception. Although the company had grown significantly each year, top management spent little energy in developing key personnel to run new business units or departments as opportunities arose.

The CEO of the company was an individual whom I will call Greg. During the first ten or so years of the company's existence, the overall attitude Greg and his management team seemed to project was that if you needed a key spot filled, you simply looked around the company. If you had someone who fit the bill, fine. If not, you went outside and hired someone. Because they lived in a world of very fast growth, their attitude was that when a key opening occurred, you get a good person and throw him or her into the situation and let the person figure out what needed to be done. Clearly, some mistakes would be made, but what was more important was to keep things moving forward. You could always repair things on the fly. The need for specific management skills was not high on their list. They just looked for strong people to jump into situations and take charge.

That strategy works fine for small and midsize organizations. But when a company is big enough that it has several business units, a network of regional units, and key departments that help make the place operate, it needs a pool of talent experienced in the complexities of the organization. You need to be able to reach out to a key individual who is experienced in several areas of the company, knows how the company gets work done, and has proven him- or herself to be a consistently excellent performer. That kind of management development can save you from losing momentum due to a lack of experience.

Greg was feeling frustrated by the need for experienced, multitalented individuals. He could see that his business was a heck of a lot different from what he had experienced just five or so years earlier. Parts of the business were mature and fairly complicated from a business standpoint, making it hard to manage for an individual who didn't understand the competition and the company's channels of distribution.

Greg typically would sit down with HR and go through long lists of people within the company who might meet Greg's needs. But most of these employees' experience and skills were quite narrow. They didn't have a broad exposure to the company or the industry, and they didn't have the experience to manage a large and relatively stable part of the business.

Yet Greg knew that if he went outside to fill key positions, he would be dealing with people who didn't know the company culture, didn't know how to get work done within the company, and would need to go through a steep learning curve before they were really effective. He vented his frustration on the human resources organization. So they began to look at what other companies were doing to develop talent.

Based on such benchmarking, Greg and his HR head instituted a top management development process, borrowing from other companies. It consisted of a biannual meeting where the top management team spent two hours with the head of each department and business unit. They asked each of these leaders to discuss two or three backup candidates for each of the key jobs within their particular unit. For each key job, the managers had to indicate who would be ready within 6 months, who within 12 months, 24 months, and 36 months. This forced each of the units to think about and discuss those candidates who were ready now, as well as identify those who were the rising stars and what they needed to work on to be considered for further responsibilities.

As I've discussed earlier, the format chosen to execute this kind of plan is not as important as the basic decision on top management's part to do it on a regular basis. That's the tough part.

When top management takes the lead in developing and maintaining the talent pool at a variety of levels in the company, it makes it difficult for fiefdoms to hoard people. Rotating personnel regularly makes a big difference in making sure fiefdoms don't gain traction.

3. MAKE STANDARDIZATION A REALITY

Nothing retards the formation of a fiefdom or breaks up an existing fiefdom better than the existence of standardized data available to all the appropriate people in the organization.

Following are the key principles to make standardized data a reality.

PRINCIPLE 1. Each department or functional area of the company (finance, human resources, marketing, manufacturing, etc.) must assign a group of two or three veterans/experts to design and manage the implementation and maintenance of company-wide processes and systems.

This group should not rely on committees to do their work. They need to view the CEO as the customer for their efforts. The leader of each group should report directly to the head of the department. The people selected to be in the group should be highly talented development prospects who understand the department and the kind of data and measures it needs to make available.

Organizations seldom delegate this kind of responsibility to a small group of people familiar with their particular area. Too often organizations let everybody provide input, creating heated debate among people who do not understand the details and workings of these areas.

Because the individuals selected to be in the small group should be extremely talented and capable, don't expect them to remain in these jobs for more than two or three years. As they move on to bigger and better things, you will need to staff these jobs once again with equally talented, confident, and aggressive developmental prospects.

PRINCIPLE 2. The data and terminology in each department must be standardized across the entire company. There should be no exceptions.

For example, finance should have one "chart of accounts," or general ledger, for the entire organization. There should be standard definitions for all employee information, standard definitions for customer information, for purchase orders, etc.

The experts assigned to design the processes/systems for each department should be able to define the key data and terminology in a few days, given how familiar they are with the department. That is why strong, experienced performers are needed.

PRINCIPLE 3. The business processes and templates in each department must be standardized on a company-wide basis. There should be no exceptions.

For each department, the small group of veterans assigned to design the processes/systems knows how to make the key business processes lean and effective and understands the kinds of questions asked by top management and within the business and regional units. They should be able to simplify and standardize the key business processes and define the templates that will answer 98 percent of the questions that come up on a regular basis.

The templates should be able to be easily pulled up on a PC screen from an employee's office, home, or hotel room, providing all the basic measures needed to understand and analyze the health of each business or regional unit. Templates relating to personnel should be available so managers can quickly access information on key talent. The marketing organization should have standard templates to capture market share trends for your products and your competitors' products, marketing budgets and actual spending levels, consumer research on the effectiveness of your products versus competition, etc.

By having each department define the key business processes, and create the templates that answer the majority of questions and give a thorough description of the health of the business and its key issues, executives basically have the core knowledge of the corporation at their fingertips.

PRINCIPLE 4. The head of each department needs to winnow down the number of information systems used to a very small number company-wide. I suggest using off-the-shelf packaged software for core processes.

For most departments, great commercial software exists that can be used with virtually no customization. What is important is to not allow modifications of that software.

PRINCIPLE 5. Minimize the number of people with access to the packaged software. Direct most users to data warehouses via simple menu-driven intranet pages.

The users within the organization need only see simple menus that they pull up on their PCs that allow them to access key financial information, key HR information, etc. These menus are nothing but Web pages that are connected to the database. The Web-based menus call up the requested information from the database. The packaged software updates the database whenever it receives input. Basically, the software sits behind the scenes as the information engine feeds the data warehouse, obtaining data that has been input by the users.

PRINCIPLE 6. Don't build bridges to old systems. Eliminate old systems and methods.

One of the things you need to watch out for are employees who protect the legacy systems. These legacy people will fight hard to keep such systems in place, offering to build bridges to the old legacy systems to "retain the old reports that people are used to."

It is vitally important to fight off these requests. Huge savings and efficiencies come from cleaning house, and that should be the focus of this exercise.

PRINCIPLE 7. In each department, the department head needs to drive down the size of the IT organization and the number of IT systems developers serving that particular area.

It is important to make sure that as you eliminate systems, you eliminate systems developers. The more systems developers you have, the more systems you will get.

PRINCIPLE 8. No paper allowed. Period.

Users should see simple-to-understand reports on their PC screens.

They should be able to input data into simple forms and extract data from key reports that relate to their job. If there is a need to print things occasionally, fine. But the core process needs to assume that absolutely no paper is needed.

One useful exercise that I've seen is to ask the information technology people to get a list of the paper forms that the procurement organization buys. Then make that the "hit list" to create PC screens/templates that will drive the use of paper to zero.

PRINCIPLE 9. In each department (e.g., finance, IT, HR, manufacturing, etc.), the department heads should streamline the size of his or her staff in the corporate group and in the regional and business units.

This exercise helps to make the company lean, fast, and agile. Once the systems have been cleaned up and the company has eliminated unnecessary information systems, bloated staffs need to be trimmed. Fiefdoms love to build up the number of people who work for them. A staff-reduction exercise is an opportunity to really drive that number down. I've seen IT organizations in regional subsidiaries grow to 70 or 80 people. That's preposterous. Business units or regional divisions may need a few IT people to develop/maintain a few databases or small sales, marketing, or financial systems to reflect the "uniqueness" of that business, but "a few" means "a few."

PRINCIPLE 10. The CEO must be 100 percent behind this effort.

Without his or her strong support, the fiefdom mentality is sure to take over. I can't underscore this enough.

I've recounted numerous examples that demonstrate the importance of the CEO or the head of the organization driving standardization. He has to be able to withstand pressure from the heads of the fiefdoms.

Following the above principles will lead to an organization that has the key data at its fingertips and the ability to make comparisons across business units, subsidiaries, and departments. It'll be able to inspect overall performance and to probe the details behind that performance.

This should in no way undermine the responsibility and leadership of the business and geographical units. They need to call the shots in achieving the performance the organization expects. But now they will have an incredible arsenal of data that they can reach for to guide and judge their own performance.

They also know that they can't keep that information to themselves. Their management chain, too, will be capable of pulling up this information. But management will be looking to them to do the analysis and make the decisions that will improve overall performance of the department or unit.

8

FOSTERING CREATIVITY

JUST AS THERE are tools to enhance discipline in an organization, there are specific tools that can be used to foster creativity. I have come up with eight separate approaches to help an organization or an individual generate fresh, creative ideas.

As I've noted earlier, fiefdoms dampen creativity and innovation. Because of fiefdom members' inflated self-assessment of their work, they tend to underplay the need for improvement. In essence, they think they already are good enough, so why the rush in trying to improve?

Fiefdoms also tend to have an insular view of the world. Understanding the dynamics outside the fiefdom usually isn't a high priority. They are less driven to study competitors and understand consumers in order to figure out ways to achieve superior products and services.

So how does an organization take steps to foster creativity in its employees and divisions?

1. SHOCK THE SYSTEM: REORGANIZE

Where creativity is desirable, it is important to organize people around the task. When left too long in the same positions, people tend to approach tomorrow with the same priority, mind-set, and energy as today. Sometimes a dramatic shock, or reorganization, is needed to jar people's expectations about their work and their results.

It is important to put top-quality people into leadership positions in the new groups. They need to be given challenging goals over a short period of time. Reorganizing work groups or business units around strong people, and establishing clear goals, sends an important signal to the organization—that these goals are vitally important and will set a new direction for the company. For talented people stuck in static fiefdoms, they will see they aren't part of the action and will seek ways to escape the fiefdom they've been trapped in.

Another important advantage of reorganizing is that a *lean* group can be assembled, focused on a *single* important objective. Fiefdoms tend to associate large groups with success. When top management reorganizes around a key initiative with a lean group, it is signaling that speed, agility, innovation, and adding value to the overall organization are what is important.

We faced this issue at Procter & Gamble in the liquid Tide launch discussed in the last chapter.

Since Tide liquid detergent was superior to other liquid detergents in cleaning ability, we wanted to make the most of that competitive edge. What we had to decide was whether the existing Tide brand manager, Tim Cawley, and his brand group, which was focused exclusively on Tide powder, should also manage the Tide liquid product, or whether we should form a separate brand group.

Tim viewed himself as the keeper of the Tide franchise. He and his team argued strongly that they represented Tide and should be the ones to manage this new Tide liquid initiative, while also continuing to manage Tide powder. They argued passionately about the importance of keeping the Tide trademark focused on superior cleaning and that the advertising for both forms needed to be consistent with that of our overall Tide strategy. He raised a good point. He also talked about creating efficiencies in their marketing program that would enable the total Tide franchise to improve its profitability, by achieving economies of scale. Frankly, that was worrisome to us. The last thing we wanted to do was shortchange Tide liquid in our attempt to make it the leading liquid detergent. But we needed to make this decision quickly. People were already spending too much time debating it and getting emotionally involved in its outcome.

Associate advertising manager Tom Moore spent hours with me discussing the pros and cons of the two approaches. The thing we feared most was, given the exclusive focus the Tide brand group had on Tide powder in the past, would they be able to put aside their fundamental bias toward Tide powder and make sure that Tide liquid emerged as the leader among the liquid detergents in the marketplace? We worried about what that kind of compromising would mean to both forms of Tide.

After discussing the issue at length and reviewing it with Steve Donovan, the vice president of the package soap and detergent division, we decided we didn't want a single brand group deciding how to allocate marketing efforts between Tide liquid and Tide powder. We wanted the consumers to decide which of the two forms they preferred. As a result, we decided it would be best to create a separate Tide liquid brand group and let each of the two Tide brand groups do their best to grow market share. The management approved that arrangement, and that's what was executed.

The key to our decision was to have both of the Tide brand groups report to the same associate advertising manager, Tom Moore. It was Tom's job to make sure that the Tide trademark was treated identically by both brand groups from the standpoint of what the Tide trademark represented in the mind of the consumer.

The fundamental principle here is that when you have a new initiative, it's important to bring together a fresh, talented team to execute with excellence and exceed objectives. Assigning it to a person or group with preexisting responsibilities virtually guarantees that that new effort will be treated as a second priority.

2. AVOID LAYERS OF WISDOM: DELEGATE

What often happens in organizations is when an individual gets an idea, the chain of command makes suggestions about how to change the idea to make it more effective. These suggestions often are made in such a way that they come across as requirements. Feeling the pressure, the employee goes along with changing things even though he or she might not agree. That is the way good, creative ideas get watered down, or killed off entirely.

Creative people need to feel they have the responsibility for their ideas and plans. They should feel that the ultimate judge should be the consumer, not their chain of command. While they should certainly listen to their management, they must be allowed to decide which suggestions the group thinks make sense from a consumer perspective.

And when management wants to know the status of the effort or some details about the project, it should be the leader of the group or department that speaks, not some higher-level executive in the group's chain of command.

It is critical that creative groups understand what is expected of them. If there are constraints in terms of their creativity, they should know them up front.

The CEO of a large financial services company hired me at one point to consult with them about the launch of a set of creative new services. The CEO, whom I will call Eric, went on at length about the importance of the launch and how strong he thought these new services would be in the marketplace. The group that had developed these ideas, and was putting together the basic marketing plans to launch them, was led by an individual named Tom. I was hired by Eric to assist with this effort to make sure that the group maximized the launch's potential. I was not hired by Tom, the leader of the group (and someone who appeared to be doing a very good job in creating strong marketing initiatives to get these new services off to a very fast start).

Tom and his group had already done the hard creative work and come up with some very good thinking. But it was Eric who explained to me the importance of this launch—they did not want to screw it up. Over the next couple of months, I saw various levels of management in the company taking an opportunity to critique the work of Tom's group and to make suggestions on how to modify the original creative approach.

After several visits in which I got up to speed, I had a meeting with Tom and his group. They were in the midst of making significant changes to their marketing approach for this new set of financial services. When I asked why, the best rationale they could give me was that people at very high levels had made all sorts of suggestions and that Eric felt their suggestions had to be reflected in their plans to push the project through. When I asked Tom if he thought the suggestions genuinely improved the services and the marketing plan used to launch them, he said no. In fact, when Tom and I critiqued all the various suggestions, we agreed that overall the plans had taken a step backward.

I went to Eric and explained what I saw. He reiterated just how important the launch was, and that in his view, it simply made sense to take into account all of the accumulated knowledge of the seasoned veterans in other departments who were being given an opportunity to provide input on the new services and the launch. In fact, Eric himself indicated that he was not satisfied with one approach the group had come up with and was meeting with them in a couple of days to make sure his thinking was incorporated into their approach.

At that point, I called for a time-out. I told Eric what was happening here was that the basic services and marketing approach, which was so exciting to everyone at the outset, was being watered down. I strongly suggested that he go to Tom's group and charge them with testing their original approach using some standard market research tools. They should also test the alternate approach that reflected the accumulated "wisdom" that was being thrown their way.

At first, Eric was a bit insulted. But when I described what was going on, he began to see that they had too many chefs in the kitchen and that the worst thing that could happen to a creative "recipe" of this sort was to have a bunch of people whack away at its distinctive edges. That's what degrades a creative idea down to an average idea.

Eric took my suggestion. About four weeks later, I checked in with Eric and Tom and found out that the original set of services and marketing approach had been far more interesting and persuasive in the marketplace. The original services and plans that Tom's group had put together were officially approved by Eric and his management team.

This company was exhibiting what I call the "layers-of-wisdom" model. Under this kind of model, the people who are charged with studying the problem and generating new, creative ideas end up feeling like all they are doing is floating ideas up the layers of management and watching the ideas get harpooned, modified, and shaped in a variety of ways before being blessed for implementation.

This makes the group feel as if management is the one who has all the answers and is ultimately responsible for creativity rather than the group that was assigned full-time to the task. They feel like mere drones, powerless to effect significant change.

This diffusion of responsibility slows things significantly and kills off creativity. Worse, the "layers-of-wisdom" approach causes the original group charged with being creative to constantly second-guess those above them rather than focus on the consumer. That is a terrible disease for a company to catch. If a group charged with being innovative has to work within certain constraints, it needs to know those constraints up front. On the other hand, everyone should question why the constraints exist.

Now let me give you a positive example. This is a case from Microsoft, which does a great job of delegating. The product is called SQL (pronounced "sequel") Server, a database tool that competes with database products from Oracle and IBM. SQL Server runs on servers based on Intel microprocessors, as opposed to IBM and Oracle products, which are used primarily on traditional high-end servers. As a result, in the past, SQL Server was seen as a tool for small-to-medium databases. But with Intel-based servers growing in power each year, the plan was (and still is) to increasingly take on the large databases at a much lower price than IBM or Oracle.

This SQL Server team was vintage Microsoft. Their area of performance was clearly laid out: the database business. The expectation was also clear: Study the database business, then innovate and innovate. The long-term goal was to create a product that was rated better than the competition's by customers and the trade press. They were told this would be a long-term effort, and the goal was to achieve steady market share gains each year.

The SQL Server team was staffed with very strong people. Anytime there was a question in regard to the progress in the database area, the head of the SQL team was called upon for the answer. In other words, the SQL leader's boss, or top management, did not speak for the group; it was the leader of the group who was responsible.

Since then, SQL Server has grown in market share virtually every year and at last has become a serious competitor to Oracle and IBM, two very entrenched and strong competitors. Yet each year, SQL Server seems to get rated better and better by the trade press as Intel microprocessor capabilities have skyrocketed.

When people feel responsible, and the objective is clear, amazing things happen.

3. DON'T PREJUDGE PEOPLE

Whether we like it or not, we all make prejudgments about people. But it is dangerous. This is particularly true when looking for real innovation and creativity. Often it is the individual who marches to a different drummer who is the most creative. Yet these are often the very people management wants to put constraints around. As the individuals charged with being creative try to second-guess what management wants them to do, they become internally focused, as opposed to being genuinely creative in addressing their consumer needs.

Fiefdoms make lots of prejudgments about people. They've already decided how they want or expect the folks in the organization to act. If anyone steps out of line, they are made to feel ostracized. That doesn't mean they get kicked out of the organization. Rather, it usually means they're left to do whatever they want, and no one pays much attention to them.

Let me give you an example from my own life where I realized I was operating with preconceived notions that I needed to put aside.

After twenty-six years at Procter & Gamble, I pretty much knew how people should look and dress in the business world. For twenty-six years, I saw a lot of white and blue dress shirts and dark suits. P&G has changed a lot in this regard since I left to join Microsoft in 1994, but historically it was a very formal place. That's not a knock against Procter & Gamble or people who wear suits. It's just that it helped to shape my impression of what business success should look like.

I had been at Microsoft for a couple of weeks when I attended my first Microsoft board of directors meeting. Bill Gates had me schedule a team from one of the product units to come in to talk about a new and creative approach in e-mail architecture and network directories.

Into the boardroom walked three energetic young guys who looked more like graduate students in a university computer science department rather than the brain trust of one of the most important product groups at Microsoft. All were wearing blue jeans, and most were wearing T-shirts or sweatshirts that I could swear they had slept in for the previous three days. I was wearing a blue dress shirt (from my P&G wardrobe) and slacks (I left my blazer in my office when I saw the other board members were dressed in slacks and sport shirts).

I'm sitting there thinking, "Oh, man, have I really screwed up; these guys didn't understand that I was inviting them to speak to the board of directors."

After forty-five minutes of absolutely first-class presentation and dialogue, I began to see how crazy it was to prejudge others before giving them a chance to show their ability. The Microsoft board loved these guys and their work, and it made absolutely no difference how they looked.

When you prejudge others, you are forcing on the other party a set of constraints that are irrelevant with regard to the task of generating innovation and creativity.

The example above, as well as a dozen others during my first four or five weeks at Microsoft, quickly taught me the importance of focusing on the person and their work rather than on prejudging them.

4. AVOID UNNECESSARY COMMUNICATIONS AND TRAINING

We've all seen examples of organizations that have an incredible list of training courses that they put people through, as well as a system of internal communication that overloads employees with excess information—in many cases with e-mails or "cc'd" materials that are sent only "for your info" or out of courtesy.

All of this can end up being an incredible overload on employees, which can create artificial constraints on how tasks should be done.

Over the years, I have found that the most talented individuals don't want to be trained at all. They want to be given clear responsibilities and expectations, and then they want to be free to discover what they believe is the best set of steps to take to accomplish their objectives. Such folks tend to turn up very creative ideas on how the organization can approach particular tasks differently, massively improve how work is done, and how to change products and services to generate consumer excitement and satisfaction.

It is easy for corporate training to become a ritual, one often led by top management, as opposed to a valuable training exercise for the troops.

The key point to remember is that the best employees don't want to be saddled with a bunch of worthless rituals. They want to be directed toward the challenge and work to achieve some kind of greatness. They'll live within your constraints if you explain them up front, but they'll also charge hard to generate good ideas and results. What fiefdoms do is constantly load people down with excess training and communication, handicapping them with the mediocrity that the group has become comfortable with. Strong performers tend to see what's going on pretty quickly and work to get out of that environment.

In my experience, the person who best exemplifies a focus on excellence is Bill Gates. I learned a fundamental lesson from him very early on—one that Bill would consistently remind the organization of. Namely, you need to constantly ask the following questions: What currently isn't going well? What disadvantages do we have versus competition? How can we quickly prioritize those areas where we are falling short and not only get them fixed but pull ahead of the competition?

This value was expressed in virtually every meeting and every conversation at Microsoft.

We tried to avoid excessive formal training, and a lot of FYI kinds of e-mail. We also avoided e-mail on what we had done *right* and unnecessary reviews designed primarily to please bosses, as opposed to uncovering insights. The real focus was on what wasn't going well and how we could fix these things to gain a competitive advantage.

Our value system focused on areas where innovation was badly needed, and it provided clarity about what the result was supposed to look like.

To a certain extent, this is the same message that Andy Grove described in his book *Only the Paranoid Survive*. You need to continually isolate the areas where you are behind, organize around those areas, and drive the expectation that real innovation must occur. An excess of training and wasted communications slows this process down.

5. DON'T OVERCOMPLICATE THE PROCESS

One thing I learned over the years is that you can't develop a process to generate innovation. Many companies have attempted to put together a series of specific steps involving consumer interaction, consumer testing, and product experimentation to improve their batting average with respect to creativity and innovation. I pointed this out in Chapter 6 with respect to Six Sigma. In most cases, the results are disappointing. The reason is that you simply can't break into logical steps the way the innovative mind of a human being contemplates and generates creative new ideas. The individuals who excel at innovation typically have a finger on the pulse of what will excite or please the consumer and what won't, based on years of experience with consumers and personally submerging themselves in the changing habits, practices, and cultural trends of their market.

We need to be very careful of the constraints that we put in place—sometimes without even realizing that we are putting them in place—around people whom we expect to be innovative.

In the late '80s and the early '90s, there was a tremendous push for what was called total quality. It originated in Japan as a powerful analysis/improvement tool when applied to structured processes. In the late 1980s, the rage among management in the U.S. was to apply it corporate-wide. To some extent, total quality was the precursor of Six Sigma. The implementation of total quality involved meetings, committees, or task forces designed to improve the process being studied.

Total quality became a high priority at Procter & Gamble when I was senior vice president of marketing in the early 1990s. As part of that effort, a multifunctional team (involving manufacturing, R&D, finance, marketing, etc.) developed a process designed to "qualify" any product/marketing initiative before it was placed into the test market. This process was based on a thorough analysis of past test market successes and failures. A project had to pass several "hurdles" before it was recommended to top management to test-market.

At P&G, the brand management personnel were expected to participate in those "qualification" meetings along with people from purchasing, finance, HR, product development, and manufacturing.

It wasn't long before I began to get some incredibly emotional complaints from the various brand groups regarding the frequency of these "qualification process" meetings. They were eating up big chunks of time. More important, they faced enormous group pressure in those meetings to slow things down and to make changes in their marketing efforts and in their product directions to make it easier for sales to implement them with a higher degree of certainty, as well as to make it easier for manufacturing to modify production lines to meet the needs of a particular new product initiative. In essence, the group was becoming a lot more risk-averse, which tended to handcuff our marketing efforts.

One particular brand manager, whom I will call John, burst into my office one day when I was chatting with a few folks from sales. John had a new package with him that consumers really liked. It was a shampoo bottle that made it a lot easier to control the flow of the shampoo out of the bottle as well as to measure the correct amount to use. It was quite innovative. John and a few of his creative friends in product development had been working on it for several months. John's face was a brilliant red, and he couldn't hold himself back. He said to me that he had to get together with me in the next couple of hours—he'd had an experience that was so exasperating that he felt it was hurting business. Naturally, I was intrigued, as were the sales folks who were sitting there with me. I asked my sales guests if they minded if we took ten minutes to hear what was on John's mind. They said they would be very eager to hear what was going on. John then unloaded. Now, John was the essence of what brand management was all about at Procter & Gamble. He had a strong sense of urgency; he did his homework well in regard to what would excite consumers in the marketplace. He was determined to get this particular idea out into the marketplace as fast as possible because his market research indicated he could generate real excitement.

The manufacturing folks, it turned out, wanted to make modifications in the bottle, and product-development management thought more work was needed with regard to the design of the innovative cap. In each case, employees in other departments were following the practices of the "qualification process" involving all kinds of data-collection and concurrence requirements that they claimed John needed to go through in order to properly qualify this new package. John's point of view was that we know it excites the consumer and we know we can make enough of these to get the new design into the test market; we can make modifications on the fly. So let's get going.

I heard several of these kinds of complaints over the next few months, and it was becoming clear to me that on some subjects, such as those involving the design of products and the development of marketing plans, "qualification" meetings were not serving a useful purpose. I told the CEO that brand management personnel were no longer going to go to these meetings to "qualify" their projects. I indicated they would go only if the topic was well defined around a problem and marketing personnel were clearly needed.

One thing I had confirmed from that experience at P&G was that teams and complicated processes don't do a very good job of generating creativity. Individuals can be highly creative. But when those creative ideas are exposed to a "clearance" committee or a complicated multi-hurdle process, the creativity—the unique aspects—are bled out of it, leaving an idea or product or modification that is acceptable to many, but not one that is provocative or distinctive.

6. FOCUS ON CUSTOMER NEEDS, NOT MEETINGS AND MEMOS

Too often in organizations, things get proceduralized to an excessive degree, and you end up with more focus on the process than on the marketplace.

It serves no real purpose to generate an elegant, superbly written memo, or an incredible presentation, or to hold a meeting where lots of things are discussed and thrashed out, if no real creativity occurs that will improve the company's overall business.

If you want to foster meaningful creativity that's going to have a big impact in the marketplace, the focus of the discussion has to be on understanding consumers, probing for areas of consumer dissatisfaction, and looking for areas where you can surprise consumers with new capabilities.

Make sure that the individuals responsible for such creativity know that you don't want fancy memos and you don't want well-orchestrated meetings or a streamlined process; you want great ideas that are going to have a huge impact with the customer. It's not about form, it's about substance.

With twenty-six years' experience at Procter & Gamble, about half of that in brand management and marketing management, I am an expert on the subject of elegant memos! Procter & Gamble is famous for the one-page document. But it also is famous for the four- or five-page document with seven or eight exhibits, which some assistant brand manager spent weeks drafting and revising.

Now let me qualify what I'm about to say by explaining that the example below reflects my experiences at Procter & Gamble in the 1980s and early 1990s, not P&G today. I know things have changed quite a bit there. But those older practices taught me a powerful lesson.

I recall once spending about half my time over a two-month period putting together a detailed analysis of the antiperspirant/deodorant industry. Preparing such an industry review was an annual practice for the upcoming budget season, where each of the brands proposed its strategy and marketing plans for the next fiscal year. After weeks of effort, we forwarded this document to our associate advertising manager, who provided a ton of suggestions on how we could modify the document to make it more thorough and persuasive. He also suggested how we could better prepare management for the kind of budget we would be asking for on our brand. We had two or three meetings with him to finally agree on the kinds of changes we would make. Juggling my many other responsibilities in the brand group, it took me a couple of weeks to make those changes.

Once the changes were made, we again forwarded this to the associate advertising manager, who put a cover note on it and sent it to the advertising manager. After another week, we finally got fifteen minutes with this person. He had scribbled all over the document, explaining to us that he wanted to restructure it (back to what we had before we talked to the associate advertising manager) and that we needed to take the material related to budgeting out of it and keep the document pure with respect to studying the industry and what we thought it would take to catch up with key competitors.

Back to the drawing board! I spent a few weeks making the modifications, amid my other responsibilities, and eventually the document went up to the associate ad manager again, and then to the advertising manager, and then he forwarded it to the vice president of the division. We didn't hear from the VP for a couple of weeks. Eventually, he responded with a brief note indicating that he liked the analysis but that we needed more historical perspective in the background section in order to be able to draw some analogies to how we had faced similar conditions in the past.

A few more weeks were taken hunting up historical facts and incorporating them into the document and getting ready to launch it again. Three weeks later, it went all the way to the CEO. About two weeks later, the memo came back with a small handwritten note in the upper right-hand corner that said, "Good memo. It is clear that we have some work to do in catching up with competitor X." I looked at it and thought, "Is that all we get?!" I already knew we had work to do to catch up with competitor X. And I would have been far better off spending time on how to do that instead of revising this document fifteen times. Yet, it worried me a bit just how much I valued his comment: "Good memo." Was I becoming too internally focused?

You can't argue with Procter & Gamble's success. The thoroughness of the company's approach and the focus on the consumer leaves a life-long mark on employees with regard to how to think about marketing problems and business problems in general. But I am glad to hear from their current top management that a lot of things have changed, because a lot of human effort was wasted on memos and meetings as opposed to thinking about how to beat the competition.

7. REWARD RESULTS

People who are true achievers want to be acknowledged. This means treating them well financially, but it also means taking the time to do the small things that signal that their work is acknowledged and appreciated.

Many experts who have studied the public K-12 education system in the U.S. believe that one of the problems in attracting talent to the American teaching profession is the lack of ability to provide rewards for people who excel. Typically, the salary systems in the K-12 school systems provide very little flexibility to reward outstanding performers. Nor are there ways to promote these people.

This is in stark contrast to private industry. For example, at Microsoft, we not only gave pay increases to strong performers through a well-designed, quantitative performance-appraisal system, but we also acknowledged individual contributors with promotions.

At Microsoft, there was a set of titles for individual contributors that acknowledged experience and expertise in technological innovation. The titles were intended to motivate individuals who were primarily technical contributors, to show them that you didn't have to become a manager of people to succeed. Each technical level had an appropriate salary and benefit range similar to the managerial hierarchy. The top technical title was "distinguished engineer," and those folks were treated as vice presidents. This title was given to individuals who had a long and impressive track record of solving problems and coming up with unique ideas that were valuable to the company.

Creating ways to make sure you are appropriately rewarding important contributors to the company is vitally important. Sometimes these rewards should be in the form of money; sometimes they should be in the form of titles, or support, or other things that signal to the rest of the company that the individual in question is highly valued.

8. PAINT THE DREAM AND
ASK THE ORGANIZATION TO INVENT IT

In recounting my Sam Walton story in Chapter 1, I showed how he painted a picture for top management at Wal-Mart and Procter & Gamble of a world where the Wal-Mart computers were hooked to the Procter & Gamble computers, automatically replenishing inventories.

It is a good example of a CEO describing a dream and charging the organization to somehow figure out how to make it happen.

Sam had the ability to describe what he thought might be possible and excite the group to believe they could make it happen.

Another example of a key executive knowing how to motivate a group to create something fresh and exciting involves John Smale, the CEO of Procter & Gamble during the 1980s. John was in brand management, responsible for Crest when that product got the ADA seal of approval. To a large extent, it was John's hard work with the ADA that resulted in that endorsement. In a short period of time, that endorsement took the Crest brand from nowhere to about a 40 percent market share.

I worked on the Crest brand group in the early '80s, and later as an associate advertising manager, the Crest brand group reported to me. Whenever Crest's market share dropped a point or two below the 40 percent level, John Smale would personally invite the brand group to his office for a "discussion."

He made it clear that Crest was a 40-percent-market-share toothpaste. He talked about the importance of keeping up that tradition—how we had the finest product-development resources you could imagine and that he was confident that our team would be able to bring the brand back to that 40 percent level quickly. He opened up his corporate wallet in the context of marketing dollars if he thought the brand group had a good idea on how to productively spend that marketing money.

What John was really saying to the group was: "OK, you have the responsibility to make this happen. But I want you to know that I'm watching carefully, and I am confident that you will innovate and create in order to keep this prize brand where it belongs."

To some extent, John was like a great football or basketball coach; he knew how to motivate the group when it needed a kick in the pants.

Another example of painting the dream occurred at IBM, a troubled company in the early '90s. Lou Gerstner, despite his statement to the media shortly after arriving at IBM that "the last thing IBM needs is a vision," in fact painted the dream for all the organization to see. Within six months of his arrival, he began telling the employees, day in and day out, that IBM's new strategy was going to revolve around his belief that "the unique opportunity for IBM . . . our distinctive competence . . . was an ability to integrate all of the parts for our customers." Lou was convinced that customers were faced with such a barrage of technology from so many different vendors that there was a gigantic opportunity to focus all of IBM on that task. And that is exactly what he did throughout the late 1990s. He created the dream for IBM employees—he told them how they should act in order to get the company back on a success track.

These tools to foster creativity, coupled with those for achieving discipline throughout an organization, help to eliminate fiefdoms and allow a company to define an exciting strategy and execute it with discipline and excellence.

PART IV

MAJOR CHANGE AND THE FIEFDOM SYNDROME

9 HOW FIEFDOMS AFFECT STRATEGY AND EXECUTION

THERE IS PROBABLY no task more important to a company or organization than getting its long-term strategy right. Once the strategy is hammered out, the company needs aggressive and detailed two- or three-year plans to make sure its strategy is well executed. Unfortunately, fiefdoms can prevent an organization from forming strategy and setting direction because they inhibit insight, creativity, aggressive marketing, and superb execution.

In any for-profit organization, a strong strategy ideally will make enough of a splash to set a new tone and direction for the company and increase its market value significantly as the marketplace recognizes your dynamic new direction.

The best strategies—the ones that set the direction for the future of an industry—are usually surprisingly simple and fundamental. For example, Southwest Airlines identified pairs of cities where it felt there was sufficient air-travel demand for it to operate low-cost, high-volume, point-to-point service.

At the start, management agreed that Southwest would establish enough of those routes to create a steady business, and that's exactly what happened. Southwest had come up with a new and fresh strategy, one that stood in stark contrast to the old hub-and-spoke model utilized by most airlines. This unique strategy, along with its low and flexible cost structure (unlike the high-cost, unionized structure of its competitors), eventually gave Southwest a market value bigger than that of all the other major U.S. airlines combined.

Fiefdoms can prevent the implementation of a new strategy. Why? They believe that their current approaches and execution are good enough. Consequently, they won't foster the creativity or sense of urgency necessary for tackling new directions with gusto and figuring out a long-term leadership strategy.

To gauge whether fiefdoms will hamper *your* company's strategy, look to top management first. Do you have strong leadership? Without it, a fiefdom mentality can take hold and make it impossible to drive major change.

STEEL, COMPUTERS, AND COFFEE

The fiefdom syndrome can impact the best of brands as well as entire industries. I'm going to discuss three cases—in the steel, computer, and coffee industries—where fiefdoms had a dramatic negative impact on seemingly healthy organizations. As these examples demonstrate, no company is immune, no matter its size or balance sheet. In fact, in some instances, the more successful the organization, the more likely a fiefdom will grow and prosper.

To prevent fiefdoms, management must constantly push to create an industry-leading strategy backed by simple planning procedures— practices all fiefdoms are sure to hate.

FIEFDOMS AND THE STEEL INDUSTRY

My first example stems from the steel business. The '60s were the glory days of the U.S. steel industry, when virtually all steel came from huge, integrated steel mills. Adrian Slywotzky describes in detail (in his book *Value Migration*) the slow decline of "big steel," a great case study of how the fiefdom syndrome caused one industry to lose its strategic edge over decades, little by little. Here are parts of Slywotzky's story, focusing on the strategic blunders.

In the 1960s, eight American companies—US Steel, Bethlehem,

National, Republic, Armco, Jones and Laughlin, Inland, and Youngstown—dominated the U.S. steel market, with an estimated total market value of almost $60 billion and over 450,000 employees.

In those days, the U.S. steel industry was seemingly invincible. The process started with mining iron ore in Minnesota, loading it onto freighters, carrying it across the Great Lakes to the steel furnaces of Pittsburgh and Cleveland. There the ore was crushed, then fed into the huge blast furnaces, which produced enormous quantities of high-quality steel ingots. The ingots were later melted down again to make individual steel products.

In 1966, a steelworker named Ken Burns, who worked for US Steel, opted to use his vacation time to travel to Japan to examine its steel industry. His colleagues discouraged the trip. Burns was undeterred. He was curious—he'd heard Japan had some of the world's most efficient and technically advanced steel mills in the world.

What he discovered in Japan was that their blast furnaces had significantly greater capacity, they had an improved basic oxygen process, and their straight-line configuration of handling raw material made it more efficient. Situated on deep-water harbors, their plants enabled quick and easy transport overseas, and their broad adoption of continuous casting allowed them to skip the intermediate step of creating steel ingots, saving time and money.

Burns realized he was looking at the next generation of integrated steel business design, one with impressive cost advantages. But when he returned to Pittsburgh and communicated this to US Steel's leaders, they had very little interest. They reacted as a fiefdom, reasoning that the U.S. market hadn't yet been impacted by Japan's mills and that strong lobbying in Washington, D.C., would significantly restrict the imports of foreign steel.

A healthily paranoid management would've jumped all over what Burns was describing and quickly gotten detailed information on how to use Japan's ideas to improve its own factories and give them a much stronger leadership position on the global stage.

The U.S. steel industry stumbled again in the next decade, when they lost business to mini–steel mills.

In the early '70s, construction companies found that U.S. mini–steel mills were offering attractive prices on low-end steel bars used for reinforcing concrete (often called rebar). These mini-mills were unique. They operated without unions, and they used scrapped steel for raw materials—usually crushed automobiles. They also operated regionally and used relatively inexpensive and small-capacity electric arc furnaces, often utilizing old warehouses as their manufacturing sites.

All of this added up to huge cost efficiencies for a product like rebar. As a result, they took that business away from big steel.

Big steel's reaction? They reasoned that rebar wasn't that important anyway, since they didn't make much money on it (because of their high costs in all parts of their business). So they didn't worry about the mini-mills. This is another typical fiefdom reaction.

After taking virtually all the rebar business away from big steel, mini-mills like Nucor realized they couldn't build a business on one product alone. So they began looking at other options to generate revenue. The most aggressive mini-mills got into the continuous-casting business, enabling them to produce flat rolled steel for use in construction, appliances, automobiles, and other manufacturing applications. Once again, big steel didn't pay much attention. Even as their business continued to be siphoned off by mini-mills, they refused to recognize them as serious competition. In essence, the entire big steel industry had become a fiefdom, closing its eyes to the changing world around it.

By the mid-1980s, the aggregate market value of the publicly traded mini-mills was growing at 15 percent per year, while the "big steel" companies were declining about 9 percent annually.

While part of big steel's decline was due to mini-mills and foreign production, it was also hurt significantly as beer- and soft-drink-can manufacturers moved from steel to aluminum.

To make matters worse, plastics companies began to look at automobiles, realizing that many of the parts could be made with a lot less weight and a lot more durability by using plastic rather than steel. By the mid-1980s, plastics had displaced 15 percent of the steel in auto production and aluminum had displaced 95 percent of all steel for beer cans and 70 percent for soda cans.

So what happened to the steel business throughout these decades as it watched this go on? Its market value declined from the near $60-billion level of the 1960s to roughly $13 billion in the mid-1990s. Big steel employment, which peaked at about 470,000 in the late 1960s, had fallen to about 135,000 by the mid-1990s.

This is a classic story of an entire industry that became so fascinated with its strong position that it made no attempt to face up to or cope with changes in the marketplace. Mini-mills, foreign mills, the aluminum industry, the plastics industry—all were pecking away at big steel, and big steel did nothing in response. Why? Because the huge success of the 1960s had gone to its head, it refused to explore different production methods others were exploiting; its pride and egotism blocked it from seeing reality. Today, many of those big steel players have either gone bankrupt or are in the process of doing so.

The key lessons here? Be paranoid about what is going on in your industry and always test bright new ideas (yours and others'). An idea may look small at the onset, but watch out, because someday it might just supersede your current methods. This holds true even if you're highly successful and profitable.

FIEFDOMS AND THE COMPUTER INDUSTRY

Given the high speed with which the information technology industry moves and the enormous success its companies can have over a short period of time, it's not surprising that it's been a hotbed for fiefdoms.

In the mid-'70s, IBM's market value reached the $100-billion range as a result of its enormously successful mainframe business. But in the late '70s, its market value decreased by $40 billion due to the emergence of the Amdahl and Hitachi mainframe clones.

IBM's fundamental problem lay in its continued reliance on the mainframe for its revenue and profitability, though competition was inevitable. The surprising element, however, was that it failed to come up with any innovations that could make up for the maturing mainframe business. Its mainframe profitability caused IBM to become a classic fiefdom, blocking innovation and preventing that healthy sense of paranoia.

In the early '80s, at the strong urging of a small internal group, IBM launched a personal computer project. IBM top management viewed it as a minor initiative that would never generate much revenue compared to its mainframe business. Were they ever wrong. Lo and behold, the emergence of the IBM personal computer resulted in a strong surge in IBM's market value, from $70 billion to almost $130 billion in just a few years. In fact, in 1984 IBM had a 37 percent share of the personal computer business. Things were looking up. But then this business suddenly began to unravel.

IBM signed historic contracts with Microsoft and with Intel, allowing Microsoft and Intel to sell their software operating system and microprocessor, respectively, to other PC manufacturers. And, unfortunately for IBM, they came along very quickly. The growth of the personal computer saw the emergence of numerous "clones" of the IBM PC, each featuring Microsoft software and Intel chips. Most industry experts believe IBM didn't include exclusivity in those deals because they believed it wouldn't matter; the PC wouldn't be a big deal. Before long, however, the personal-computer business was growing like a weed. It branched out into many hardware vendors, and almost all of them were also using Microsoft's operating system and Intel's microprocessors.

Then IBM ran into more trouble in the form of the Digital Equipment Corporation VAX minicomputer (which I discussed in Chapter 2). The minicomputer was all the rage in the early to mid-1980s, representing an incredibly cost-efficient alternative to mainframe computers.

The minicomputer was a brilliant strategic move for DEC and caused big problems for IBM. As explained earlier, however, DEC would go on to have problems of its own—the success of the VAX caused the fiefdom syndrome to emerge at the company. DEC could not imagine a world where the minicomputer would be eclipsed. Yet, with the advent of networked PCs and servers in the late 1980s, that's exactly what happened. Networked PCs and databases residing on servers connected to the network represented a strategic shift in the industry. And both IBM and DEC missed it.

In the late '80s and early '90s, the market value of IBM dropped $90 billion and the company was on the verge of being split up. DEC's market value dropped from a high of $25 billion back to $5 billion, its level before the VAX.

The IBM decline was viewed as a national disaster, one that rocked the computer industry. Never before had a company that had a proprietary, vertically integrated business model become so completely fragmented. IBM's failure was blatantly evident as personal computers and powerful servers became available from a variety of vendors, along with an explosion of great software applications. It seemed only natural to go in this direction, as it enabled companies to piece together technology and craft solutions that uniquely fit their needs.

As I cited in Chapter 1, Lou Gerstner, in his book *Who Says Elephants Can't Dance?*, commented extensively on how fragmented the company was when he joined in 1993. All its separate fiefdoms were completely incapable of envisioning IBM's future. They were all so completely focused on their own businesses that John Akers, the previous CEO, was seriously considering breaking up the company.

There's never been a clearer example of a company fragmenting itself into fiefdoms and becoming unable to mount a unified strategy for the organization.

IBM was at a crossroads. The most important question: Was there a strategy that could pull the company out of the tailspin, or was it headed for oblivion?

As I mentioned in the last chapter, after six months, Gerstner developed a strong belief "that the unique opportunity for IBM—our distinctive competence—was an ability to integrate all of the parts for our customers," which he declared to be the company's new strategy.

Gerstner spent the next few years implementing that strategy, which focused on solving customer problems and building a huge global services organization. This new services organization led the charge, while also creating opportunities for IBM's various products and services.

During Gerstner's tenure, the market value of IBM increased by $150 billion. His challenge had been to face the fact that IBM was composed of different fiefdoms, all of which had to be broken up. He did it by driving a unique new strategy through the organization—one that affected not only the company but the entire industry.

FIEFDOMS AND THE COFFEE REVOLUTION

In his book *Value Migration*, Adrian Slywotzky discusses how, back in 1987, traditional coffee brands sold in grocery outlets represented more than 90 percent of the $8-billion coffee market. Over the course of the next fifteen years, however, the new gourmet segment of the coffee industry took a chunk out of that market. Leading the charge, creating many billions of dollars in shareholder value, was Starbucks.

Onlookers scratched their heads. How could major players like Procter & Gamble (Folgers) and General Foods (Maxwell House), each of which held roughly 25 percent of the coffee market, stand by and watch as Starbucks became an incredible success and the gourmet coffee brands gained significant market share?

In the late '80s, both General Foods and Procter & Gamble were the dominant players in the coffee industry. Their products were based on coffee-bean blends that were relatively inexpensive compared to the gourmet beans beginning to take hold. Little by little, the fancier brands at prices two or three times higher than Folgers and Maxwell House gained market share.

But Folgers and Maxwell House showed little if any reaction. It became clear from their lack of marketplace initiatives during the late '80s and early '90s that they believed the premium gourmet brands and coffee shops wouldn't amount to much.

These two dominant brands were used to waging price wars, and, consequently, they focused on getting the costs of their products down as much as possible. By focusing primarily on the price point, both companies implied there was very little taste differentiation between brands. This traditional approach differed starkly from that of the gourmet brands and Starbucks. These new brands used arabica beans, which were expensive but also very aromatic and flavorful, making for a better-tasting coffee.

By early 2004, Starbucks had over 6,500 retail outlets around the world, with an annual revenue rate of $5 billion and a market value of $15 billion. During this huge strategic shift in the coffee industry, Folgers and Maxwell House played the role of spectators.

So what's the lesson in terms of the fiefdom syndrome?

Procter & Gamble and General Foods were attached to an outdated success model. Like US Steel and IBM, they had been very successful, and paralysis set in, thanks to the self-interest of fiefdoms within the companies. They were slow to think of alternatives in the new world of coffee. Obviously, had they jumped quickly into the marketplace with a luxury brand like Starbucks, they would have been better off. They certainly had the marketing muscle and corporate funding to execute a major assault in the late 1980s against this brilliant new idea. But they didn't do that. My assessment of why they didn't (and I was at P&G at the time, but not in the coffee area) is: 1) they were enamored of their own success; and 2) they were playing defense instead of offense.

What I find interesting about this example is that General Foods and Procter & Gamble are both generally thought of as being incredibly focused on the consumer. Unfortunately, they missed the boat on this one. The consumer had become bored with bland, weak-tasting coffee and could afford a minor luxury such as a great-smelling and great-tasting cup of coffee flavored with a spoonful of mystery and a dash of style.

These stories are classic examples of opportunities that giant consumer-product companies should jump all over. But the leading companies were too proud of their market leadership positions (Folgers and Maxwell House had very large and very similar market shares), intensely focused on battling each other, and had little interest in contemplating an alternative market structure. Hence, they had little interest in entering the gourmet market.

These examples highlight just how much damage fiefdoms can cause. In the case concerning steel, an entire industry was disabled by fiefdoms. IBM risked fracturing the company, and DEC lost it all. Consumer brand giants General Foods and Procter & Gamble lost billions in potential revenue.

With strong leadership, you can fight off such fiefdom-like behavior and achieve an aggressive, industry-leading strategy. Making that strategy a reality requires careful planning and execution. In the following pages I will identify some methods that small, medium, or large organizations can use to make that happen.

THE KEY TO GREAT EXECUTION

Fiefdoms arise in the absence of planning. Business units that have morphed into fiefdoms resist disciplined planning because they hate sharing data. They would rather not confront reality or make promises about future performance.

By planning, I mean the development of an actionable, medium-term (usually three years) business plan that will utilize some very simple exhibits (standardized charts and descriptions of assumptions) that must be uniformly filled out by all business divisions. These exhibits will constitute the business plans the divisions are expected to execute. But this process has to be driven from top management, or it won't work.

Well-developed fiefdoms will fight this exercise with every excuse imaginable. They will claim this is a bad time to plan, or explain why the exercise doesn't fit their business model, or tell you that key people are on vacation and ask you to delay the review for several months.

Planning has to be a regular exercise (typically, every six months) so progress can be evaluated and future plans can be modified with the latest information.

Fiefdoms will try to tailor-fit the planning process to suit their own unique approach, which will create more complexity in the organization. If successful, they will compromise a plan's overall value.

Top management must drive the use of standardized templates or exhibits in the planning process and indicate how to define the data—for example, the source of the market-size estimates, how market shares should be defined, what costs should be included in cost of goods sold, how to handle part-time employees and contractors in headcount data, etc. Without this standardization, fiefdoms will likely present management with a set of exhibits crafted to defend the current business plans and thinking as opposed to stretching the organization.

It is often best to get a neutral third party, like the finance organization, to craft these standardized templates and define the data and then get approval from top management.

DEVELOP A THREE-YEAR PLAN

A key exhibit in a three-year plan (and you should have such an exhibit for each product or service or business unit) summarizes the business impact of the product; it typically becomes the focal point of discussion when reviewing the plan. This chart should include the following entries down the left side: market size, market share, revenue, cost of goods sold, gross margin, R&D expense, sales expense, marketing expense, general and administrative expense, other expenses, total operating expense, and total operating income.

Across the top, from left to right, list nine columns: three columns representing the last three years; three columns representing the current fiscal year plan, year-to-date results, and current fiscal year estimate; and three columns representing the next three years.

This chart should fit virtually any product, service, or business unit, whether you're in the cosmetics business or the auto parts business.

Every product is part of a market, and this exhibit is infinitely useful in getting a handle on your place in that market. It asks for the market size in dollars for the last three years; your estimate for the current year (your full-year estimate when you put the plan together, year to date, and your current full-year estimate); and your estimates for the next three years. It also asks for market share for the same time periods for revenue, costs, etc. This simple chart captures all the essential information in a uniform language, accurately representing past performance and the promise that the general manager is making for the future.

AVOID THE R&D "GEE WHIZ" TECHNOLOGY SHOW

The typical fiefdom will look at an exercise like the creation of a three-year plan and try to avoid giving specifics. Instead, it will work to turn the planning exercise into a research and development review of all its great new product directions or technologies and its brilliant R&D staff.

While the fiefdom members brag about their great *ideas* for the future, they will attempt to dodge making any hard *commitments* about the future.

The real goal of such fiefdoms is to avoid being held responsible for a specific three-year plan. They would rather just come to an agreement on next year's budget without making any further promises or commitments.

Fiefdoms that attempt to turn the planning exercise into an R&D review usually succeed because top management often becomes excited about some of the new product dreams or technologies being described. The questions are will those ideas or technologies make it to the marketplace, and when?

REQUIRE OBJECTIVITY

One of the most difficult parts of this planning exercise is obtaining an objective analysis of business over the past three years and a reasonable projection for the future, given past performance and the product's performance against the competition.

Each business unit must make concrete projections about the competition, and top management needs to probe the reasonableness of those projections. Those projections will play a key role in estimating their products' success in the marketplace.

You will always be working from projections and judgments when you estimate your future business performance versus that of the competition. That's why it is critical to prevent the unrealistic optimism of a fiefdom from controlling the process.

AVOID THE HOCKEY STICK CHART

Back in the spring of 1997 at Microsoft, we were going through three-year plans of the various Microsoft products. During this process, Bill Gates consistently challenged the excessive optimism in the reports. In response, the product groups would attempt to defend their projected growth. The back-and-forth dialogue went on for a while. Finally Bill jumped in, sarcastically saying we must have a hidden feature in our Excel spreadsheet that causes a relatively flat set of numbers to suddenly explode upward on a graph to show the kind of growth they were projecting. Everyone in the room broke into laughter, including Bill, who then turned to ask one of the product managers how you activated that feature of Excel.

Everyone has seen these kinds of hockey stick charts. The fact is that unless there is some very significant product or marketing breakthrough, it is simply incomprehensible to grow significantly in the future after a mediocre three years. You need hard data to support estimates of future market shares, such as product tests versus the competition, data from prior product launches in the category, and statistical analysis of recent growth trends and their impact.

It's a good idea to ask the business unit to fill out the three-year chart in three separate ways: with an optimistic set of projections, a pessimistic set of projections, and a best-guess set of projections.

DEMAND FACTS, NOT ANECDOTES

During these three-year-plan meetings, top management must demand hard facts and data behind the projections.

Too often, however, these planning meetings turn into storytelling sessions where members of sales or R&D discuss the positive reaction of customers to new approaches or the reactions from a focus group to some of the concepts the business unit hopes to execute in the next year or two. Some of this may be useful, but it's important to push hard on basic questions such as:

▓ What is the basis for the projected market share gain?
▓ What is the data from historical launches of similar products by the business unit or by the competition?
▓ Why are we increasing marketing spending faster than revenue?
▓ What do you think the competition will do to counter our efforts? Did we build their reaction into our forecast?
▓ Has any product or service in this category ever experienced the kind of growth we are forecasting?
▓ Why isn't the cost of goods sold, as a percent of revenue, decreasing as revenue increases?

HOLD A SPECIFIC PERSON ACCOUNTABLE

At the completion of the three-year-plan meeting, it is crucial to assign specific tasks to specific individuals. Most fiefdoms will avoid this like the plague. In order to combat fiefdoms, select these individuals (responsible for particular tasks) carefully—these assignments can be crucial to the development of rising stars, who will gladly embrace the opportunity to make important contributions.

Given this opportunity for staff development, top management and the division's general manager should be the ones to evaluate the "people aspects" of what is being planned.

Ask key questions like:

* Do we have the right people in place to achieve this plan?
* Are there folks in key slots who we don't believe can deliver?
* Should we make staff changes in personnel now to make sure that we deliver these results later?

INSPECT, INSPECT, INSPECT

Once this three-year planning exercise is completed, it is vitally important to put a system into place to routinely check on execution. Too often with planning exercises, big binders full of data are generated, and once the meeting is over, those binders are put in a credenza, never to be opened again. Often, in six or twelve months, when it's time to do the exercise once again, the promises of the last meeting are not addressed.

These three-year plans are useful only if they are treated as the basic blueprint that management expects the team to execute.

As Larry Bossidy observed in *Execution*, company management must pay close constant attention to its business units and probe for possible improvements. Only then can the group achieve and exceed the three-year plan.

Track the three-year plan carefully. Each element of the exhibit should be continually scrutinized. Ask the following questions: Is the market share target being achieved? Is the revenue goal being met? And are the costs coming in at or below projections? Top management must stay on top of those measures and check a timetable regularly to see what should be happening—and when.

Following these guidelines will not only help to eliminate fiefdoms, it will also make an organization more agile and more able to grow.

HOW FIEFDOMS HAMSTRING MERGERS AND ACQUISITIONS

WHEN A COMPANY acquires a new company or technology, it must do so as smoothly and quickly as possible in order to gain the expected advantages. Management must be able to seamlessly integrate the company/technology into the existing organization, gaining the synergies and the business bump expected. Unfortunately, fiefdoms compromise an organization's ability to do both these things well.

Because they prefer to be left alone and do things as they please, fiefdoms are threatened by the idea of an acquisition and how it might impact them. And such fiefdoms are often found in both the acquiring and the acquired companies.

There are two ways to battle a fiefdom's effect on acquisitions. The first is to make sure that the key functional areas of the acquiring organization have standardized systems that are easy to use and modify, unburdened by systems protected by fiefdoms. With such standardized systems, it is much easier and faster to make the necessary modifications when the business rules change or when acquisitions are integrated.

Unfortunately, organizations typically can take nine to twelve months to modify information systems. From a technology perspective, this is a clear sign of antiquated architecture. When a company's staff and systems are up-to-date, reorganizations and acquisitions take place more smoothly.

The second method for achieving agility and allowing the smooth integration of acquisitions is to reorganize groups around the task at hand. This sends a clear signal that the organization must change. People must learn to use new tools, assume new responsibilities, and work with a new team. If people are not removed from their old responsibilities and reassigned to new tasks full-time, their first priority tends to be to focus on the comfort of the familiar—the tasks they had been responsible for before.

Reorganizing represents a powerful opportunity to keep people fresh and on their toes while signaling to the corporation that it is embracing a new world.

Using these two methods—reorganizing around desired changes and using standardized key functional systems that are easy to modify—enables an organization to stay agile. It will be better prepared to implement new business approaches and integrate acquired businesses, talent, and technology needed for future success.

ACQUIRING A FIEFDOM

Acquisitions can result in funny behavior. This is especially true when the acquired company is reluctant to give up control or independence. Let me give you an example. A well-established chemicals company that I will call BigChem acquired a small chemicals company (LilChem) whose products were unproven in the marketplace but that utilized exciting state-of-the-art technology.

When the acquisition was made, the CEO of LilChem—whom I'll call Bob—made sure that he would remain as the head of LilChem while reporting to a BigChem exec.

LilChem executives made a fair amount of money as a result of the acquisition. Because of this, Bob and his top employees stayed fiercely loyal to their own goals and vision—whether or not they agreed with the goals of BigChem.

What occurred during the next twelve months shocked BigChem. Bob fought any attempt by BigChem to integrate his products and technologies with BigChem.

Soon after the acquisition, BigChem scheduled a meeting between Bob and the business unit management team whose products were similar to his. The goal was to have both organizations explain their current thinking on product direction in order to develop synergies between the two organizations. It was important to decide on how the existing products from the two organizations could coexist in the marketplace and how they could evolve over time with minimal duplication and maximum impact on customers.

At the last moment, Bob decided to skip the meeting. He said he had a conflict and asked his lead technical person, Paul, to explain their current situation and goals for the future. But instead, Paul spoke in broad generalities that failed to give a detailed description of LilChem's products and the future of their technologies. To hear Paul speak, you'd never guess that LilChem had been acquired. Paul made no reference to working together to strengthen their lineup.

About six months after the acquisition, BigChem's CEO, Chris, set up a review of a product Bob's team had developed. Bob led the discussion; he talked about LilChem's products and their superb technology. Bob was a real charmer and a skilled technologist with strong feelings about the future of his products. In fact, Chris received quite a tutorial—Bob detailed LilChem's technology and eventually convinced Chris to follow his advice about how to approach some very exciting technological opportunities.

Chris became a real fan of Bob's and started asking questions about why he wasn't seeing that kind of technical leadership coming out of BigChem's product-development efforts.

What Chris failed to notice, however, was that Bob had fought off any ideas about integrating the sales forces of BigChem and LilChem. For all his innovative technological expertise, Bob was extremely protective of his products and unwilling to try a new approach to reaching customers. He had all kinds of reasons for slowing that process down and in subsequent sessions successfully convinced Chris that the risks were just too high to rush that process.

This kind of problem is not unusual. LilChem had great pride in its products and did everything possible to remain an independent fiefdom. Because BigChem exerted no discipline to integrate the company they acquired, LilChem simply defended the status quo.

Chris and the rest of BigChem's executives eventually remedied the situation. But Chris delayed dealing with Bob for another twelve months, and the tension only got worse. Bob was let go eventually, and, unfortunately, many of his technical team went with him. BigChem integrated the remaining personnel into various departments, but the two years of wasted time cost BigChem dearly.

LilChem was no longer state of the art; in fact, new systems had emerged that were much more efficient than LilChem's.

This story illustrates a classic top-tier fiefdom. Bob had an incredible amount of charisma and was the emotional godfather of the employees of LilChem. Everyone—including key members of BigChem's staff—adored him. He was viewed as a technical giant; he had made everyone at LilChem quite wealthy—and it was hoped he would do the same for BigChem. But Bob was so arrogant that he treated his relationship with BigChem as a game.

One of the reasons this dragged out so long was that BigChem feared losing Bob's talented team if they confronted him. They also regretted their inability to capitalize on the incredible technical capabilities of Bob and his team. Ultimately, this was a bad acquisition.

These types of personnel problems and difficulties in integrating an acquired company into an existing culture must be thought through up front. While one can argue that it's very difficult to predict the behavior that will occur after the acquisition, there usually are some very good indicators in the due-diligence stage. In this particular case, a little research would have revealed that Bob had gone through a similar kind of acquisition several years earlier, when he was CEO of another technology company. It turns out he acted similarly.

The lesson here is that fiefdoms do not die easily. Fiefdom leaders like Bob will do everything possible to maintain them. Only by dealing with the leader can the fiefdom be overcome.

What if you find yourself caught inside such a fiefdom? The sooner you can get out, the better. Who wants to be trapped in a ship whose captain would rather sink than give up the wheel? You should begin searching for opportunities outside the fiefdom—otherwise, you might find yourself without a viable career after the blowup occurs. And believe me—it will.

WHEN THE ACQUIRING COMPANY IS THE FIEFDOM

In another example of an acquisition, a fairly large company, which I'll call Silverside, acquired another company, Zoom, about a third of its size. Both operated in the electronics industry, but Zoom was clearly the most cost effective in that industry—and produced the best products to boot.

Silverside wanted to capitalize on Zoom's strengths. It hoped to quickly learn how such efficiency and high quality were achieved—and how to implement those practices throughout the merged organization.

The CEO of Silverside, whom I will call Carol, underestimated the power of the fiefdoms in her business units. Since Silverside was much larger and much older than Zoom, her employees felt they should be emulated. They were proud of their size, had grown comfortable as a large player in the industry, and felt no sense of urgency to change.

Carol's business units felt confident that the acquisition would make Silverside even larger and more powerful in the industry. They saw no reason to learn from Zoom. Life was comfortable—why change?

During the first year of the acquisition, Carol made numerous trips out to the field in order to understand how the integration was going. On one particular trip to visit the sales organization on the West Coast, she discovered that Zoom operated with about half as many people per $100,000 of sales revenue as Silverside. She marveled at their leanness. She encouraged her national sales management team to capture this valuable learning. As you might guess, however, Silverside was teeming with fiefdoms, and sales was no exception. While her sales force indicated to Carol that they understood her point, they felt no sense of urgency, and the integration of the sales arm got pushed to the background.

After a few months, Carol checked in with sales again on its progress. Fred, the western division sales manager, pointed out that his people were doing the kind of benchmarking Carol had requested. Carol replied that benchmarking had already been done; when were they going to get the efficiencies? Fred pointed out that Zoom's sales team lacked professionalism, and he indicated that a lot of work needed to be done to bring these people up to the standards of his own salespeople.

After this interaction with Fred, Carol took it upon herself to call a couple of the major accounts in the western division. She learned that the sales personnel of Zoom were viewed as genuine problem-solvers. Though they approached their business in a very informal manner, they always went out of their way to make sure their offerings meshed well with their customers' needs and that their solutions were well executed. Carol also learned from these accounts that her own sales force were generally viewed as highly professional but very formal and afraid to get their hands dirty in helping an account solve problems. It became clear to Carol that her sales organization was acting much like an impenetrable fiefdom.

Carol also did some detailed probing in the information technology area about five months after the acquisition. She requested data on the number of IT personnel prior to the acquisition in Silverside as well as in Zoom, and the number of information systems used to run each business. She also hired a consultant to interview her IT personnel. She discovered that Silverside lacked the skills to deal with the more up-to-date technologies of Zoom. Additionally, it appeared that the number of Silverside's personnel and information systems dwarfed that of the ultralean and very profitable Zoom. She had uncovered yet another fiefdom. Silverside's IT organization was unable to make dramatic and quick changes. They did things their way, with no real sense of urgency to seize the obvious savings that would come with upgrading.

In the personnel department, Carol found that too many of the "old guard" kept key jobs six months after acquisition. Silverside had waited too long to reassign Zoom's employees to these positions, wasting the valuable talent they had purchased through acquisition.

The integration took years, and the synergy was never fully achieved. The fiefdoms were too strong, causing all kinds of compromises. No one decided which people were best for certain jobs and how different practices would be refined as the two organizations began to work together.

There were a few examples of placing Zoom's key leaders in meaningful positions. However, these leaders experienced problems as well; the Silverside troops dragged their feet, having never received a clear message from Carol and her management team that they should adopt Zoom practices.

Silverside's top management had hoped its troops would see these obvious opportunities. But in reality, the Silverside managers were reluctant to move to these practices because they felt it would be admitting their own inferiority. And Carol never forced the issue. Consequently, the acquisition was a failure.

The lesson here is that fiefdoms occur in organizations large and small. Too often management attempts to adopt new practices before addressing problems within the existing organization. Acquiring a profitable company is not a substitute for strong leadership at the top.

ENTERING A NEW BUSINESS
THROUGH ACQUISITION

When a company with stagnant growth in its core industry decides to enter a completely new industry, its first step often is to acquire a company in that area. But the success rate in entering a new industry is not high.

Members of the acquired organization often think, "This new management knows nothing about our industry. We'd better keep them out of our activities or they're going to screw up our business."

Even worse, the acquiring company often believes that because it doesn't know a lot about the new business, it should allow its acquisition to remain independent (in other words—become an insular fiefdom). The acquiring company simply works with it in a superficial way, hoping over time to learn what kinds of resources are necessary for growth. But such thinking is simplistic. The acquired company typically has no interest or ownership in the kinds of businesses the acquiring company has experience with. Hence, it will feel both isolated and like a second-class citizen in its new organizational setting.

All of this often leads the most valuable people in the acquired company to feel ignored. Many will leave for another company that works exclusively in their industry; the best people are often lost this way.

I experienced one such situation where this kind of separation between the acquiring and the acquired companies went on for almost ten years. Looking back, I now realize one could have guessed this was going to happen right from the onset.

The acquired company, Siberion, a computer hardware design firm, was headquartered about a thousand miles away from the headquarters of the acquiring company, Centro, a consumer electronics firm. It was so physically isolated and hard to travel to that nobody wanted to visit the place. However, because the CEO of Siberion, Jim, was a research scientist who had been picked to be the CEO about five years before, the company was viewed as a leader in innovation. Jim was a man of few words, and while he knew the R&D part of the business extremely well, he approached the business and marketing issues in a very analytical manner. He ran a solid operation, though it was certainly not flashy. Centro was looking to his attributes—his analytical approach to innovation—as a way to break into a new line of business that had a solid footing in the industry.

While Centro played very much of a hands-off role during the first few years after the acquisition, it soon became clear that Siberion didn't really have as strong an innovation engine as Centro had first thought. Centro didn't know what to do about it. Its CEO, whom I will call Rick, preferred to pretend things were A-OK, since he didn't want to admit that maybe he'd acquired a dud.

Rick also felt very uncomfortable probing into the key inner workings of Siberion with Jim. Rick knew he couldn't talk Jim's technical language, and on the rare occasion that Rick asked where the real growth opportunities were, Jim would simply point to the steady track record and predict that R&D would continue innovating.

What you have here is two individuals dancing around the issue, both of them afraid to confront it. Jim was comfortable being left alone; he hadn't wanted to be acquired anyway since he was something of an introvert. Rick knew he had to break Centro into some new areas in order to generate growth, but once he did, he was afraid to confront the fact that the acquisition had not lived up to expectations.

About five years after this acquisition took place, Rick retired and was replaced by a new CEO, whom I will call Stan. Stan never understood why the company had acquired Siberion. During his first year as CEO, he made a few long trips to get a sense of what Jim and his people were doing, but he found he couldn't get excited about it. On the other hand, Siberion wasn't hurting Centro; it continued to enjoy a steady— though unspectacular—revenue growth. But the growth could have been so much greater. Siberion's growth was disappointing because Centro never really learned about the industry they had acquired and therefore never took the steps necessary to make this new area a key growth generator.

Clearly what was missing was strong leadership on the part of the two Centro CEOs, Rick and Stan. Neither of them had the nerve to explain their vision to Jim. Neither of them challenged Siberion. And so Siberion operated as a fiefdom for almost a decade. Just before the tenth anniversary of the acquisition, Stan finally had the nerve to deal with this situation. He sold off 80 percent of Siberion and force-fit the remaining staff into an existing business unit. The rationale given was that Centro had decided to focus on its core consumer electronics business. Basically, they were back to square one!

After an acquisition, top management of the acquiring company must set the tone by explaining the reasons for the acquisition and the goals and expectations they hold for everyone involved. The management team and department heads need to make their objectives very clear. Ideally, the two organizations should become one quickly, taking full advantage of the strengths of each and overcoming the weaknesses of each. If this doesn't happen, the acquired company will remain a fiefdom, growing more insular, more concerned about itself, and, consequently, less able to drive the business ahead.

THE FLAWLESS ACQUISITION

In another situation, a large pharmaceuticals company, Goliath, acquired a much smaller one, Davidson (about 8 percent of its revenue). Davidson fit quite well into one of Goliath's business units, and they did a marvelous job of making the acquisition go smoothly.

Harry, the head of the business unit driving Goliath's acquisition, was simply outstanding. He was in his early thirties, had a marvelous personality, and was doing very well in the company. He was not a fancy dresser and saw no need to be flashy. He was extremely friendly, smart, and had a clear sense of urgency to get things done. He always had a smile on his face and was ready to tackle any kind of problem thrown his way. He was also a great communicator, but his style was warm and informal rather than polished and professional.

Harry made numerous trips to Davidson during the negotiation phase. He sat down with its top team and told them up front how things would operate, making it clear they would experience an open, performance-focused environment. He explained where each person would be working and how they would be quickly integrated into his business unit at Goliath. He told them Goliath's benefits package differed from their previous package and truthfully explained that in some cases they would feel they were taking a step backward and in other cases a giant step forward.

Harry excelled at describing how certain elements in his business unit could be paired up with Davidson's products to create a powerful force in the marketplace. Second, he mentioned some R&D resources within his organization that he believed could work well with Davidson's—strengthening their products significantly and leading to much greater success in the marketplace. His honest and simple presentation of his goals for the acquisition genuinely excited Davidson's employees.

In essence, he laid all his cards on the table, making it very clear to Davidson's team what to expect and why. He also made it clear that things would happen very quickly. Davidson was told that while the names of their products would be retained, the Davidson name would disappear. Additionally, they were expected to take on Goliath's value system—or start looking for another job.

Harry was businesslike and positive but also very frank. He made sure there was absolutely no room for a fiefdom to occur.

One of the toughest elements of this acquisition was that Davidson was expected to abandon its pride and joy—an information system it had developed that tracked customers and provided sales leads. Keeping it, however, Harry explained, would lead to tons of duplication in the information technology area; eventually, Davidson's data center and systems would have to be put aside. He explained the new systems to Davidson in detail and described how the transition would go. Harry asked a few people from Goliath's IT department to explain their integration plans. This was quite an emotional issue for the Davidson team, but Harry made it much more digestible by being extremely up front about the process.

Harry also explained that additional R&D resources would be made available, and that additional marketing dollars would be provided to drive their products to the level they had all dreamed about.

Harry arranged several meetings to introduce Davidson's team to the top management of Goliath and help them understand how the company ran its business.

All in all, Harry presented the most clear-cut explanation I've ever heard of as to why an acquisition took place and how to make it a financial, organizational, and marketplace success.

Harry is a fine example of a leader who decided exactly what should happen during reorganization, made his vision clear to everyone involved, and got things moving right away. This example shows why strong leadership and a focused explanation of expectations can prevent the formation of an acquired fiefdom.

FORMING A NEW BUSINESS UNIT FROM WITHIN

It is common for companies with a bright new idea about a product, a service, or a major change in business practices (such as a new logistics approach or a new set of financial systems) to assign the initiative to a group of people who already have responsibilities.

It's not hard to imagine what this leads to. When a fiefdom is asked to take on something new, beyond its normal tasks, it often goes in one ear and out the other. The fiefdom members may say they will assist, but in reality their goal is often to maintain the status quo. They feel no sense of urgency to take on additional work or do things differently. They've probably fine-tuned their excuses as to why they are busy and may even require more resources just to complete their ongoing tasks.

In one consumer electronics company I am very familiar with that I will call Innovate, the top management team was very enthused about a new line of cellular phones they were launching, and they wanted to make it happen fast. The company was not acquiring a new company or system but, rather, launching a new product direction and building a talented team to make it a success. Because Innovate excelled in reorganizing around key tasks, they were confident that experienced talent and fresh new organization would lead to a big win.

The CEO of Innovate, whom I will call Adam, strongly believed that in order to make a splash in the marketplace, you had to reach out to your very best people and make your expectations crystal clear. To get things rolling, Adam went to his board of directors and told them about his aggressive plans for the new division. The very next day, he made a Webcast announcement to every staff member's PC detailing his plans. He explained that he would be drawing 300 strong performers from existing business units to create a team that could make his product a quick marketplace success.

This kind of clear, company-wide communication sent a powerful signal that something new and exciting was taking place in the company and that the company would be putting top talent behind it. It made the project seem important, one that the company was working hard to make successful.

In his Webcast, Adam announced that Catherine would head up the new business unit. She was one of the most respected business leaders in the company, currently at the helm of the company's fastest-growing division. Her involvement sent an incredibly powerful signal to the organization that this was a big deal.

Within the next three weeks, Adam and Catherine hand-picked the 300 people who would form this business unit and asked HR to move those people from their existing jobs and replace them.

Adam not only formed the business unit quickly and made it clear to the entire organization what he was doing, he also told the business unit that he wanted the new product in the marketplace within six months. He set a goal of a 10 percent market share by the end of eighteen months. These were very aggressive goals, but the company had backed the project with its best people. When that happens, the results are usually quite positive.

What Adam did was prevent any chance of fiefdoms slowing the company's efforts. He avoided the involvement of preexisting fiefdoms that would take on new responsibilities only in a part-time manner. Adam knew that if he delegated the responsibility full-time to the strong performers, great things could happen.

The results were phenomenal. The new business unit became the envy of the company. The new product was in the market by month five and had a 14 percent market share by month eighteen. By the end of that eighteen-month period, other strong performers were clamoring to get into the new business unit.

As a result, Adam and his top management team learned that they had been too passive with the other business units when laying out expectations. When people understand what is expected of them, they perform beyond anyone's wildest expectations. But without that clarity, those human instincts of territoriality, arrogance, and complacency, the bases of the fiefdom syndrome, take over. It's human nature. Comfort, pride, and an inflated assessment of one's work sets in. Before long, fiefdoms eat up even more resources and grow even more bloated and bureaucratic.

A HOT NEW BUSINESS UNIT EMBARRASSES ITSELF

I once consulted with a relatively new business unit in a large, mature retail/general merchandise company that I'll call Nova. The new unit consisted of an upscale catalogue service for a line of medium-to-high-end women's clothing. This new service was very exciting to its high-end customers but very punishing financially to the company. Nova wanted to get into this new business despite the fact that the start-up would be expensive. However, as things got rolling, management didn't monitor the new business unit closely enough to ensure its frugality.

This hot new group got off to a fast start, gaining significant awareness among targeted consumers of their service via huge marketing promotions and ad budgets. They achieved a respectable and growing market share. However, the financials were worse than expected; Nova was burning through cash at an unbelievable rate, and the loss was twice the budgeted level. The main culprits: exploding marketing costs and sloppy inventory management.

This new business unit was headed by a person I will call Joan. She had assembled a strong team of direct reports and was very creative herself, but she was also quite disorganized. And while she was charming and articulate, she was massively overconfident. She and her team would fight off top management anytime they began to ask questions of her. The team's fast start falsely convinced them that they could excel at just about anything. Joan had built a very strong and impenetrable fiefdom that hid behind its impressive initial revenue growth and its uniqueness.

The unit's business needed an intricate consumer account management system to keep consumer profiles and collect revenue from tens of thousands of users (some ordered from the catalogue via phone and credit card, some online, and some sent orders and personal checks). The team members felt their unique business model forced them to operate very independently. To further justify their independence, they stressed that in their world, what drove revenue and market share was the high degree of creativity and innovativeness in the service itself.

The very nature of Joan's business, and Joan herself, attracted overconfident and cocky individuals. This prevailing attitude led to many marketplace mistakes from the start. Rather than accept responsibility, the team blamed market conditions and the newness of the service.

As the business unit was being launched, Joan and her people convinced themselves that they could build their own account management system to maintain consumer accounts, handle the intricate transactions, and collect the appropriate revenue in a timely manner. The corporate information technology folks strongly encouraged the use of an experienced outsource vendor in this area, but Joan would have no part of it. She loved her independence and didn't want to be told by anyone how to run her business. She was confident her talented team would put together a sensational account management system. After all, it's just simple systems work—or so she thought.

You can probably guess what happened. They excelled in creativity and innovation but not in the strong discipline required to develop and run an account management system. They built their own system, which was incredibly fragile, and as the database grew to tens of thousands of consumers, the system regularly collapsed. Top management first became aware of the problem six months later, when it discovered revenue collection was lagging by six weeks. Joan's team fought off all the questions and forged ahead. But by the end of nine months, the unit was nine weeks behind in revenue collection. The integration with the credit card vendors was a mess, and personal checks were being lost and/or processed late. It was clear that the problem had to be confronted.

Joan was fired, and Nova's management sent in new people to run the business unit and demanded that those people outsource some of the vitally important operational tasks. It took six months to get the operational aspects of this exciting new service to an acceptable level.

The key lesson here is that with new business units or new organizations, it is vitally important to pick leaders with a balanced set of skills—and even some battle scars. These leaders need to fight off early tendencies to form fiefdoms, to become complacent about learning, and to become overconfident. A new business unit must be paranoid as it launches its products or services. Top management should pick managers who are brutally objective and will thoroughly inspect every aspect of the operation.

Whether acquiring a company or launching a new division, product, or service, companies must have a focused set of goals—and be up front with everyone involved about what is expected of them. It is, of course, natural for fiefdoms to emerge during acquisitions. People feel loyal to their supervisors and comfortable with the old way of doing things. But strong leaders can nip the problem in the bud—by learning about the company they are acquiring, foreseeing problems that may occur, and making an effort to introduce people to their new responsibilities right away.

11 COMMUNICATION AS A TOOL TO FIGHT FIEFDOMS

COMPANY-WIDE COMMUNICATION is a vitally important tool for executives in breaking up fiefdoms and avoiding their formation. When top management communicates directly with employees, it undermines the authority of the person controlling a fiefdom. Communication from the top also undercuts the fiefdom's independence. It shows those working within a fiefdom that they are part of a bigger organization. Communicating directly with the rank and file is also a powerful tool to make sure everyone understands the basic expectations within the organization. Company-wide communication also allows top management to implement change quickly. When changing conditions in the marketplace call for a company to adapt its strategy rapidly in order to stay competitive, spelling this out clearly throughout the company is an effective way to spark prompt company-wide action.

Such top-down communication also enables company leaders to reinforce the organization's long-term goals. Explaining the company's goals down the road is half the battle in making it happen. Broad-based communication is vital for breaking down complex issues into more easily understood terms.

RETAINING THE FEEL AND AGILITY OF A SMALL COMPANY WHILE EXPLODING IN SIZE

During my time with Microsoft in the 1990s and early 2000s, Bill Gates regularly informed the entire company about the direction of Microsoft products and key industry trends.

One tool Bill often used was a detailed memo delivered broadly via e-mail. Typically, it would address an overall product direction or "sea change" in the industry or in Microsoft's direction within the industry. In 1995, he crafted a lengthy memo about the Internet and what it would mean to consumers, to the software industry, and to Microsoft. The memo was distributed throughout the company via e-mail, as well as to the public. Every Microsoft employee knew instantly what the CEO of the company was thinking about this important issue and what the company would be doing to take full advantage of the trend.

Such crisp direction makes even a big organization feel small and agile. Everyone knows who is calling the shots, and no time is wasted deciding what direction to go in to keep the business healthy.

A second method Microsoft used to discuss an important event or issue was to set up a live broadcast over the company intranet to employees' personal computers so that everyone could get the announcement at the same time and learn top management's thoughts about it. Depending on the topic, the announcement might also be made available to the press and technology-thought leaders throughout the world. For employees in a different time zone, the presentation would have been sent to a server for them to see it on their personal computers and watch it as if it were a live event.

These two communication tools—e-mail and the intranet—were used on an ongoing basis to explain the company's overall product strategy and why we believed it was the right path to take. Bill would also spell out the implications for various divisions within the company, so it was clear how we were going to organize to tackle the task at hand. There's very little chance for a fiefdom to emerge with that kind of clarity.

This kind of communications approach stands in stark contrast to the tactics used by many organizations I've observed. I've seen situations where the CEO drafts a memo covering a new corporate strategy or direction for his direct reports, only to have them take the memo, put a cover note on it explaining what *they* thought it meant, and give it to their direct reports. By the time it reaches lower-rung employees, several weeks may have passed, and what they typically get is merely a summary of the original memo. Moreover, numerous people have put their "twist" on it; in many cases you'd never recognize the original message the CEO was trying to get across. Such a system breeds fiefdoms. People who control fiefdoms love it when top management communicates that way, simply because they get to control how the message is delivered to their people.

Another approach I've seen is for the CEO to tape a presentation about an issue or direction and then make thousands of copies with the expectation that the tape would be shown at group and department meetings. This can be modestly successful, but it gives the head of the fiefdom the opportunity to show or not show the tape and to "interpret" the words of top management so that they fit with the overall direction of the fiefdom.

GERSTNER COMMUNICATES HIS DREAM

In *Who Says Elephants Can't Dance?*, Lou Gerstner describes the fiefdoms within IBM and how difficult he knew it was going to be at the outset to pull these fiefdoms together. Says Gerstner: "This was a crisis we *all* faced. We needed to start understanding ourselves as one enterprise, driven by one coherent idea. The only person who could communicate that was the CEO—me."

Gerstner points out that at about the same time "I also discovered the power of IBM's internal messaging system, and so I began to send employees 'Dear Colleague' letters. They were a very important part of my management system at IBM. I sent the first one six days after I had arrived."

In this early e-mail, Gerstner acknowledged the intense loyalty of IBM employees during the very difficult recent years. He communicated his initial objective, which was to visit as many operations and offices as possible in his early months and quickly implement a new strategy that would make IBM successful.

Employees responded enthusiastically to his initial e-mail. "The reaction from IBM employees was overwhelmingly positive and, for me during the dark early days, a source of comfort, support, and energy," says Gerstner. He cites several of the e-mails he received soon after sending out that initial e-mail and how encouraged he was that company members understood the challenges he faced and supported his efforts to get IBM back on track.

Gerstner had found a powerful communication device. As I mentioned earlier, after about six months, he decided IBM's strategy should be to dedicate all employees to one key issue. This issue was the challenge of integrating various technologies to solve important customer problems and create new customer capabilities. Not surprisingly, he e-mailed all employees to make sure they understood the new strategy and what their role would be to make it happen.

Gerstner became such a believer in the importance of communicating directly to all members of the company that he included a fifty-two-page appendix of "favorite" e-mails that he'd sent to employees during his tenure. "In a crisis it is far easier for the company to emerge intact if the CEO makes sure that all employees know there is a crisis, what the management is doing about it, and what everyone must do to help," says Gerstner. Lou Gerstner's communication methods were crucial to his success in breaking up IBM's fiefdoms, implementing his unified strategy, pulling the company out of its tailspin, and making significant progress in the marketplace.

THE TOUGH TASK OF CLOSING FACILITIES

I once had an eye-opening experience working with the CEO and CIO of a large global company headquartered in the U.S. that found itself in the unfortunate position of having nine full-scale data centers scattered throughout the world. Over the years, each of the company's six geographical fiefdoms had quietly built up its own data center, using fewer and fewer of the resources from the three corporate data centers in the United States, Europe, and Japan. Each one also built its own IT systems development staff. These regional data centers were located in northern Europe, southern Europe, the U.K., Japan, South Asia, and Latin America.

The CEO was having difficulty globalizing the company. Several of its product lines were marketed around the world, but all of the data about product performance were stored regionally (in the regional data centers).

The CIO, whom I will call Brad, had a great relationship with the CEO. The CEO had hand-picked Brad about two years earlier, when it was clear that the company's investment in IT had grown significantly and needed more professional management.

The CEO had complained vehemently to Brad about the overall lack of quality analysis for the growing number of brands that were being marketed worldwide. The CEO had appointed global brand coordinators, but they had constantly told him that they couldn't get reliable data from the separate regions to put together the kind of global analysis he wanted. Consequently, the CEO put tremendous pressure on Brad to come up with a solution.

All of this was occurring at the same time that global telecommunications capabilities were skyrocketing, enabling data to be moved around the globe easily and cheaply. Given these newfound capabilities, the IT organization, under Brad's leadership, came up with a completely new telecommunications and computing architecture for the company, featuring one data center in the United States coupled with server farms in the three key regions (U.S., Europe, and Asia). Brad and his organization put the proposal together and reviewed it with the CEO. The savings would be enormous and the increased capabilities would meet the CEO's needs. The CEO gave Brad a few suggestions for the plan to better explain to the regional business managers why the reorganization was taking place. He then asked Brad to send the document to all his direct reports as well as to each of the regional business heads.

The pushback was immediate and intense. Within the IT organization, employees in the data centers throughout the world immediately saw that their jobs were being eliminated. And the regional business heads quickly realized that management would be able to stick their noses into the region's business.

One regional VP in charge of southern Europe became so incensed by the idea of closing "his" data center that he asked the CEO to "never let that computer guru get involved with any European issue." With that comment, the CEO knew he had struck gold. The CEO jumped all over the VP and followed up with a clear and thorough communication to all six regional heads indicating why this change was going to take place and what he expected from them. The CEO then e-mailed the same message to all employees at the department-head level and above.

Brad followed up with a clear, detailed memo that top management agreed to and sent it to all employees, explaining why they would go from nine data centers to one. He also described the architecture involved in being served by a single data center and what the implementation plans were. A crucial part of the announcement discussed the extensive testing that had been done to confirm that there were no technical issues in operating the company in the new way. In addition, Brad's memo carefully laid out how much equipment would be saved and how much leased space would be phased out. The savings were gigantic. Even more important, the memo explained how this new architecture allowed the company to manage the strategic direction of brands globally, while continuing to count on excellent local execution.

The direction-setting aspect of the memo was critical because it gave company leaders the opportunity to be supportive and set things in motion quickly. They could do so before the fiefdoms attempted to set up a grand debate on whether or not the plan should be implemented.

Brad and his IT team had thought the plan through very carefully and scheduled roughly one data center shutdown per six-week period. In essence, the data and systems for each regional data center were simply being moved to the global data center, with key databases placed in the regional server farms. No databases or systems were modified, but for the first time, all the key data was accessible for the kind of business analysis the CEO wanted done. Within the next eleven months, all of the data centers were closed, and their key applications were running in the global data center, with access to key databases via the U.S., European, and Asian server farms.

Technology changes have to be implemented quickly and efficiently to be successful (in this case, the plan had been tested extensively prior to the announcement, so there was little chance it would fail).

This story is another example of a company that was able to use broad-based communications to cut through its fiefdoms. The announcement that the data center capabilities were being taken over, closed down, and replaced with a new way of processing business was timed and executed in such a way that the fiefdoms didn't have time to come up with a competing plan to achieve the same kind of global analysis capability, efficiency, speed, and newfound agility.

HOW LAYERS OF MANAGEMENT
CAN OBSCURE A MESSAGE

I once got called in to do some work with a health and beauty aids company. The CEO, whom I will call Jack, was concerned that the company was not taking advantage of the breadth of its product offerings across all of its business units. Jack also was concerned that the business units were putting a lower priority on the retail trade than they should and not pushing the retailers to aggressively merchandise the company's individual brands. It was becoming clear to Jack that the balance between advertising and point-of-purchase retail presence had skewed way too far in favor of advertising.

Jack sent a memo to all of the business unit heads indicating that they needed to take retail more seriously and that he expected the business units to work together on occasion to provide the retail customers with new, exciting offerings that branched across several of the company's business units and products. The document was also sent to the senior vice president of sales, who had responsibility for all of the sales organizations within the business units. Jack made it clear that he didn't think sales was doing a very good job of executing at retail or putting pressure on the business units to collaborate more.

One problem Jack faced was that many of the company's retail customers were buying products from each of the company's business units. Each used different methods to interact with customers. The responsibility was on the customer to figure out how to best deal with the variety of approaches.

Jack's memo was designed to put in place procedures on how the individual business units should work together to avoid this problem. Unfortunately, Jack sent the memo only to his direct reports, asking them to disseminate it within their organizations. As the business unit heads forwarded Jack's memo to their people, they typically included a cover note designed to minimize changes within their fiefdom while still holding true to Jack's directives. Additionally, the senior VP of sales had his own point of view on how Jack's initiative should be implemented, with the goal of minimizing any trauma to his sales fiefdom. So he sent his own thoughts to the sales folks in the business unit fiefdoms.

In essence, each of the heads of the various fiefdoms, as well as the senior VP of sales, were gaming the system to diffuse any change that affected them while still being able to claim they were working to carry out Jack's requests as spelled out in his memo. Given that Jack failed to put in place any overall measurements to track the effectiveness of his proposed changes, the fiefdoms were generally ignoring what was intended.

Jack should have sent his memo directly to all employees in the company, outlining the problem and how he expected individual organizations, such as corporate sales, the business unit's sales staff, and management, to act. He should have also been clear about measures that would be used to track progress. Instead, the fiefdoms got to "interpret" this and feed their own plan to their groups that would protect the fiefdom and not upset the status quo.

When top management communicates with the organization, it needs to be clear and simple about the behavior it wants to see and how this behavior will be verified. In Jack's case, it took several iterations before he finally communicated how success would be gauged. The gauge would be the customers; it was their perception that mattered. Jack put a customer satisfaction measurement system in place and laid out in detail a new organizational design for sales that put a small sales team in charge of each of the large customers. Jack made it clear that these teams had the decision-making authority for implementation with the customer, that is, they could make certain modifications to promotion offers and timing of offers to better meet customer needs. They did not need to constantly check back with the business units. The plan worked. The unfortunate part was that it took a year and a half to determine how the company would solve its biggest problem. And during this time, the customer's patience was sorely tested.

TURNING IT FIEFDOMS INTO PRICING FLEXIBILITY

Let me tell you about the worst information technology–spending nightmare I have ever seen. A $8-billion chemical company I know had way too many IT people; the company was composed of literally hundreds of small fiefdoms that continually built up their own IT staff and systems. Each business unit had IT people working in finance, manufacturing, marketing, sales, etc.

The company began to have problems with pricing. Several competitors had started lowering their prices, a rarity in this segment of the chemicals industry in which they operated. Typically, the company had stable prices and fairly decent profit margins on most of the major products. The CEO, whom I will call Sam, initiated a series of cost/profit analyses to better understand how competition could take such an unusual step, cutting prices on key high-volume products.

The analyses Sam had done made it clear that his company had gotten way too fat due to all the fiefdoms and their bloated staffs. Among the problem areas, IT stuck out most prominently. Sam and the CIO, whom I will call Frank, began to realize the enormous amount of cost duplication in IT.

Sam was relatively new on the job. The financial press was starting to suggest that he wasn't reacting fast enough to the pricing changes instituted by his competitors. Also, articles had come out about the inflated cost structure of his company. Clearly, Sam had to do something drastic.

After doing a fair amount of benchmarking and analysis, Frank explained to Sam that 6.3 percent of revenue was going against IT spending, which was almost double the industry average. Sam realized that cutting the cost of IT would require him to take on the massive fiefdom structure that he inherited when he took the job. This was a company that had fiefdoms within fiefdoms. Each division had its own finance department, manufacturing department, etc. And each department had its own resources. If it weren't for the solid growth in the industry over the previous several years, and the competition's lack of aggressiveness during that period, this company would have had its day of reckoning much earlier.

Frank developed a new IT design that would bring huge savings but would require the company to create a single unified architecture for both its network and its key information systems in core areas such as finance, sales, and marketing. Frank pointed out to Sam that the only way to achieve the desired savings on a timetable that would allow them to lower their prices in the not-too-distant future would be to put all IT staff and resources under Frank's authority. They would leave the resources physically within the business units but alert the units that the IT staff would be drastically cut. In other words, Sam had to back up Frank as he attacked the fiefdoms.

The competition continued to be aggressive in its pricing, and the company's revenue continued to lag, so Sam had Frank put together—on crash timing—a presentation to be broadcast to all employees simultaneously via their internal network, explaining that cleaning up the IT area would be the company's first step in tackling its problems. The broad-based communication to all employees clearly stated that Frank was developing a single corporate IT plan. Sam noted that he backed Frank 100 percent and wanted to see the plan implemented quickly.

Frank told the company's employees that hundreds of IT people would be displaced in each of the business units and replaced by a group of ten to twelve IT professionals who would implement core corporate systems. The company would leave three or four people to support a *few* "special" information systems to handle the "unique" needs of that business unit. The displaced staff could apply for other jobs in the company (obviously not in IT, since IT was being cut significantly) or take a separation package.

Frank had done extensive homework with the head of product sup-ply, HR, and finance prior to the announcement and asked Sam to make sure all of these functional heads were actively participating in the cleanup process. The message from Sam described the company's intended decrease in the number of data centers as well as the creation of a central information-technology-systems group that would main-tain the core global information systems and databases.

The effort took sixteen months and was immensely successful, thanks to its simplicity and Sam and Frank's leadership and clear communica-tion. The financial results caused the percent of net revenue spent on information technology to decrease from 6.3 to 3.9. Those 2.4 percent-age points went directly to lowering prices. At long last, the company began to gain some ground against its competitors.

Without Sam's broad communication that sent a shock wave through the entire company, the effort would have been slowed by end-less debate about what should and shouldn't be done. The fiefdoms would've attempted to get involved in the design and, consequently, fragmented the project. It would have been a massive failure. This kind of thing happens all the time.

Within months after the IT cleanup was initiated, Sam began clean-ing up HR, and the people in finance knew they were next on the list. Sam finally had gotten the message—streamline the company or lose out to the competition.

A CENTRAL APPROACH TO DISCIPLINE, A LOCAL APPROACH TO CREATIVITY

During my years working in marketing at Procter & Gamble, I was impressed by top management's focus on having centrally managed dis-cipline in the marketing organization and locally managed creativity.

A central marketing organization at P&G served the needs of all P&G marketing people worldwide. It contained a marketing personnel group, a media group, and a few other marketing services groups. One of the small organizations within the central group was Copy Services. Let me explain how it worked, because it demonstrates the concept of central discipline and local creativity. Copy Services consisted of five people who were experts in the development of television and print advertising, the lifeblood of P&G marketing at the time.

During the early '90s, when I was the senior vice president in charge of marketing at P&G, I developed a keen appreciation for Copy Services's work. This group's job was to dictate how Procter & Gamble people would be trained to think about and develop advertising. And they did it so effectively that people in marketing units all throughout the company clamored for help from them.

The Copy Services group was always out in the field working with marketing people in various business units and locations, doing training. Part of the training involved showing brand management personnel a very disciplined approach to developing a strategy for advertising a particular brand. Other training focused on the core fundamentals, such as how to create and judge advertising, how to run an ad development meeting with the ad agency, and when to use or not use various approaches in television advertising, such as testimonials, humor, demonstrations, and music.

Everyone working in marketing at Procter & Gamble knew that Copy Services spoke regularly with the senior vice president of marketing (me, at the time) about problem areas in marketing. Consequently, the group of five was deeply respected and treated with importance.

The group would take hundreds of ads over a ten-year period in a particular category (such as detergents or cosmetics) and study which products were growing market share behind what advertising. They would analyze all the successes and failures and come up with key findings about the secrets of success for advertising in that industry.

On the other hand, both top management and Copy Services made it clear that the actual development of advertising was in the hands of the brand people locally. Copy Services did not attempt to do their job. It existed to train people to do that job well and to apply a level of overall quality control that enabled problems to be spotted early so that top management in the marketing area could deal with them quickly.

Because of this balance of discipline in the central unit and creativity out in the local offices, there was no chance for fiefdoms to develop in the marketing area. Everyone knew they were part of a marketing *community* at Procter & Gamble, which gave them a tremendous amount of pride.

It was also made clear that their progress, from a career standpoint, depended on their generating successful marketing campaigns for the brands in their individual business units. Top management communicated frequently with all employees on the importance of both their training from the central marketing organization and their local creativity.

This constant communication, coupled with the high quality of the central marketing resources (and the extensive measurement devices used to track marketing success or failure), made this whole operation very successful.

When top management communicates clearly to the organization, day-to-day operations are simpler and fiefdoms are never given a chance to emerge.

12 BEATING THE FIEFDOM SYNDROME

THE BENEFITS TO overcoming the fiefdom syndrome are not merely theoretical. Doing so produces concrete, measurable, and, in many cases, extraordinary results.

But how can you achieve the constant vigilance needed to eliminate the basic tendencies that contribute to the fiefdom syndrome?

Again, the basic behaviors behind the fiefdom syndrome are part of human nature. Human beings, left to their own devices, naturally try to control information that pertains to them, attempt to act independently and exercise control over their time and activities, and tend to overestimate their importance and performance in the organization. Consequently, the battle to keep the fiefdom syndrome out of your organization is an ongoing battle that needs constant vigilance.

■ Each organization needs a high-level "enforcer." At Microsoft, I played that role in instilling discipline in the various functional areas (finance, procurement, IT, HR, manufacturing, etc.). Steve Ballmer played a similar role in sales. And most important of all, Bill Gates, as the CEO, played a pivotal role in backing us up. We pushed for discipline across the company, while he pushed hard on the business units to achieve the creativity needed to constantly improve Microsoft's products and services.

As the head of marketing at Procter & Gamble, I played a similar "enforcer" role. My job was to make sure we had the discipline necessary to ensure that all marketing people were properly trained and that key worldwide measures were in place to judge the impact of product and marketing efforts on the consumers and thereby to judge its overall marketplace success. It was also my job to make sure that marketing personnel understood that their key responsibility was to use their creativity to excite consumers about their products and services, so that their market shares grew and their financial results constantly beat objectives.

■ To eliminate weak links in the top management team, everyone must understand the need for the proper balance of discipline and creativity in driving the company forward. Companies that balance innovation with corporate discipline do not offer the kind of fertile soil that allows fiefdoms to grow. Balancing those two different directives, however, requires strong leadership at every level. In *Execution*, Larry Bossidy talks at length about the importance of having the right people lead—at the group level, the department level, and the division level. That's why he spent a large percentage of his time getting the right people into the right positions. It is one of the primary responsibilities of every CEO.

THE ADVANTAGES OF A "FIEFDOMLESS" COMPANY

Being aware of the fundamental human behaviors that lead to fiefdoms, and taking steps to overcome them through a balance of organized discipline and creativity, offers fantastic benefits for businesses. Such awareness allows them to:

■ **DEVELOP BETTER LONG-TERM STRATEGY**—As the lessons of big steel and IBM show, you need to have a solid grasp of where you stand in your industry. You can do that only with full access to the information on how your company is doing at every level, both the good news and the bad. Only then can you adapt your current strategy to reflect where you want to be in the future. Coming up with the

strategy that will take your company to a new level is much easier
to achieve in a transparent, fiefdom-less organization.

▓ **EXECUTE FOR THE SHORT TERM**—Use what Larry Bossidy calls "robust
dialogue" between top management and business units to review
the company's or group's plans and expectations for the next two
or three years on a regular basis. Only by focusing on executing the
fundamentals well will your strategy become a reality. Making the
data about the company's performance available to managers and
conducting regular dialogue about what's going well and what isn't
will help ensure that fiefdoms never take root.

▓ **ENJOY SIGNIFICANT COST ADVANTAGES**—Implementing disciplined
company-wide systems and practices will help an organization execute tasks with a surprisingly lean staff. The secret to weeding out
the excessive costs created by fiefdoms is to implement core global
systems and practices. Management should set their sights high
when it comes to implementing company-wide practices and
measures. Microsoft decreased its procurement staff by 70 percent
while massively improving service by centralizing the procurement
process. The organization I discussed in Chapter 11 cleaned up a
messy IT department and cut IT costs from 6.3 percent of net revenue to 3.9 percent.

▓ **ADAPT TO CHANGE WITH SPEED AND AGILITY**—Having one set of global
practices enables an organization adopting a new business model
to make a single set of modifications rather than change hundreds
of "unique" practices. That agility allows an organization to constantly change and improve as new skills are learned and opportunities are seized. There's nothing worse than being bogged down
with so many systems and practices that each change requires massive adjustment—it can eat up time and resources.

▓ **WORK CREATIVELY**—Opening a dialogue between the business units
and top management, and utilizing easy-to-access business performance data, will help foster a tremendous sense of urgency and
the appropriate level of marketplace paranoia to improve the products and services so they are clearly preferred by consumers. Such
urgency is the engine that leads to invention.

FIEFDOMS AND NONPROFIT ORGANIZATIONS

I believe it's harder to break up fiefdoms in nonprofit organizations than in for-profit companies, primarily because it's more difficult to insist upon measures that reflect whether things are going well or not. Public for-profit organizations are regularly scrutinized by the marketplace and shareholders in regard to their overall performance. This rarely happens with nonprofits. This often leads to an increase in the cost of services as well as in the perpetuation of services that have outlived their usefulness. This eventually can lead to an overall lack of focus within the organization as the number of services grows. But tackling fiefdom behaviors within a nonprofit can have very significant benefits, including:

▓ **BETTER, MORE RELEVANT SERVICES**—Constantly revisiting the overall strategy of the organization and assessing the impact of individual services is an extremely healthy practice. Nonprofits must institute the same kind of strategic reviews and short-term planning as for-profit organizations, and they should expect the same constant improvement.

▓ **MORE SERVICES PER DOLLAR**—Nonprofits must push themselves to create ways to gauge the efficiency of the services they provide. I'll never forget how hard I worked on United Way campaigns over the years, constantly convincing donors of the importance of the United Way. In the 1980s I was told that for every dollar contributed to United Way, almost 98 cents went straight to the human services organizations that United Way supports. This is a good measure of efficiency. But even at United Way, which was incredibly efficient, this percentage decreased over the years. The administrative costs crept up to about 5 percent by the late 1990s.

One nonprofit I know of—a small college with a great reputation—put together a staff to increase the size of the endowment. After a slow start, the staff began to look every quarter at the amount of money it raised per dollar of fund-raising cost. After comparing their efforts with several other endowment campaigns at similar schools, they realized how weak they were. That led to coming up with creative ways to approach potential donors.

▓ **MORE MOTIVATED AND EFFECTIVE PERSONNEL**—Nonprofits tend to put less emphasis on performance appraisals than for-profits, and they seldom think about weeding out weak performers. One gets the impression at times that they think it is rude to confront poor performance and move people out of their jobs. After all, they are serving a higher purpose. But if a nonprofit is truly interested in improving its impact and its efficiency, it must have strong personnel in place. Coddling underperforming employees too often leads to low morale and sets the stage for fiefdoms to take root.

FIEFDOMS AND GOVERNMENT

There are gigantic opportunities to improve the effectiveness of government if leaders are willing to take on the fiefdoms. As with nonprofits, creating useful measures is certainly more challenging than in the for-profit sector, where organizations are required to publicly report on progress and shareholders press for constant improvement. But by tackling the fiefdom syndrome in our government bureaucracy and the basic behaviors that drive it, federal, state, and local government—and the entire country—can benefit.

▓ **BETTER SERVICES**—Fiefdoms tend to flourish in government primarily because it is difficult to eliminate or modify services that are faltering. Savings from such streamlining should be the source of funding to create new or significantly improved services.

I noted in Chapter 2 some of the fiefdom issues in the CIA and FBI that became obvious after the terrorist events of September 11, 2001. What seemed to push the public to its highest level of outrage occurred when FBI lawyer Coleen Rowley came forward with the fact that the month before the September 11 events, FBI agents in Minnesota requested FBI headquarters to approve a search of the computer files of a suspicious immigration violator who was trying to learn how to fly a commercial jet. After many delays, the request was turned down. Several months after the September 11 events, the search was approved, and information related to jetliners and crop dusters was found on the hard drive of the computer. Ms. Rowley vented her frustration at working in an "ever-growing bureaucracy" that led to risk aversion, make-work paperwork, and "seven to nine levels" of officials that impeded effective decision making. There is no doubt government departments are full of fiefdoms.

At Microsoft we held an annual Government Leaders Conference, inviting representatives from governments around the world to showcase the way they used technology to improve the services they provided their citizens. We set up a friendly competition to allow countries to try to outdo one another in coming up with creative ways to serve customers. I'll never forget the envy sensed in the audience as the representatives from the U.K. demonstrated a Web site that allowed their citizens to easily access services they once needed to wait in line for, such as renewing a driver's license and paying property taxes.

Each year, we saw significant improvements as governments jumped on the ideas they had heard in prior years and institutionalized them.

It was clear from those Microsoft conferences that governments typically lack a forum in which the ways they carry out their basic duties are "inspected" or benchmarked alongside their peers. Governments may not have shareholders to answer to, but such forums could lead to exciting ways to save money and improve the lives of their citizens.

Some of the most important services a government supplies are roads, sewer systems, water, and power. But politicians often are reluctant to spend enough money for long-term infrastructure planning and execution, given the pressure to use that money for short-term programs or services that might be more visible and advantageous to their political careers.

The key to creating great services is setting priorities in a world of limited budgets. Corporations have to do that, and the best of them do it well. But until the same pressure is put on governments, they'll continue to have difficulty phasing out old services to pay for new or improved ones. Unfortunately, in a political environment, long-term plans often sink to the bottom of the to-do list, while political survival tactics float to the top.

▪ **LOWER COST**—An efficient government needs to constantly make tough choices about which programs and services to downsize or eliminate in order to lower budgets or fund new services. Just like for-profits, they can slash costs by cleaning up their information technology, moving to simplified systems, and striving to set clear goals for driving down costs. Unfortunately, governments lack the kind of value system you'll find in a for-profit company whose financial performance is always under scrutiny. But the top management team of a government—a president, governor, mayor, chief of staff, department head, etc.—can provide that pressure. Unfortunately, this is a dangerous political move; too many politicians put their own survival ahead of what's best for the country or their constituency. Citizens should hold government leaders accountable for government efficiency via the ballot box and ongoing public vigilance.

▪ **MOTIVATING AND UPGRADING PERSONNEL**—Too often in government, it is difficult to terminate an employee for poor performance. Usually the core problem is that governments lack good performance-appraisal systems. But in order to fight off the fiefdom syndrome, a government must set goals regarding overall effectiveness and efficiency as well as measures to evaluate personnel on their ability to contribute to those goals. Government needs the same kind of performance-appraisal systems as those I discussed earlier for for-profit organizations. That requires strong government leadership.

Not long ago I was asked to consider a fairly high-level government job in Washington, D.C. The organization had significant performance problems and an absolute morass of information technology systems and databases. When I asked the government leaders what they wanted to see happen in the organization, it became clear that the employee union made it basically impossible to terminate an individual for performance reasons. As a result, many strong performers left, and the entire organization had evolved into a series of fiefdoms that looked to be almost impenetrable. The losers in this situation, in addition to the public they serve, are the dedicated and diligent government employees trapped in such a fiefdom. There is little opportunity for advancement, and morale is devastated (I ended up turning the job down because I didn't see the kind of strong backing from those in charge that would be needed to initiate major change).

The most important tasks of any organization are to set high expectations for personal performance and to create a system where employee performance is evaluated on a regular basis. Every employee needs to be aware of their strengths and weaknesses, and employees should be rewarded for genuinely excelling. There should also be consequences for repeated underperformance. Government leaders need to push hard to make these changes happen.

■ **IMPROVED EMPLOYEE ATTITUDE**—All of this leads to a higher sense of fulfillment and motivation on the part of all employees. When government employees feel better about their work and the contribution they are making, it encourages strong people to accept government positions.

For example, in the mid-1990s, I was very impressed by the way the government of Ireland worked with Microsoft to make sure that Microsoft's European Regional Operations Center in Dublin met the company's needs. The government did everything possible to remove barriers and improve infrastructure to ensure success (and as a result, many jobs were created). It was a mind-blowing attitude compared to the many less-responsive governments we had dealt with at the time!

About a year later, the Economic Development Organization of the Singapore government asked me about the possibility of entering into a close working relationship with Microsoft. They wanted Microsoft to set up an Asian Regional Operation Center in their country, and they had clearly studied what Ireland was doing. A year and a half later, that operations center for Microsoft was opened, and Singapore became our center of economic activity in the Asian region. In the cases of Singapore and Ireland, government employees had an overall mission to attract businesses and create jobs. Thanks to the creativity of these government agencies and politicians, they came up with an arsenal of tools that convinced companies around the world to set up their European headquarters in Ireland and their Asian headquarters in Singapore.

As with any organization, be it a for-profit company or a school system, when top management paints the dream or vision of what they want to achieve, and creates an environment where creativity is rewarded and excellent performance is acknowledged (and poor performance is not tolerated), great things can happen.

BENEFITS FOR EDUCATION

The K-12 public school system in the United States is in many ways the ultimate fiefdom. Back in 1983, the National Commission on Excellence in Education generated a report entitled "A Nation at Risk," which described unsatisfactory performance at K-12 public school systems throughout the country. Academic achievement in the basic skills of reading, math, and science were unsatisfactory, and high school graduation rates were unacceptable. A large percentage of high school graduates required significant remedial work before they could take on standard university curricula. In 2003, the Hoover Institution of Stanford University published a report that highlighted how little progress had been made in the twenty years since "A Nation at Risk" had been published. The summary paragraph in the Hoover Institution report demonstrates how the fiefdom syndrome has captured K-12 public education in the United States:

"A Nation at Risk" underestimated the resistance to change from the organized interests of the K-12 public education system, at the center of which were the two big teacher unions as well as school administrators,

colleges of education, state bureaucracies, state boards, and many oth-
ers. These groups see any changes beyond the most marginal as threats
to their own jealously guarded power.

If you think about the fundamental behaviors that drive the fiefdom syndrome, it's clear there are enormous problems in the K-12 public education system in the United States. For years, many school systems have fought testing and accountability standards, demonstrating a fiefdom's tendency to control data. Legislation was put in place in 2002 as part of the "leave no child behind" program by the Bush administration to get basic measures of student performance in place and regularly published to the public so parents can understand the quality of the schools to which they are sending their children. While many school systems and teachers understand a need for accountability, some school systems fought hard to avoid this measure, doubting that such testing could accurately assess improvements or drops in student performance. The emphasis on test scores led to accusations in Texas of teachers helping students pass the tests. If that isn't a fiefdom-like behavior, I don't know what is.

The U.S. Department of Education has reported that almost 50 percent of funding in K-12 public schools goes for noninstructional activities. If you look across different school systems in different states and counties, you'll see a significant difference in the amount of spending per student. Yet the research in this area suggests no correlation between costs and results. Couldn't some of this money be used to reward the best teachers and to streamline the overall approach with which we educate children?

We need look no further than the comprehensive Department of Education study called National Assessment of Educational Progress to see an inflated self-assessment at work. The study shows that in 2000, only 16 percent of twelfth-grade students are proficient or advanced (14 percent proficient, 2 percent advanced) in math. Of the remaining students, 48 percent have only a "partial mastery" of prerequisite skills and 36 percent are at the "below partial mastery" level. Why aren't K-12 public-school administrators and teachers in a panic, trying all kinds of new things, and releasing weak teachers, to improve these results? If they were a for-profit company, the shareholders would have massively cleaned house! Somehow they convince themselves that the end product seems to be adequate. This is a good example of inflated self-assessment.

How would tackling the fiefdom syndrome benefit our school systems?

- **BETTER STUDENT PERFORMANCE**—Teachers and schools must be held accountable for their results. We must institute measures of student performance that help achieve that accountability. Legislation passed in 2002 by the U.S. government attempts to tackle this very issue, and strong evidence exists that such standardized quality testing in core areas like math, science, and reading generates improvement.

- **MOTIVATED TEACHERS**—School systems need to adopt performance-appraisal systems that significantly reward top teachers and isolate poor performers. The weakest 5 to 7 percent of teachers need to be removed from their job each year and encouraged to seek additional training or pursue a new profession or another job within the school system. The constant upgrading of standards is a core requirement of any organization that wants to foster excellence. By providing strong financial rewards to the top performers, teaching will look a lot more attractive to the brightest college graduates; strong performers are more interested in working in an environment where their excellence is acknowledged.

- **BETTER USE OF EXISTING FUNDS**—As noted earlier, the Department of Education states that roughly 50 percent of school funds go to non-instructional activities, including administrative support, staff to fill out government forms, excessive IT complexity, etc. School systems must eliminate as much bureaucracy as possible and push back on activities required by governments that utilize scarce resources that do not provide adequate benefit. Education leaders on local and state levels need to take up these kinds of causes that will turn up funds to reward excellent teachers who get exceptional results.

■ **EDUCATIONAL CREATIVITY**—I recently had a discussion with a university president asking why more research hadn't been done on the best ways to insert knowledge into the heads of human beings. After twenty minutes, the president acknowledged that, in general, schools and universities have yet to update their 800-year-old business model: teachers standing in front of students, lecturing and assigning homework. I read report after report of school systems awash in technology contributed by various companies that isn't being put to use. We need more creativity in coming up with ways to more efficiently and effectively educate our children. You would think that with the incredible technology capabilities available, coupled with creative approaches on how to capture the fascination and interest of youngsters, we could see significant breakthroughs in the speed and efficiency with which we educate our children.

To improve schools, the principal and the Board of Education first need to tackle the challenges of fiefdoms. In many cases, however, the administrators themselves are part of a fiefdom. Ultimately, communities must become involved if school systems can't tackle fiefdoms on their own. This requires strong leadership on the part of parents, government officials, and citizen activist groups.

THE BENEFITS TO INDIVIDUALS OF CONQUERING FIEFDOMS

Organizations that fight fiefdoms provide greatly improved opportunities for employees to use their talents, learn new skills, and make an impact. In companies where fiefdoms exist, employees typically find themselves doing the same tasks over and over. When the fiefdom eventually is broken up by new management or a financial crisis, these employees are often left out of the organization's future plans. Sometimes this comes as a shock, especially if an employee has been receiving positive evaluations over the years.

Here are key questions individuals must ask themselves regarding fiefdoms in their own place of work:

- Am I a victim of the fiefdom syndrome?
- Do I work in a fiefdom?
- Is a fiefdom hampering my ability to contribute?
- Is a fiefdom holding back my career?
- Is a fiefdom causing me to be stuck in a dead-end job that might be eliminated?
- Am I causing a fiefdom to occur?
- Am I a one-person fiefdom?
- If so, how is it damaging me?
- How is it damaging my group, department, or company?
- What do I do to beat fiefdom behavior?

In thinking about your own performance and contribution to your company or organization, there are significant benefits to escaping the fiefdom syndrome:

1. **MAKING THE MOST OF YOUR TALENTS**—All of us want to maximize our impact on the world, taking full advantage of the God-given talents we each have. When you operate as a single-person fiefdom or remain trapped in an organizational fiefdom, you waste those talents. Your focus shifts to defending the status quo. You may begin to believe you are better and more effective than you actually are and therefore overlook ways you can improve.

2. **IMPROVING YOUR CHANCES TO BE A PART OF A SUCCESSFUL ORGANIZATION**— It is fun to be part of a successful organization, one that is having a major impact on its industry or the world. When you are stuck in a fiefdom, your ability to be a part of a successful team is greatly compromised.

3. **AVOIDING A CAREER DEAD END**—Individuals who stop learning and lose their basic sense of curiosity on how to improve themselves risk handcuffing their careers. Eventually, fiefdoms are discovered and broken up. Often when that happens, the individuals within the fiefdom have become so set in their ways and outdated with respect to their skills, they risk losing their jobs.

Individuals stuck in fiefdoms are in a very tough position. On the one hand, they want to use their skills to be the best they can be. On the other hand, the fiefdom creates a comfortable environment that can seem secure and be very attractive. Its members no longer have to worry about taking on new challenges and working hard to stay ahead of competition. They no longer have to worry about their performance flaws and how to improve them. The fiefdom helps them cover those things up. In essence, the fiefdom can lull the individual into a false sense of security, which can be much more attractive than a life spent constantly tackling the future, striving for improvement, reaching for overall excellence, and battling competitors.

Giving in to those fiefdom-generating tendencies, however, in the long run leads to potential career disaster in the form of being laid off, demoted, or ignored within your organization. But there are some simple steps individuals can take to avoid the fiefdom syndrome and utilize their talents to get ahead.

PERFORM YOUR BASIC RESPONSIBILITIES WITH EXCELLENCE—Your most important task as an employee or manager is to do your basic job well.

1. Make sure your supervisor has been absolutely clear about your responsibilities.
2. Make sure there are ways to measure your progress that you and your supervisor agree will reflect your performance.
3. If such measures aren't in place, ask your supervisor about what you can do to ensure that you are performing to his or her expectations.

LOOK FOR WAYS TO MAKE THE ENTIRE ORGANIZATION WORK BETTER—Each individual should be on the constant lookout for ideas on how to improve the organization. Present these ideas to your management and ask for feedback. People who do their current jobs well and come up with ideas to improve the organization will be rewarded with new opportunities to utilize their skills—often with higher levels of responsibility.

Individuals and organizations that strive to fight off the fiefdom syndrome are usually relatively selfless. Egocentric individuals, on the other hand, eventually fall prey to the fiefdom syndrome.

Only by fighting off the fiefdom syndrome can individuals as well as organizations be the best that they can be.

INDEX

ABOUT THE AUTHOR

Robert J. Herbold is an authority on business operations, marketing, and the dynamic relation between the two. During his eight years as the COO of Microsoft, the company experienced a fivefold increase in revenue and a ninefold increase in profits. Previously, he spent twenty-six years at Procter & Gamble, where he revolutionized product distribution. He recently launched Herbold Group LLC, which consults with CEOs on strategy and profitability issues.